ZENESCOPE ENTERTAINMENT PRESENTS

Grimm Fairy Tales

UNLEASHED

Volume Two

zenescope

UNLEASHED

Grimm Fairy Tales

Volume Two

STORY
PAT SHAND
RAVEN GREGORY
JOE BRUSHA
RALPH TEDESCO

WRITER
PAT SHAND

ART DIRECTOR
ANTHONY SPAY

TRADE DESIGN
CHRISTOPHER COTE

EDITOR
RALPH TEDESCO

THIS VOLUME REPRINTS
THE COMIC SERIES GRIMM
FAIRY TALES UNLEASHED ISSUES
#4-6 PUBLISHED BY ZENESCOPE
ENTERTAINMENT.

WWW.ZENESCOPE.COM

FIRST EDITION, OCTOBER 2013
ISBN: 978-1-939683-17-5

ZENESCOPE ENTERTAINMENT, INC.
Joe Brusha • President & Chief Creative Officer
Ralph Tedesco • Editor-in-Chief
Jennifer Bermel • Director of Licensing & Business Development
Raven Gregory • Executive Editor
Anthony Spay • Art Director
Christopher Cote • Senior Designer/Production Manager
Dave Franchini • Direct Market Sales & Customer Service
Stephen Haberman • Marketing Manager

GRIMM FAIRY TALES CREATED BY
JOE BRUSHA AND RALPH TEDESCO

zenescope
WWW.ZENESCOPE.COM
FACEBOOK.COM/ZENESCOPE

GRIMM UNIVERSE

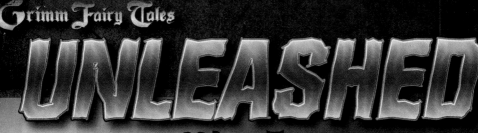

Grimm Fairy Tales

UNLEASHED

Volume Two

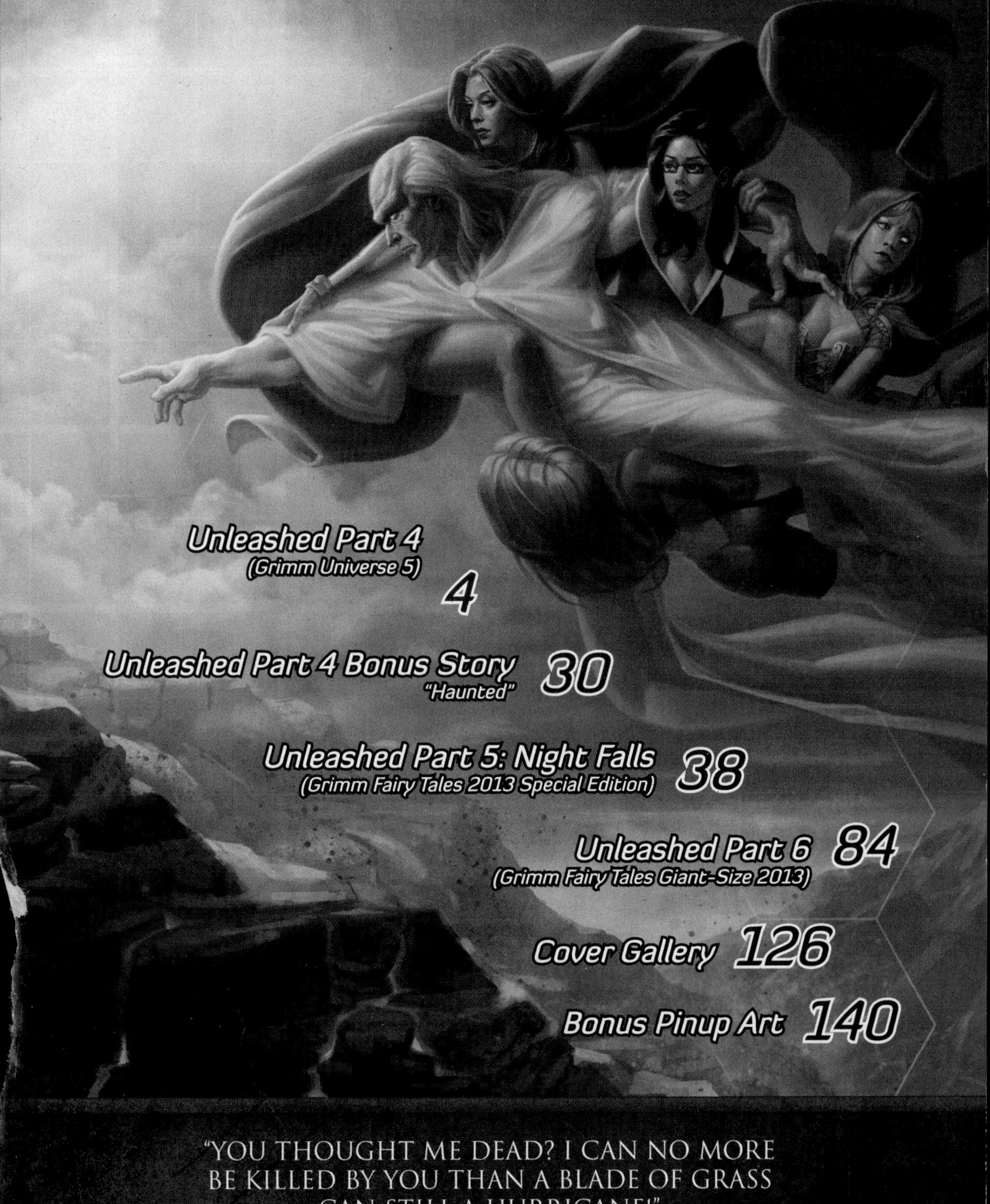

"YOU THOUGHT ME DEAD? I CAN NO MORE BE KILLED BY YOU THAN A BLADE OF GRASS CAN STILL A HURRICANE!"

—THE BEING

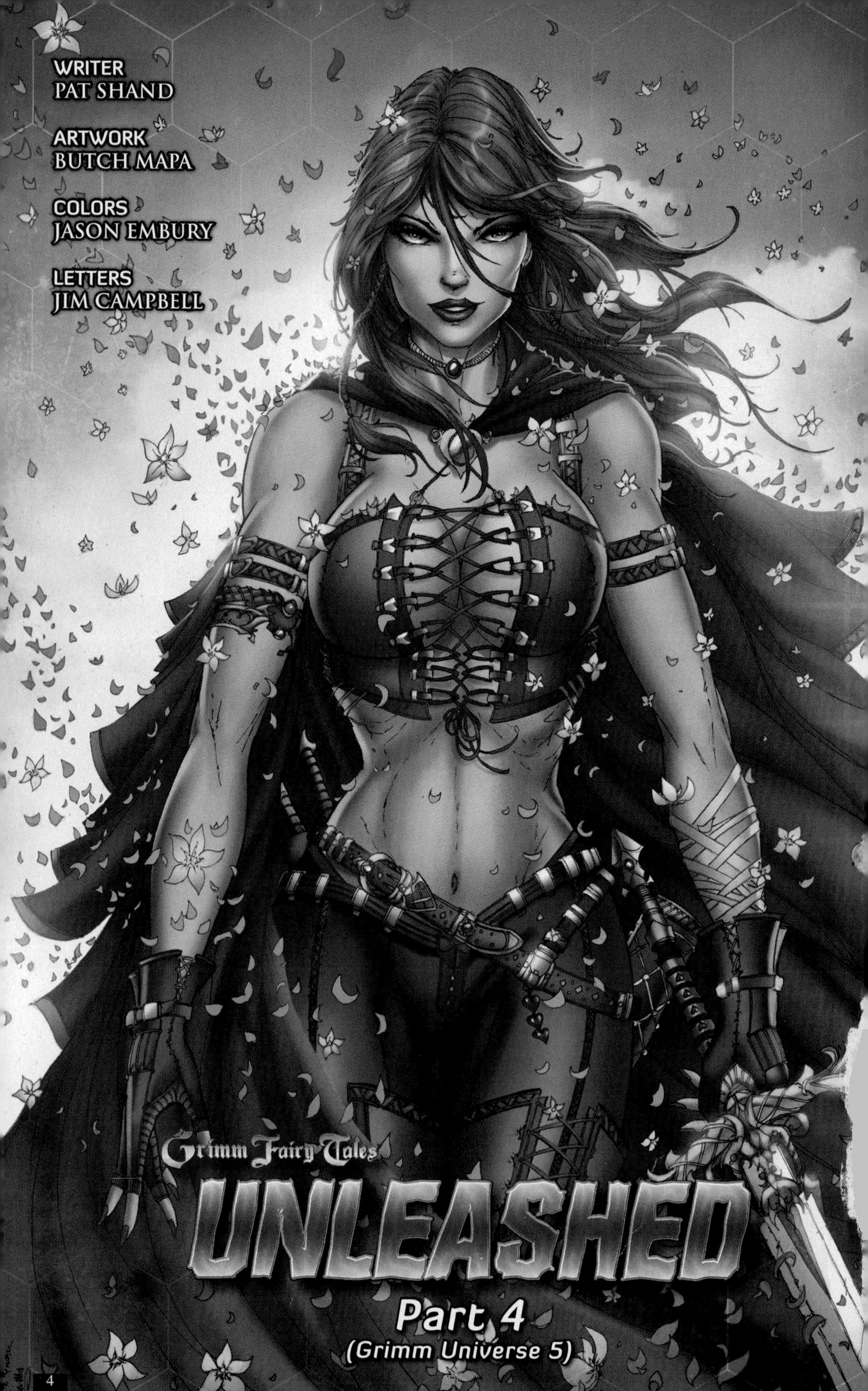
WRITER
PAT SHAND
ARTWORK
BUTCH MAPA
COLORS
JASON EMBURY
LETTERS
JIM CAMPBELL
Grimm Fairy Tales
UNLEASHED
Part 4
(Grimm Universe 5)

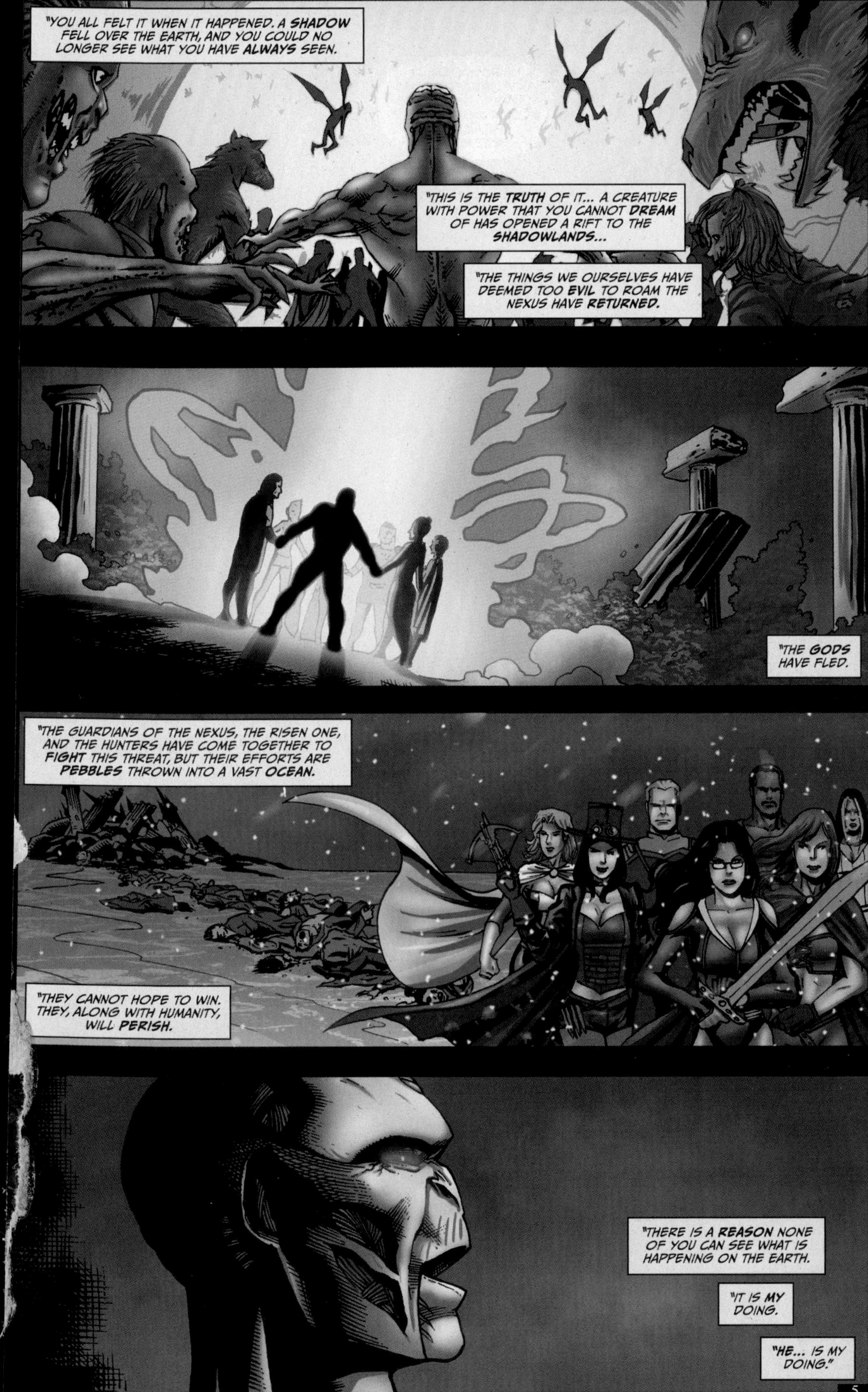
"YOU ALL FELT IT WHEN IT HAPPENED. A SHADOW FELL OVER THE EARTH, AND YOU COULD NO LONGER SEE WHAT YOU HAVE ALWAYS SEEN.
"THIS IS THE TRUTH OF IT... A CREATURE WITH POWER THAT YOU CANNOT DREAM OF HAS OPENED A RIFT TO THE SHADOWLANDS...
"THE THINGS WE OURSELVES HAVE DEEMED TOO EVIL TO ROAM THE NEXUS HAVE RETURNED.
"THE GODS HAVE FLED.
"THE GUARDIANS OF THE NEXUS, THE RISEN ONE, AND THE HUNTERS HAVE COME TOGETHER TO FIGHT THIS THREAT, BUT THEIR EFFORTS ARE PEBBLES THROWN INTO A VAST OCEAN.
"THEY CANNOT HOPE TO WIN. THEY, ALONG WITH HUMANITY, WILL PERISH.
"THERE IS A REASON NONE OF YOU CAN SEE WHAT IS HAPPENING ON THE EARTH.
"IT IS MY DOING.
"HE... IS MY DOING."

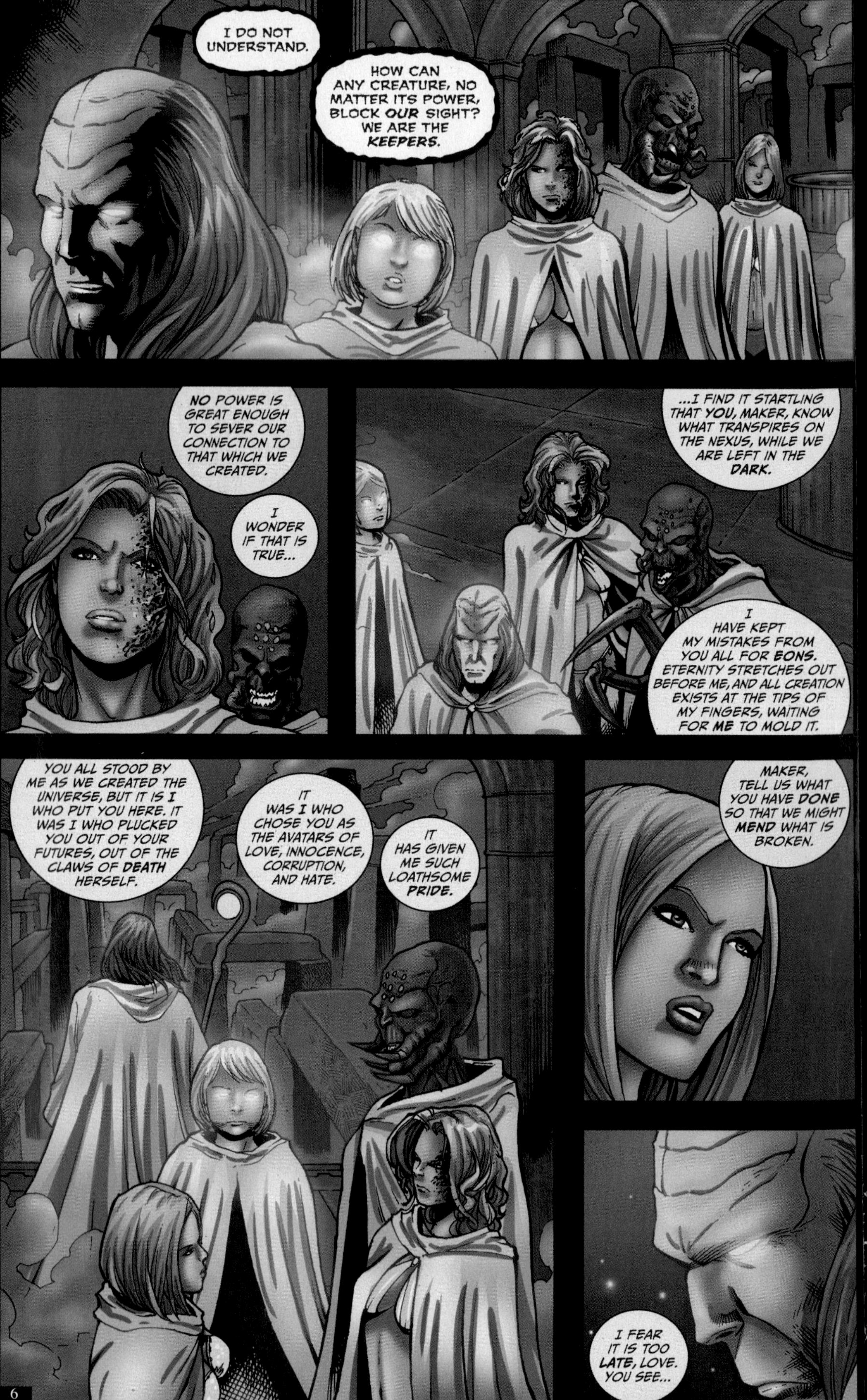
I DO NOT UNDERSTAND.
HOW CAN ANY CREATURE, NO MATTER ITS POWER, BLOCK OUR SIGHT? WE ARE THE KEEPERS.
NO POWER IS GREAT ENOUGH TO SEVER OUR CONNECTION TO THAT WHICH WE CREATED.
I WONDER IF THAT IS TRUE...
...I FIND IT STARTLING THAT YOU, MAKER, KNOW WHAT TRANSPIRES ON THE NEXUS, WHILE WE ARE LEFT IN THE DARK.
I HAVE KEPT MY MISTAKES FROM YOU ALL FOR EONS. ETERNITY STRETCHES OUT BEFORE ME, AND ALL CREATION EXISTS AT THE TIPS OF MY FINGERS, WAITING FOR ME TO MOLD IT.
YOU ALL STOOD BY ME AS WE CREATED THE UNIVERSE, BUT IT IS I WHO PUT YOU HERE. IT WAS I WHO PLUCKED YOU OUT OF YOUR FUTURES, OUT OF THE CLAWS OF DEATH HERSELF.
IT WAS I WHO CHOSE YOU AS THE AVATARS OF LOVE, INNOCENCE, CORRUPTION, AND HATE.
IT HAS GIVEN ME SUCH LOATHSOME PRIDE.
MAKER, TELL US WHAT YOU HAVE DONE SO THAT WE MIGHT MEND WHAT IS BROKEN.
I FEAR IT IS TOO LATE, LOVE. YOU SEE...

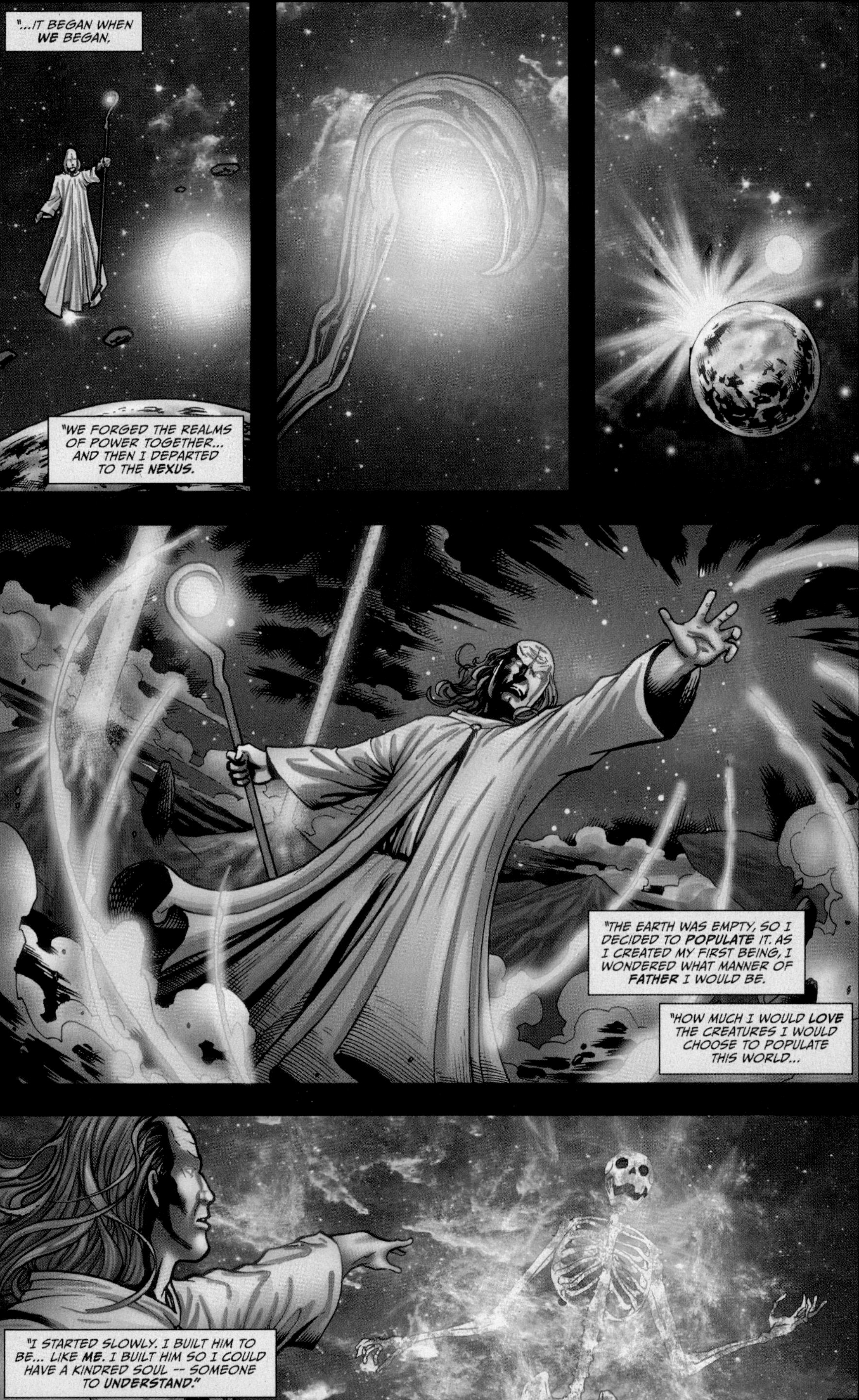
"...IT BEGAN WHEN WE BEGAN.
"WE FORGED THE REALMS OF POWER TOGETHER... AND THEN I DEPARTED TO THE NEXUS.
"THE EARTH WAS EMPTY, SO I DECIDED TO POPULATE IT. AS I CREATED MY FIRST BEING, I WONDERED WHAT MANNER OF FATHER I WOULD BE.
"HOW MUCH I WOULD LOVE THE CREATURES I WOULD CHOOSE TO POPULATE THIS WORLD...
"I STARTED SLOWLY. I BUILT HIM TO BE... LIKE ME. I BUILT HIM SO I COULD HAVE A KINDRED SOUL -- SOMEONE TO UNDERSTAND."

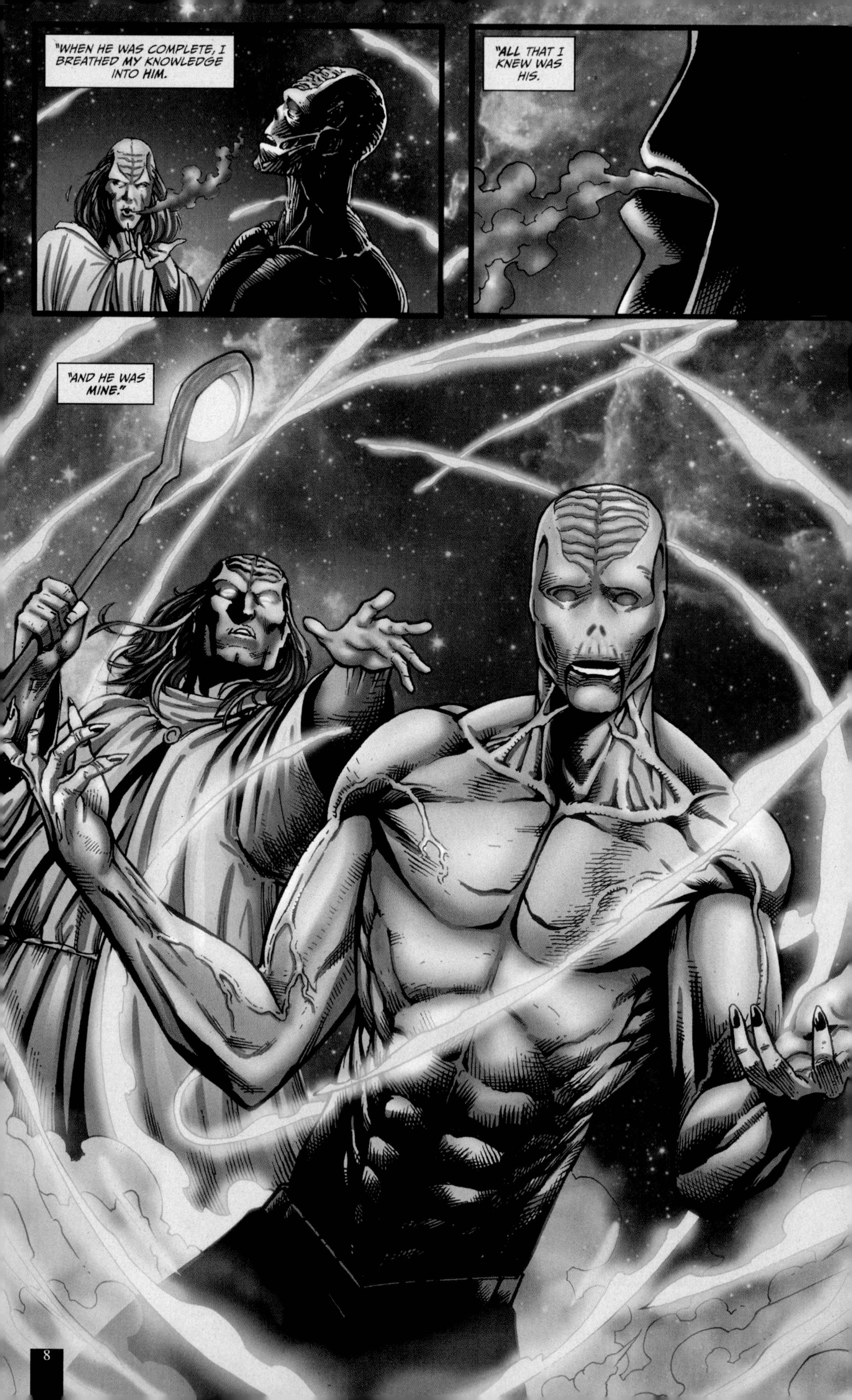
"WHEN HE WAS COMPLETE, I BREATHED MY KNOWLEDGE INTO HIM.
"ALL THAT I KNEW WAS HIS.
"AND HE WAS MINE."

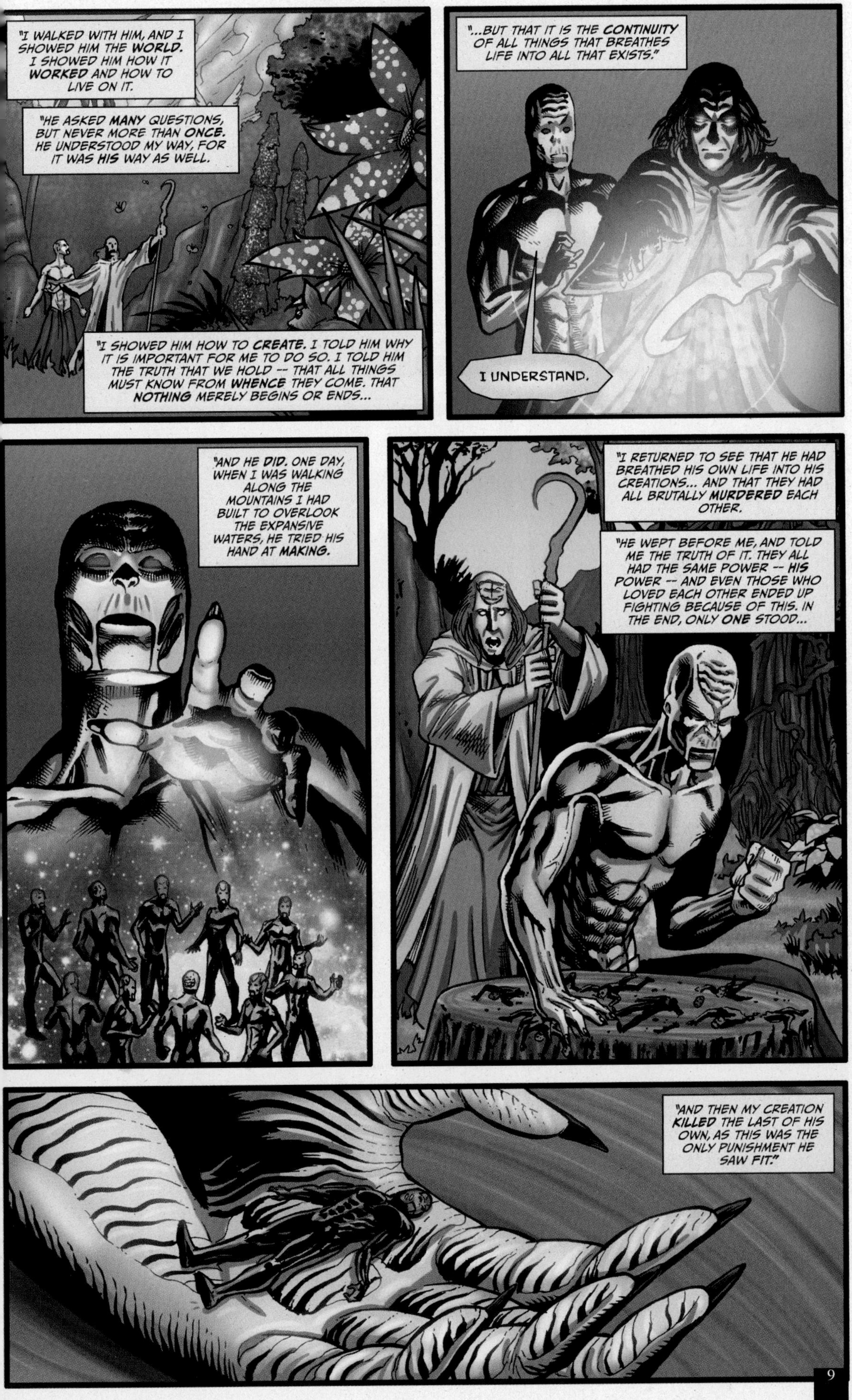

"I WALKED WITH HIM, AND I SHOWED HIM THE WORLD. I SHOWED HIM HOW IT WORKED AND HOW TO LIVE ON IT.
"HE ASKED MANY QUESTIONS, BUT NEVER MORE THAN ONCE. HE UNDERSTOOD MY WAY, FOR IT WAS HIS WAY AS WELL.
"I SHOWED HIM HOW TO CREATE. I TOLD HIM WHY IT IS IMPORTANT FOR ME TO DO SO. I TOLD HIM THE TRUTH THAT WE HOLD -- THAT ALL THINGS MUST KNOW FROM WHENCE THEY COME. THAT NOTHING MERELY BEGINS OR ENDS...
"...BUT THAT IT IS THE CONTINUITY OF ALL THINGS THAT BREATHES LIFE INTO ALL THAT EXISTS."
I UNDERSTAND.
"AND HE DID. ONE DAY, WHEN I WAS WALKING ALONG THE MOUNTAINS I HAD BUILT TO OVERLOOK THE EXPANSIVE WATERS, HE TRIED HIS HAND AT MAKING.
"I RETURNED TO SEE THAT HE HAD BREATHED HIS OWN LIFE INTO HIS CREATIONS... AND THAT THEY HAD ALL BRUTALLY MURDERED EACH OTHER.
"HE WEPT BEFORE ME, AND TOLD ME THE TRUTH OF IT. THEY ALL HAD THE SAME POWER -- HIS POWER -- AND EVEN THOSE WHO LOVED EACH OTHER ENDED UP FIGHTING BECAUSE OF THIS. IN THE END, ONLY ONE STOOD...
"AND THEN MY CREATION KILLED THE LAST OF HIS OWN, AS THIS WAS THE ONLY PUNISHMENT HE SAW FIT."

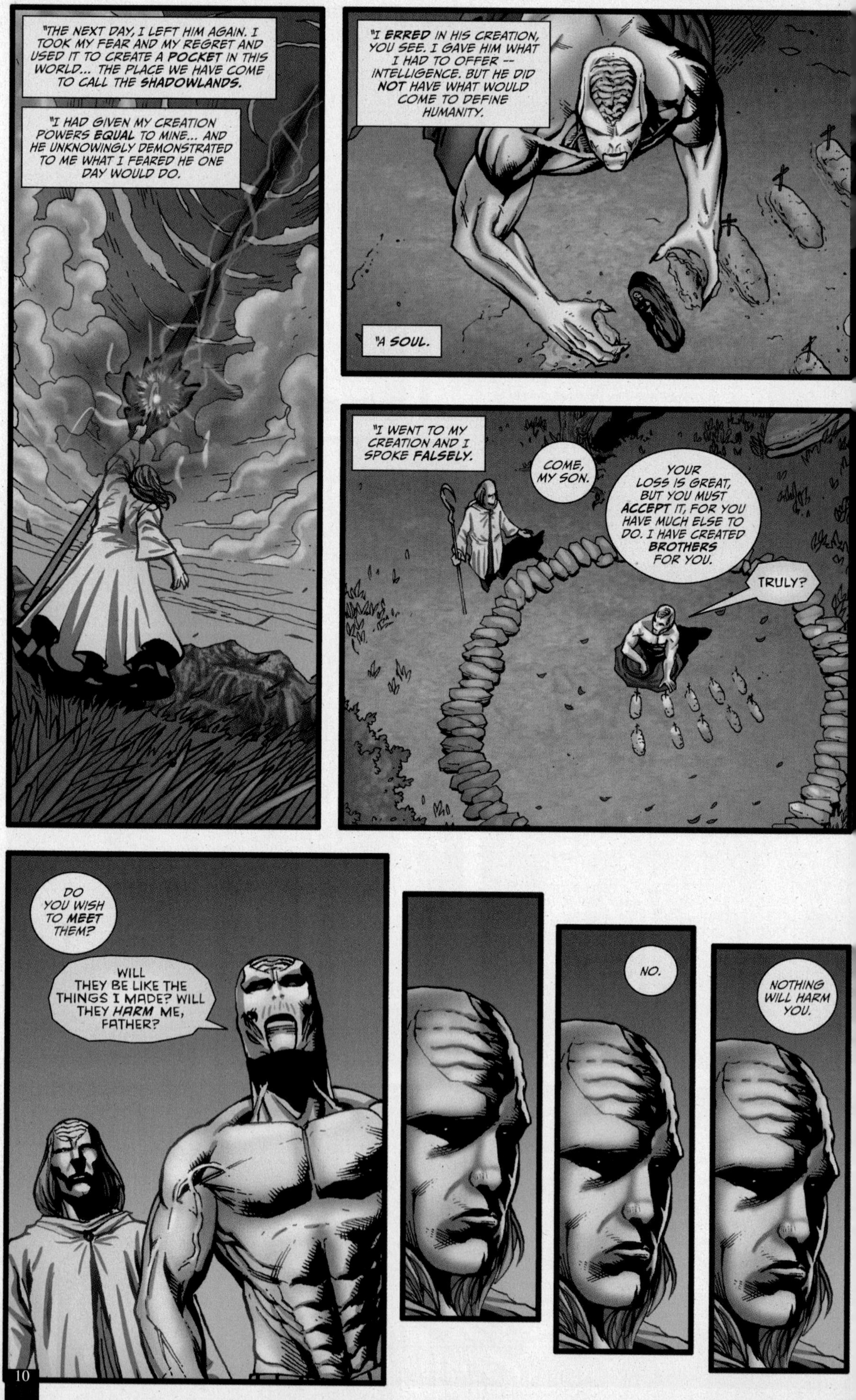
"THE NEXT DAY, I LEFT HIM AGAIN. I TOOK MY FEAR AND MY REGRET AND USED IT TO CREATE A POCKET IN THIS WORLD... THE PLACE WE HAVE COME TO CALL THE SHADOWLANDS.
"I HAD GIVEN MY CREATION POWERS EQUAL TO MINE... AND HE UNKNOWINGLY DEMONSTRATED TO ME WHAT I FEARED HE ONE DAY WOULD DO.
"I ERRED IN HIS CREATION, YOU SEE. I GAVE HIM WHAT I HAD TO OFFER -- INTELLIGENCE. BUT HE DID NOT HAVE WHAT WOULD COME TO DEFINE HUMANITY.
"A SOUL.
"I WENT TO MY CREATION AND I SPOKE FALSELY.
COME, MY SON.
YOUR LOSS IS GREAT, BUT YOU MUST ACCEPT IT, FOR YOU HAVE MUCH ELSE TO DO. I HAVE CREATED BROTHERS FOR YOU.
TRULY?
DO YOU WISH TO MEET THEM?
WILL THEY BE LIKE THE THINGS I MADE? WILL THEY HARM ME, FATHER?
NO.
NOTHING WILL HARM YOU.

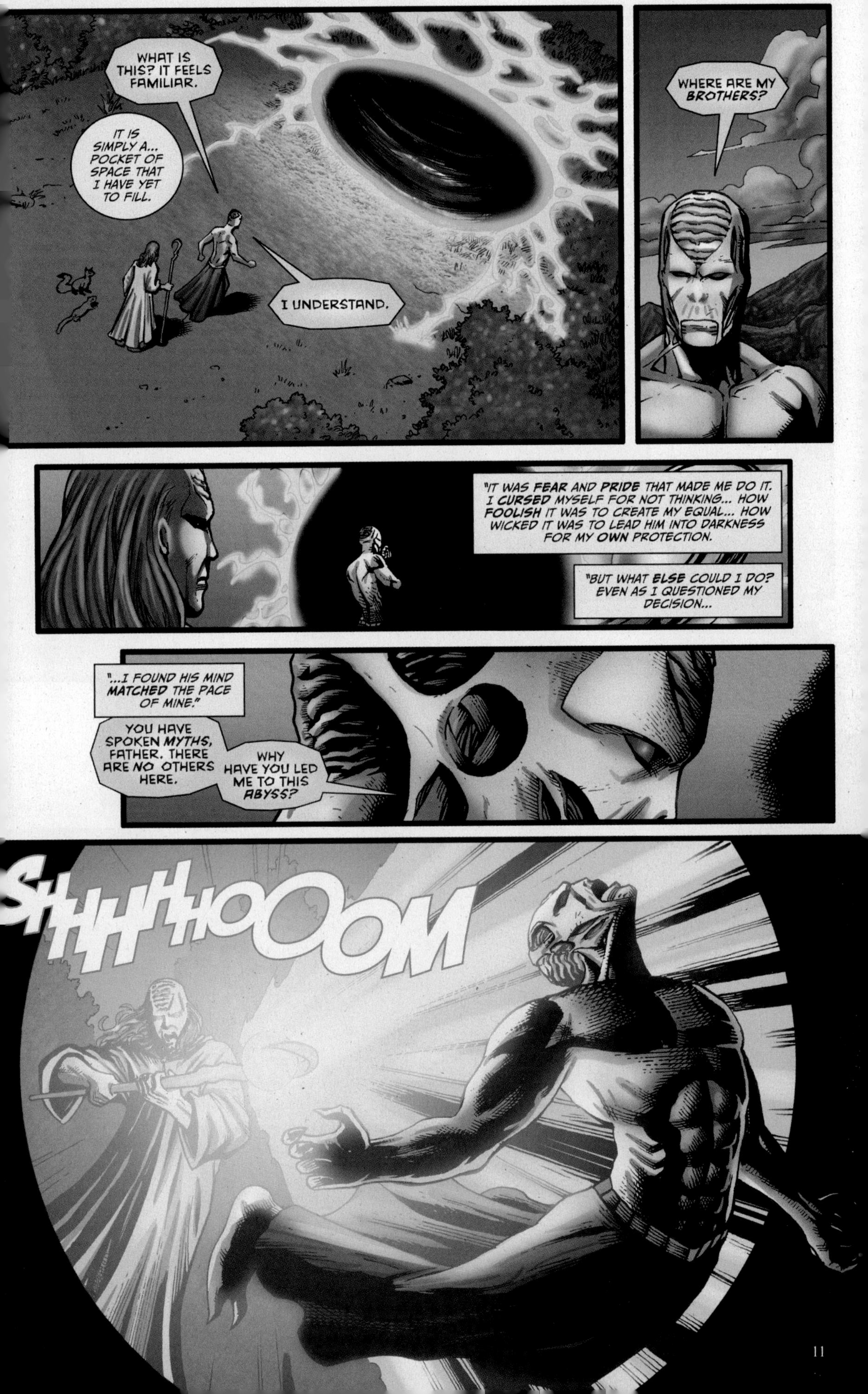
WHAT IS THIS? IT FEELS FAMILIAR.
IT IS SIMPLY A... POCKET OF SPACE THAT I HAVE YET TO FILL.
I UNDERSTAND.
WHERE ARE MY BROTHERS?
"IT WAS FEAR AND PRIDE THAT MADE ME DO IT. I CURSED MYSELF FOR NOT THINKING... HOW FOOLISH IT WAS TO CREATE MY EQUAL... HOW WICKED IT WAS TO LEAD HIM INTO DARKNESS FOR MY OWN PROTECTION.
"BUT WHAT ELSE COULD I DO? EVEN AS I QUESTIONED MY DECISION...
"...I FOUND HIS MIND MATCHED THE PACE OF MINE."
YOU HAVE SPOKEN MYTHS, FATHER. THERE ARE NO OTHERS HERE.
WHY HAVE YOU LED ME TO THIS ABYSS?
SHHHHOOOOM

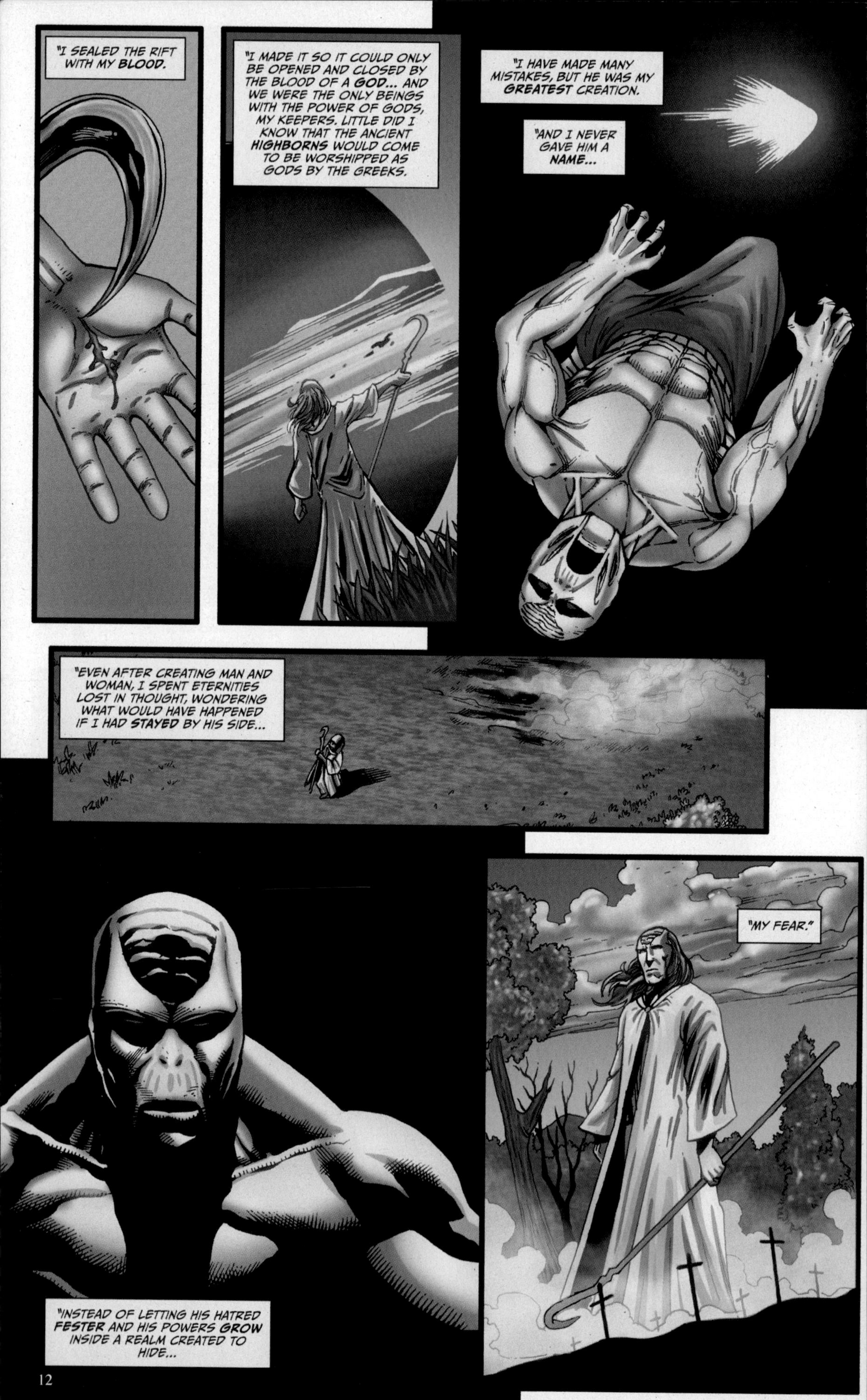
"I SEALED THE RIFT WITH MY BLOOD.
"I MADE IT SO IT COULD ONLY BE OPENED AND CLOSED BY THE BLOOD OF A GOD... AND WE WERE THE ONLY BEINGS WITH THE POWER OF GODS, MY KEEPERS. LITTLE DID I KNOW THAT THE ANCIENT HIGHBORNS WOULD COME TO BE WORSHIPPED AS GODS BY THE GREEKS.
"I HAVE MADE MANY MISTAKES, BUT HE WAS MY GREATEST CREATION.
"AND I NEVER GAVE HIM A NAME...
"EVEN AFTER CREATING MAN AND WOMAN, I SPENT ETERNITIES LOST IN THOUGHT, WONDERING WHAT WOULD HAVE HAPPENED IF I HAD STAYED BY HIS SIDE...
"INSTEAD OF LETTING HIS HATRED FESTER AND HIS POWERS GROW INSIDE A REALM CREATED TO HIDE...
"MY FEAR."

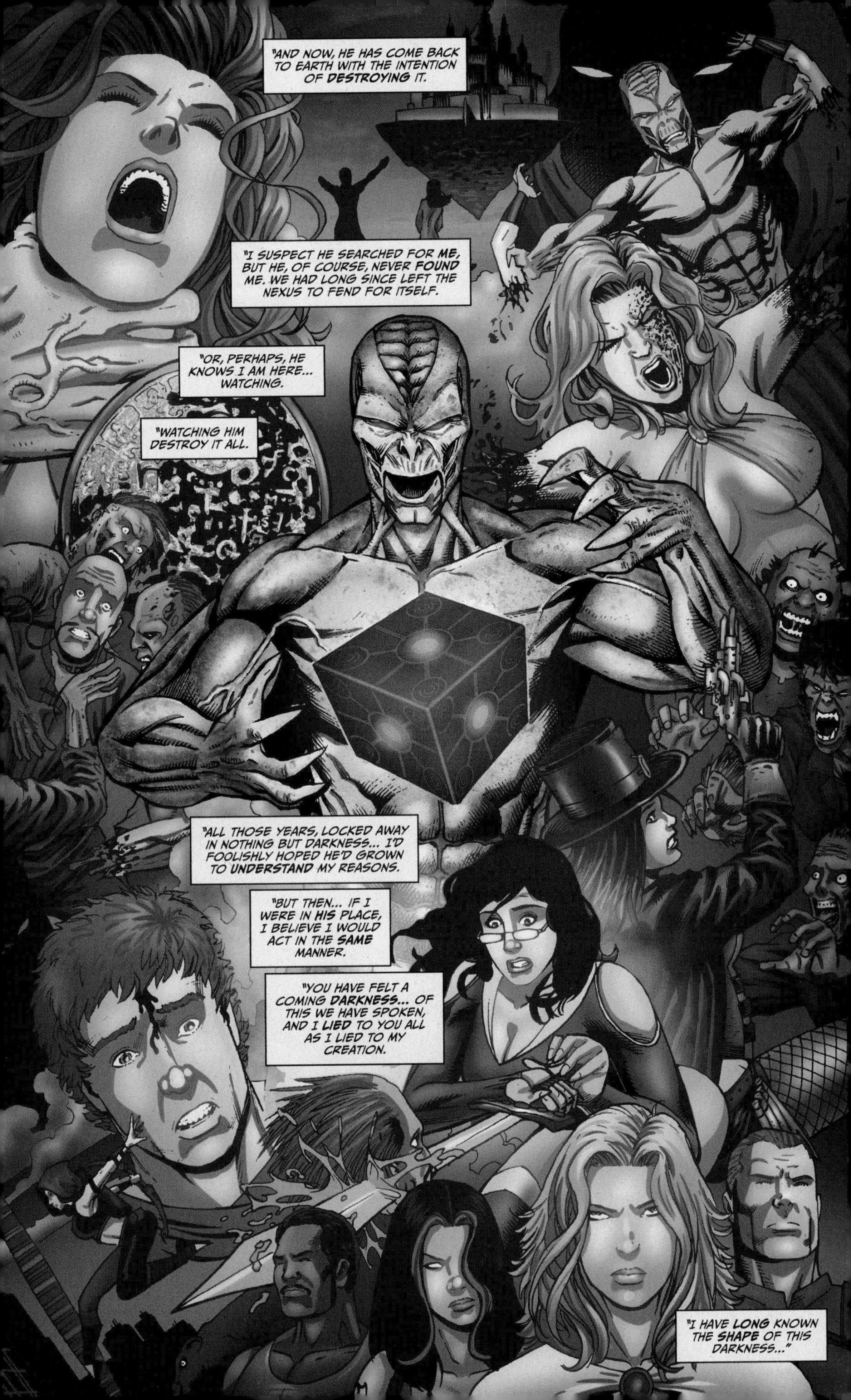

"AND NOW, HE HAS COME BACK TO EARTH WITH THE INTENTION OF DESTROYING IT.
"I SUSPECT HE SEARCHED FOR ME, BUT HE, OF COURSE, NEVER FOUND ME. WE HAD LONG SINCE LEFT THE NEXUS TO FEND FOR ITSELF.
"OR, PERHAPS, HE KNOWS I AM HERE... WATCHING.
"WATCHING HIM DESTROY IT ALL.
"ALL THOSE YEARS, LOCKED AWAY IN NOTHING BUT DARKNESS... I'D FOOLISHLY HOPED HE'D GROWN TO UNDERSTAND MY REASONS.
"BUT THEN... IF I WERE IN HIS PLACE, I BELIEVE I WOULD ACT IN THE SAME MANNER.
"YOU HAVE FELT A COMING DARKNESS... OF THIS WE HAVE SPOKEN, AND I LIED TO YOU ALL AS I LIED TO MY CREATION.
"I HAVE LONG KNOWN THE SHAPE OF THIS DARKNESS..."

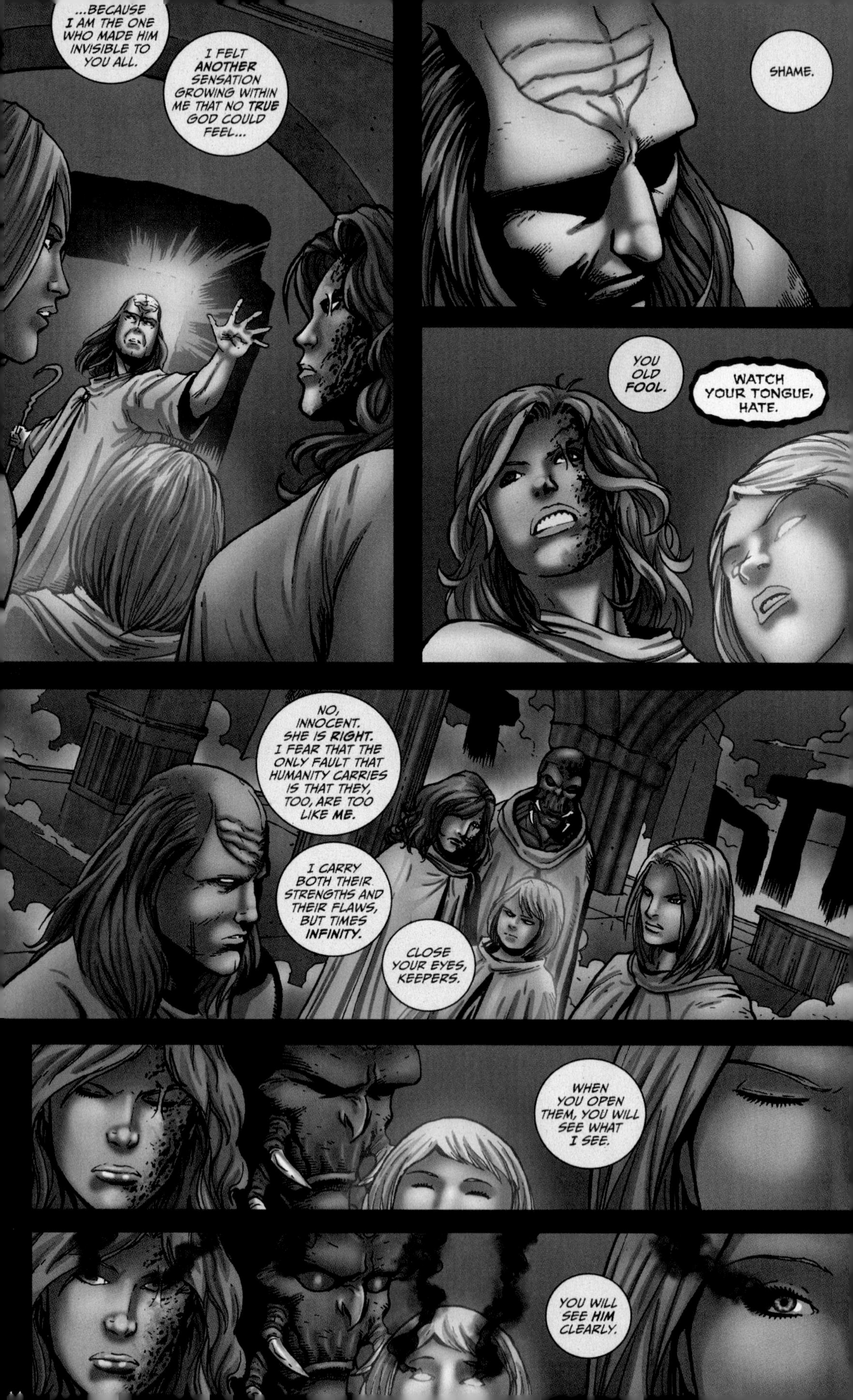
...BECAUSE I AM THE ONE WHO MADE HIM INVISIBLE TO YOU ALL.
I FELT ANOTHER SENSATION GROWING WITHIN ME THAT NO TRUE GOD COULD FEEL...
SHAME.
YOU OLD FOOL.
WATCH YOUR TONGUE, HATE.
NO, INNOCENT. SHE IS RIGHT. I FEAR THAT THE ONLY FAULT THAT HUMANITY CARRIES IS THAT THEY, TOO, ARE TOO LIKE ME.
I CARRY BOTH THEIR STRENGTHS AND THEIR FLAWS, BUT TIMES INFINITY.
CLOSE YOUR EYES, KEEPERS.
WHEN YOU OPEN THEM, YOU WILL SEE WHAT I SEE.
YOU WILL SEE HIM CLEARLY.

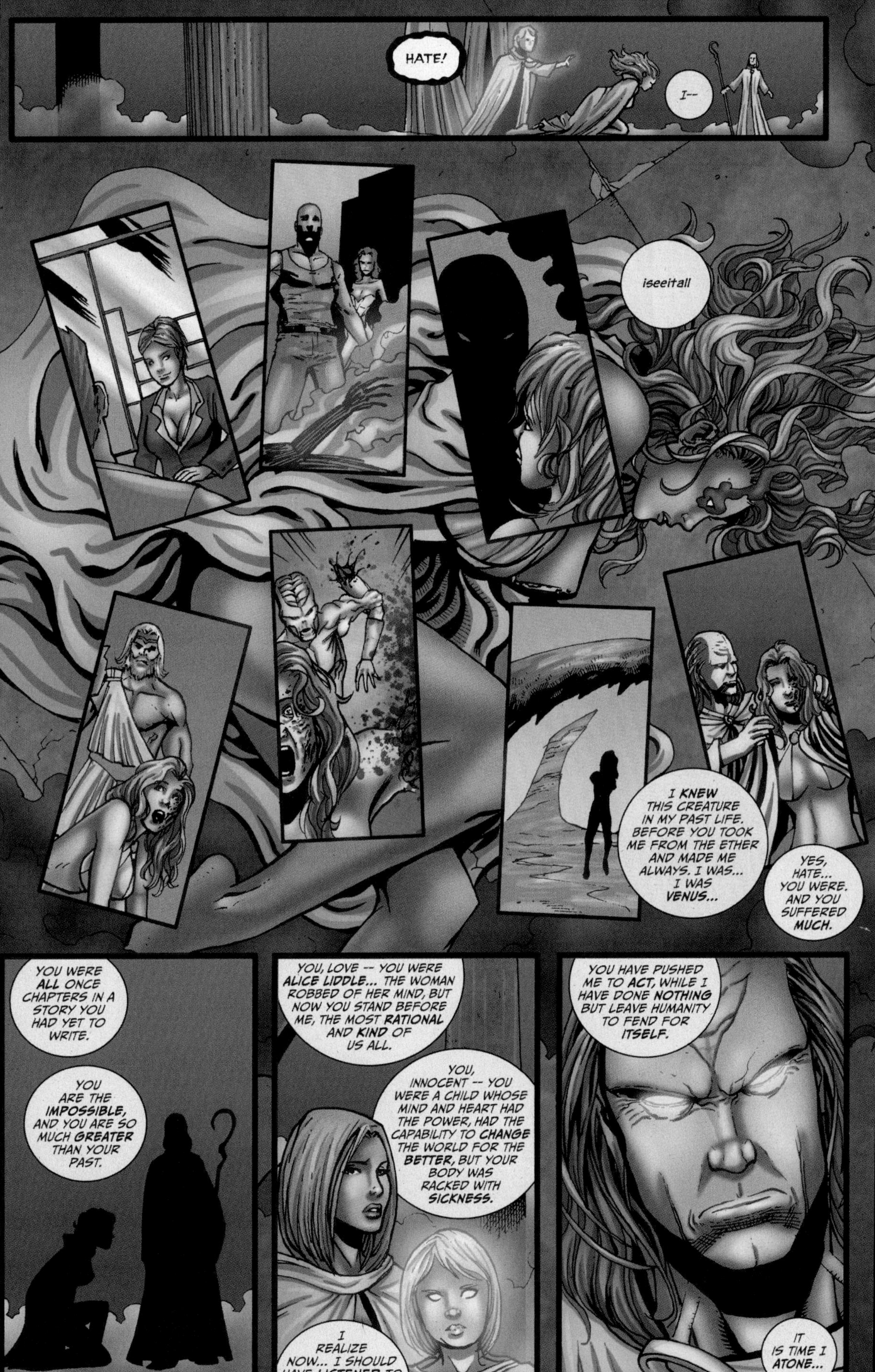
HATE!
I--
iseeitall
I KNEW THIS CREATURE IN MY PAST LIFE. BEFORE YOU TOOK ME FROM THE ETHER AND MADE ME ALWAYS. I WAS... I WAS VENUS...
YES, HATE... YOU WERE. AND YOU SUFFERED MUCH.
YOU WERE ALL ONCE CHAPTERS IN A STORY YOU HAD YET TO WRITE.
YOU ARE THE IMPOSSIBLE, AND YOU ARE SO MUCH GREATER THAN YOUR PAST.
YOU, LOVE -- YOU WERE ALICE LIDDLE... THE WOMAN ROBBED OF HER MIND, BUT NOW YOU STAND BEFORE ME, THE MOST RATIONAL AND KIND OF US ALL.
YOU, INNOCENT -- YOU WERE A CHILD WHOSE MIND AND HEART HAD THE POWER, HAD THE CAPABILITY TO CHANGE THE WORLD FOR THE BETTER, BUT YOUR BODY WAS RACKED WITH SICKNESS.
I REALIZE NOW... I SHOULD HAVE LISTENED TO YOU ALL ALONG.
YOU HAVE PUSHED ME TO ACT, WHILE I HAVE DONE NOTHING BUT LEAVE HUMANITY TO FEND FOR ITSELF.
IT IS TIME I ATONE...

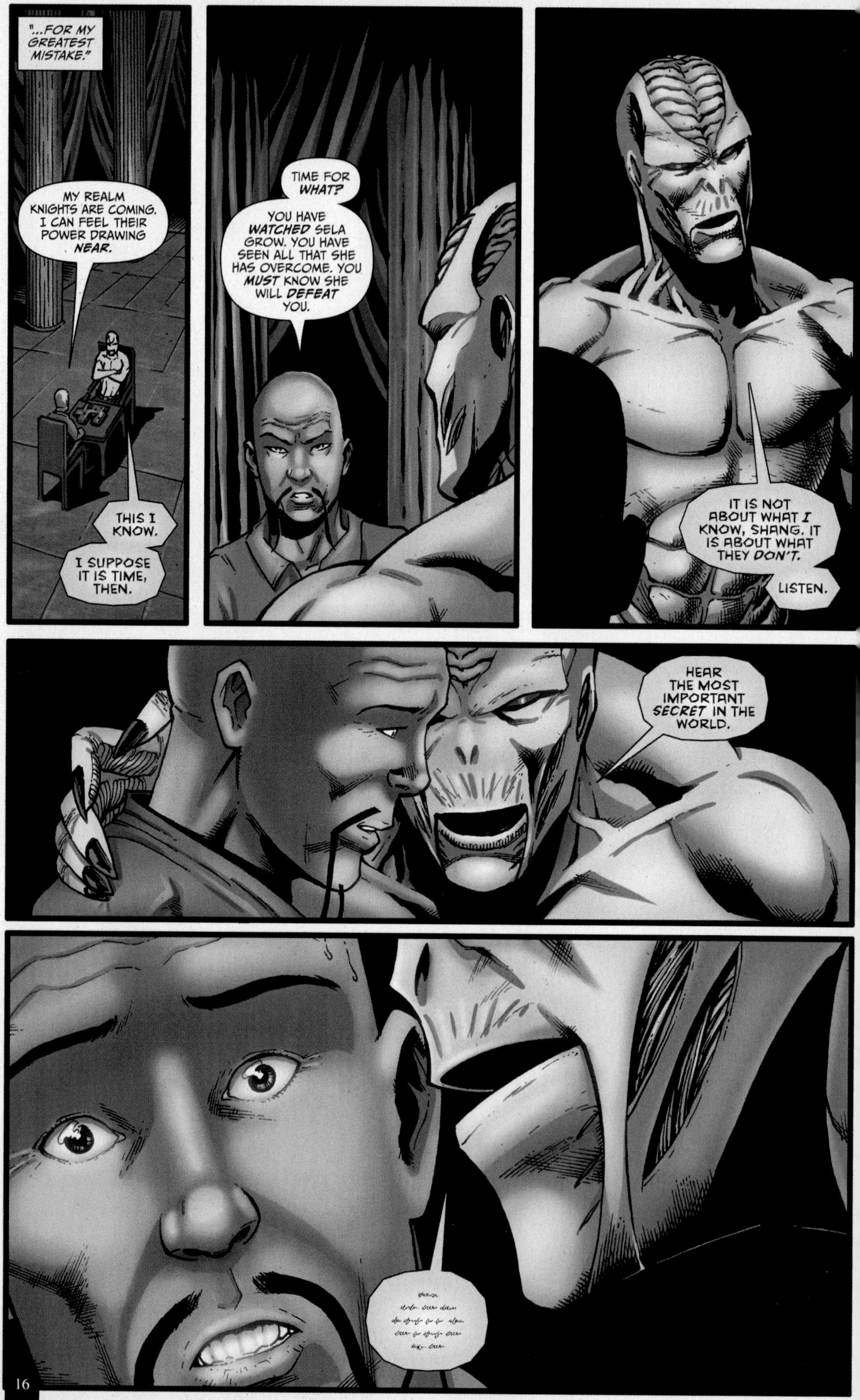
"...FOR MY GREATEST MISTAKE."
MY REALM KNIGHTS ARE COMING. I CAN FEEL THEIR POWER DRAWING NEAR.
THIS I KNOW.
I SUPPOSE IT IS TIME, THEN.
TIME FOR WHAT?
YOU HAVE WATCHED SELA GROW. YOU HAVE SEEN ALL THAT SHE HAS OVERCOME. YOU MUST KNOW SHE WILL DEFEAT YOU.
IT IS NOT ABOUT WHAT I KNOW, SHANG. IT IS ABOUT WHAT THEY DON'T.
LISTEN.
HEAR THE MOST IMPORTANT SECRET IN THE WORLD.

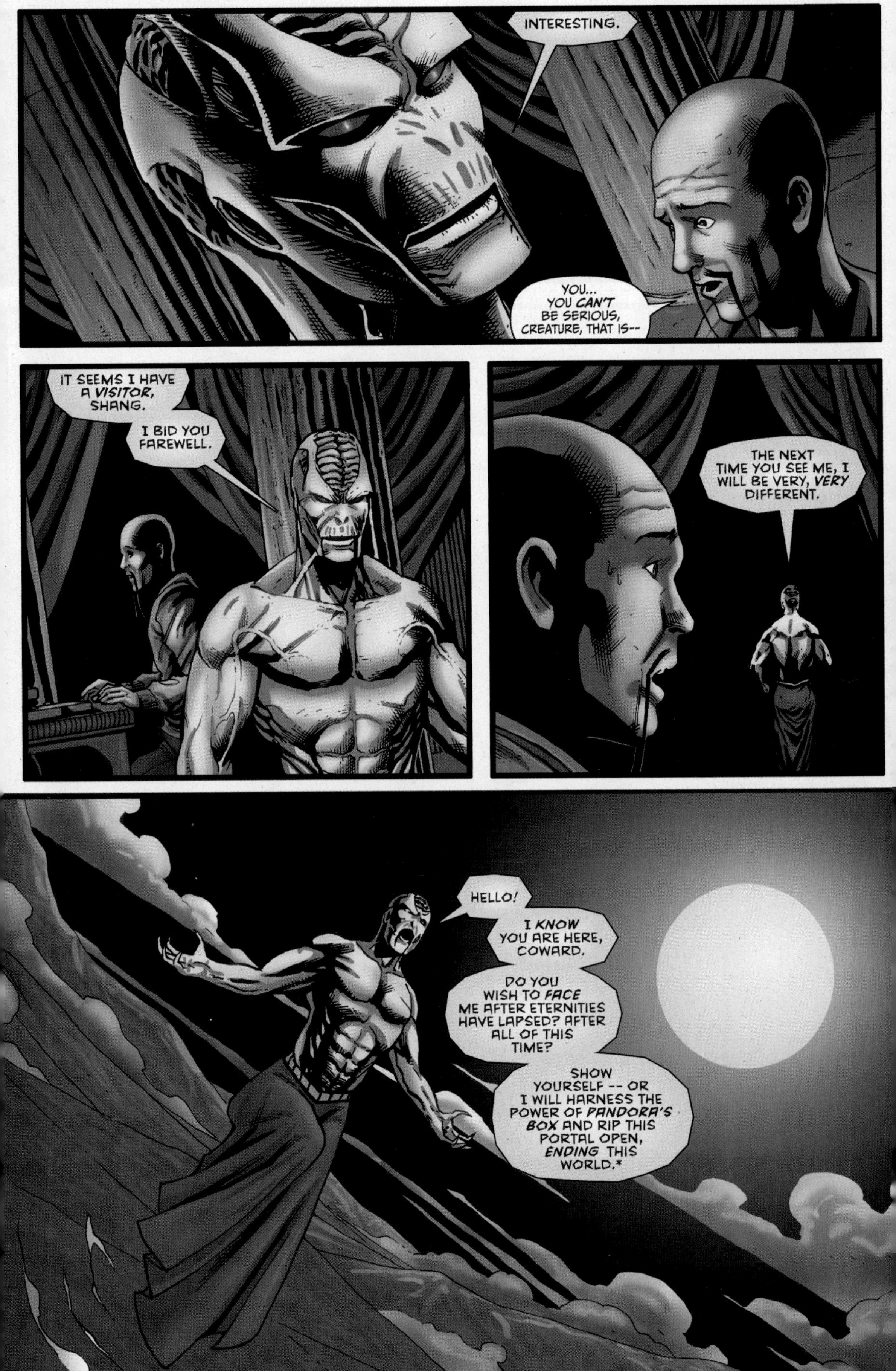
INTERESTING.
YOU... YOU *CAN'T* BE SERIOUS, CREATURE, THAT IS--
IT SEEMS I HAVE A *VISITOR*, SHANG.
I BID YOU FAREWELL.
THE NEXT TIME YOU SEE ME, I WILL BE VERY, *VERY* DIFFERENT.
HELLO!
I *KNOW* YOU ARE HERE, COWARD.
DO YOU WISH TO *FACE* ME AFTER ETERNITIES HAVE LAPSED? AFTER ALL OF THIS TIME?
SHOW YOURSELF -- OR I WILL HARNESS THE POWER OF *PANDORA'S BOX* AND RIP THIS PORTAL OPEN, *ENDING* THIS WORLD.*
*See last issue.

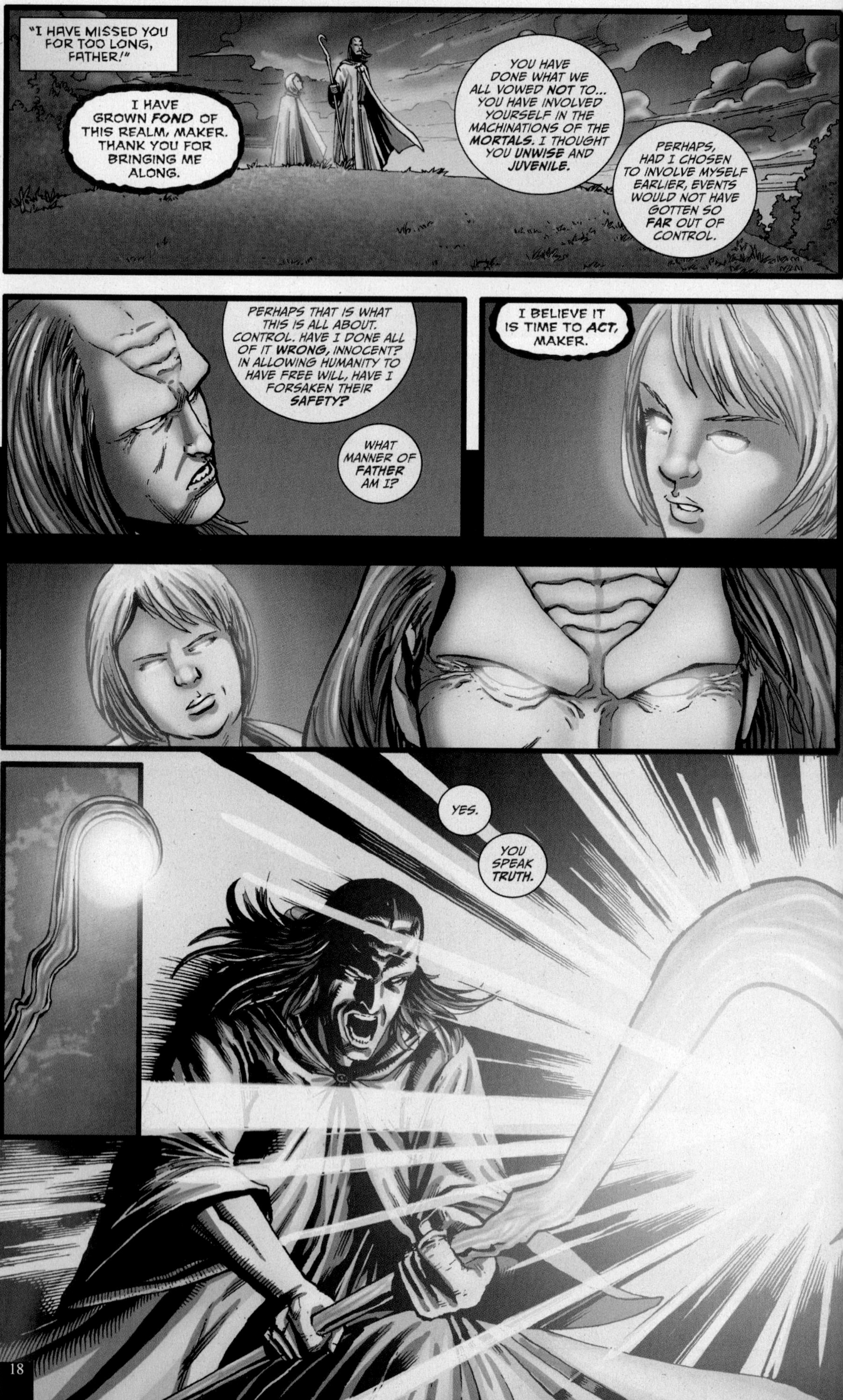
"I HAVE MISSED YOU FOR TOO LONG, FATHER!"
I HAVE GROWN FOND OF THIS REALM, MAKER. THANK YOU FOR BRINGING ME ALONG.
YOU HAVE DONE WHAT WE ALL VOWED NOT TO... YOU HAVE INVOLVED YOURSELF IN THE MACHINATIONS OF THE MORTALS. I THOUGHT YOU UNWISE AND JUVENILE.
PERHAPS, HAD I CHOSEN TO INVOLVE MYSELF EARLIER, EVENTS WOULD NOT HAVE GOTTEN SO FAR OUT OF CONTROL.
PERHAPS THAT IS WHAT THIS IS ALL ABOUT. CONTROL. HAVE I DONE ALL OF IT WRONG, INNOCENT? IN ALLOWING HUMANITY TO HAVE FREE WILL, HAVE I FORSAKEN THEIR SAFETY?
WHAT MANNER OF FATHER AM I?
I BELIEVE IT IS TIME TO ACT, MAKER.
YES.
YOU SPEAK TRUTH.

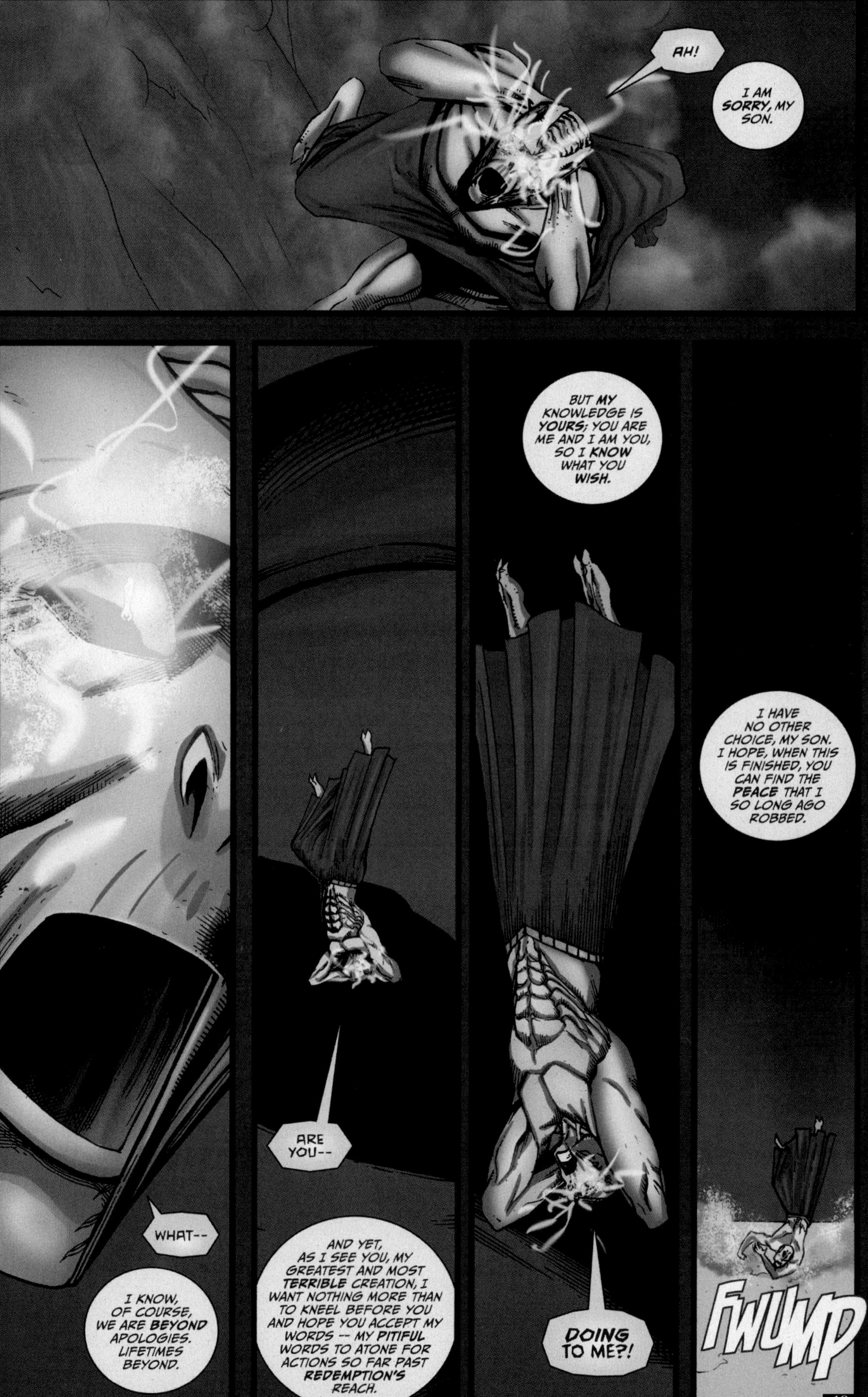
AH!
I AM SORRY, MY SON.
WHAT--
I KNOW, OF COURSE, WE ARE BEYOND APOLOGIES. LIFETIMES BEYOND.
ARE YOU--
AND YET, AS I SEE YOU, MY GREATEST AND MOST TERRIBLE CREATION, I WANT NOTHING MORE THAN TO KNEEL BEFORE YOU AND HOPE YOU ACCEPT MY WORDS -- MY PITIFUL WORDS TO ATONE FOR ACTIONS SO FAR PAST REDEMPTION'S REACH.
BUT MY KNOWLEDGE IS YOURS; YOU ARE ME AND I AM YOU, SO I KNOW WHAT YOU WISH.
DOING TO ME?!
I HAVE NO OTHER CHOICE, MY SON. I HOPE, WHEN THIS IS FINISHED, YOU CAN FIND THE PEACE THAT I SO LONG AGO ROBBED.
FWUMP

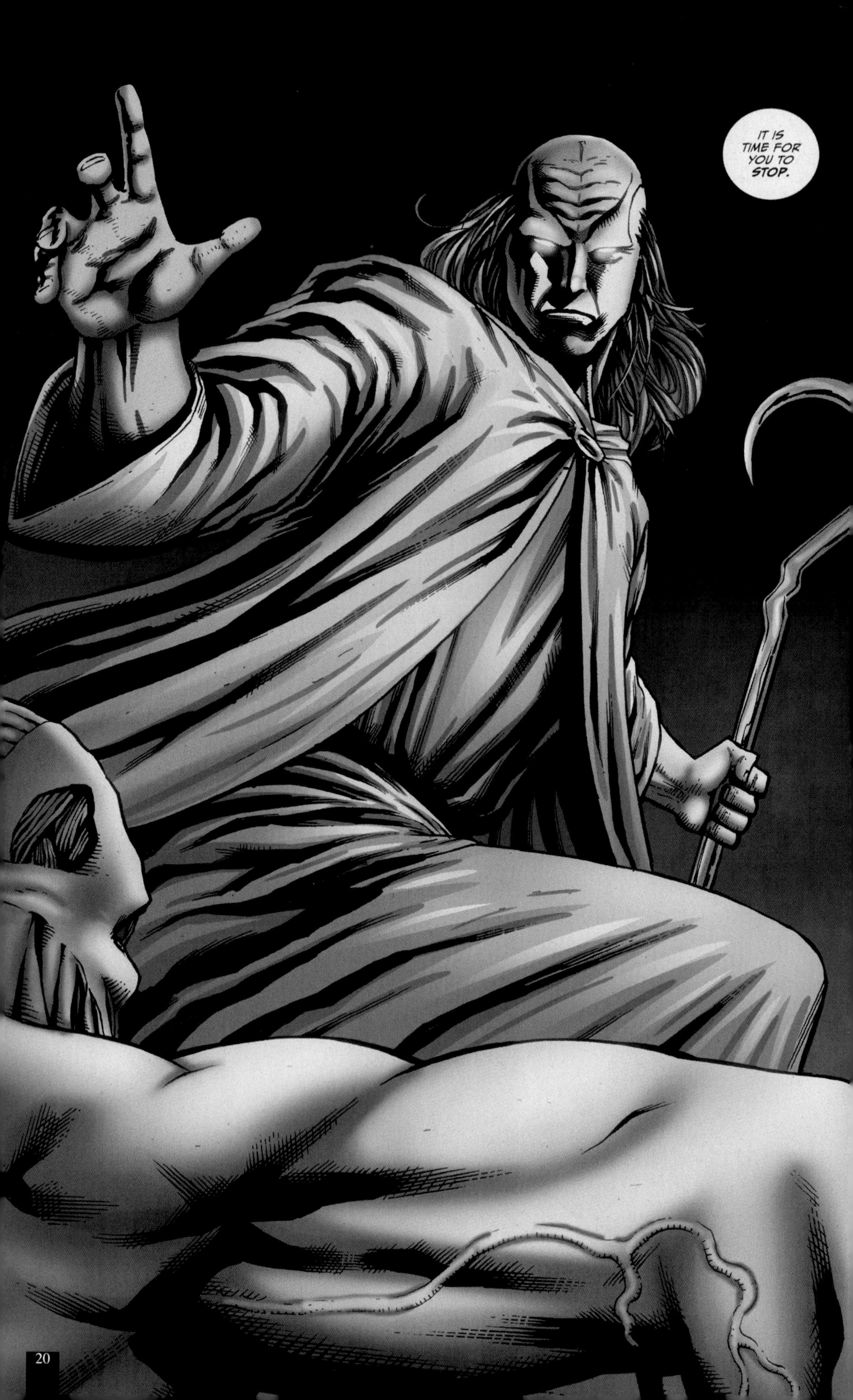
IT IS TIME FOR YOU TO STOP.

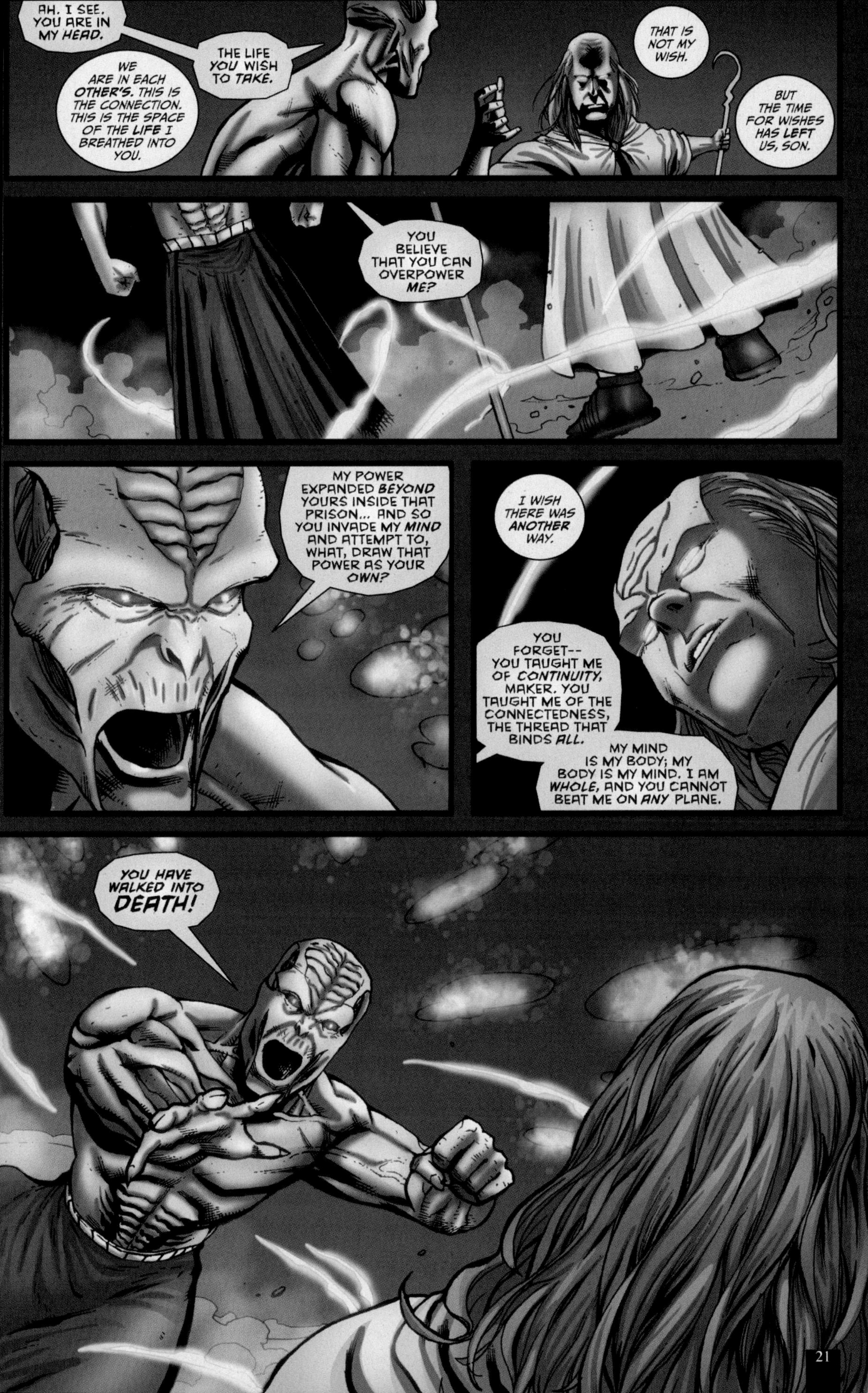

AH. I SEE. YOU ARE IN MY HEAD.
WE ARE IN EACH OTHER'S. THIS IS THE CONNECTION. THIS IS THE SPACE OF THE LIFE I BREATHED INTO YOU.
THE LIFE YOU WISH TO TAKE.
THAT IS NOT MY WISH.
BUT THE TIME FOR WISHES HAS LEFT US, SON.
YOU BELIEVE THAT YOU CAN OVERPOWER ME?
MY POWER EXPANDED BEYOND YOURS INSIDE THAT PRISON... AND SO YOU INVADE MY MIND AND ATTEMPT TO, WHAT, DRAW THAT POWER AS YOUR OWN?
I WISH THERE WAS ANOTHER WAY.
YOU FORGET-- YOU TAUGHT ME OF CONTINUITY, MAKER. YOU TAUGHT ME OF THE CONNECTEDNESS, THE THREAD THAT BINDS ALL.
MY MIND IS MY BODY; MY BODY IS MY MIND. I AM WHOLE, AND YOU CANNOT BEAT ME ON ANY PLANE.
YOU HAVE WALKED INTO DEATH!

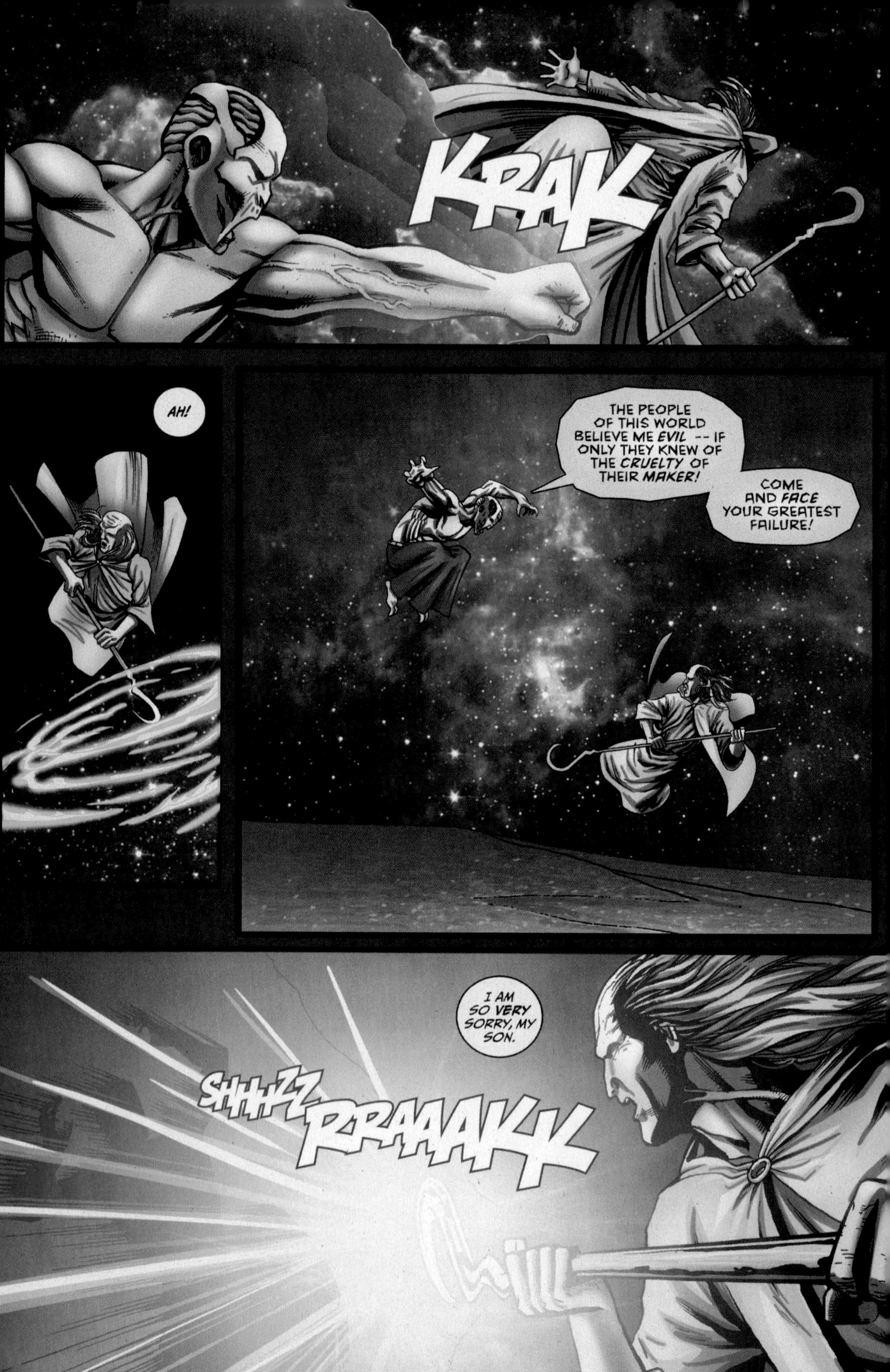
KRAK
AH!
THE PEOPLE OF THIS WORLD BELIEVE ME EVIL -- IF ONLY THEY KNEW OF THE CRUELTY OF THEIR MAKER!
COME AND FACE YOUR GREATEST FAILURE!
I AM SO VERY SORRY, MY SON.
SHHHZZ
RRAAAKK

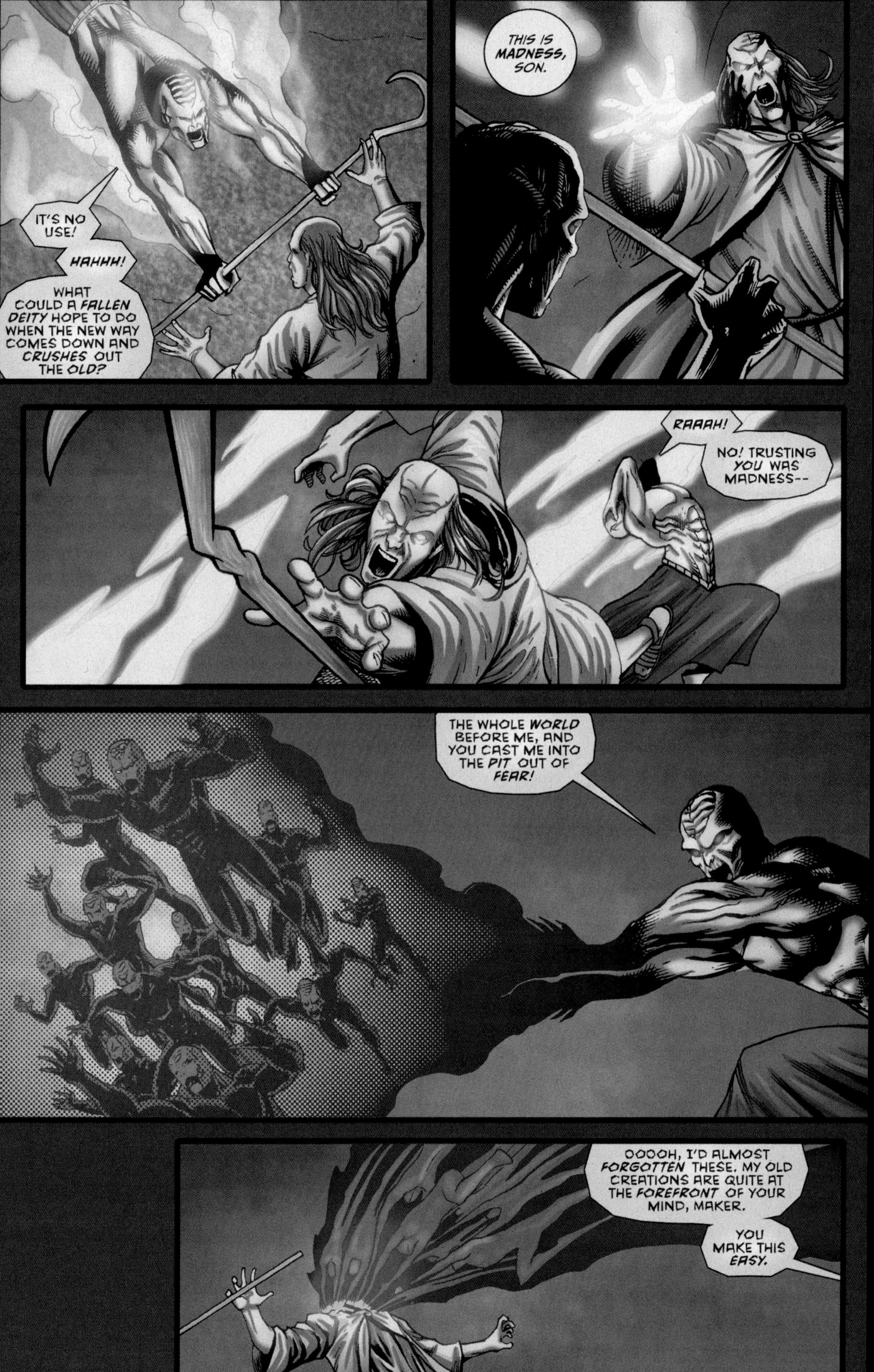
IT'S NO USE!
HAHHH!
WHAT COULD A FALLEN DEITY HOPE TO DO WHEN THE NEW WAY COMES DOWN AND CRUSHES OUT THE OLD?
THIS IS MADNESS, SON.
RAAAH!
NO! TRUSTING YOU WAS MADNESS--
THE WHOLE WORLD BEFORE ME, AND YOU CAST ME INTO THE PIT OUT OF FEAR!
OOOOH, I'D ALMOST FORGOTTEN THESE. MY OLD CREATIONS ARE QUITE AT THE FOREFRONT OF YOUR MIND, MAKER.
YOU MAKE THIS EASY.

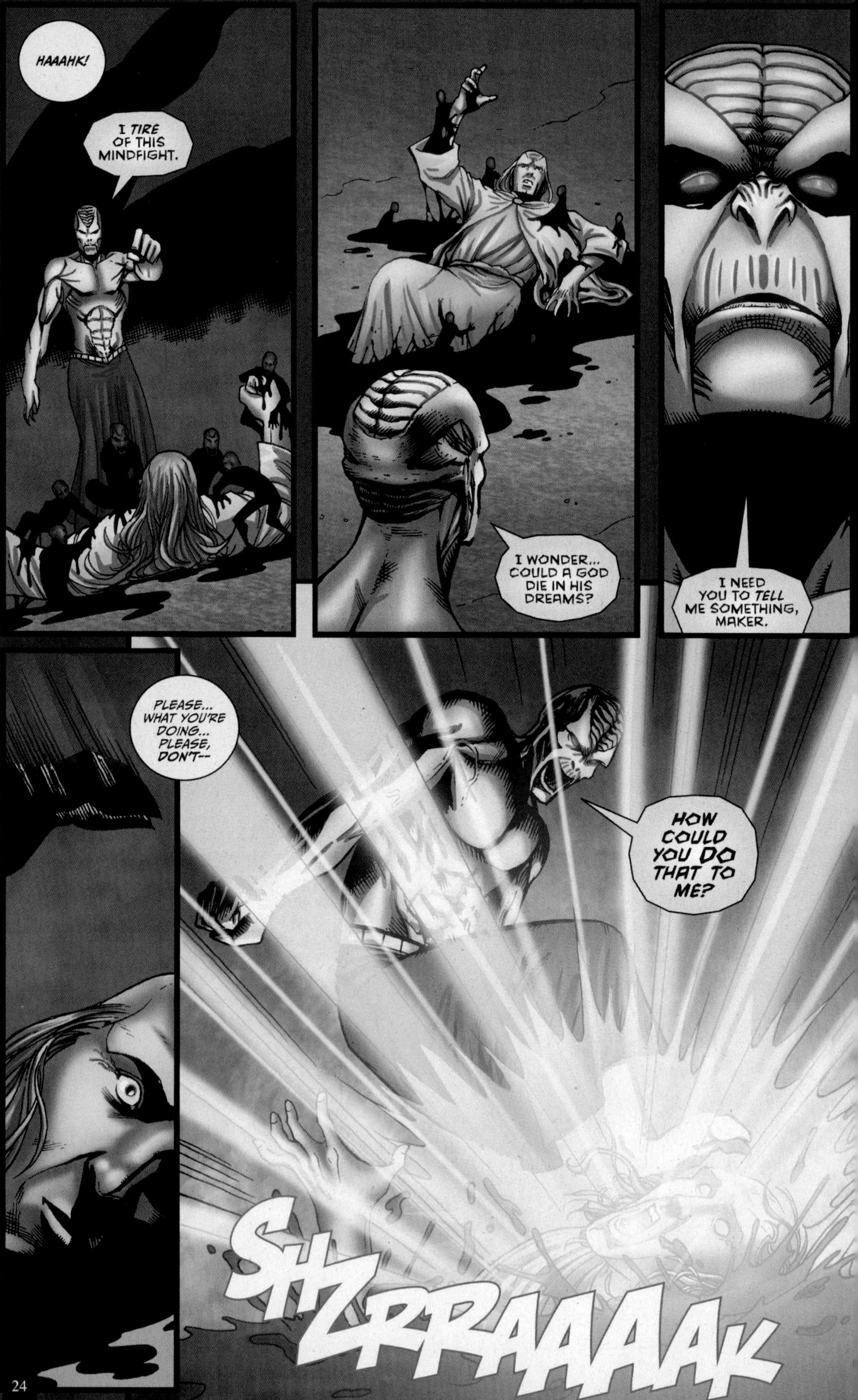
HAAAHK!
I TIRE OF THIS MINDFIGHT.
I WONDER... COULD A GOD DIE IN HIS DREAMS?
I NEED YOU TO TELL ME SOMETHING, MAKER.
PLEASE... WHAT YOU'RE DOING... PLEASE, DON'T--
HOW COULD YOU DO THAT TO ME?
SHZRRAAAAK

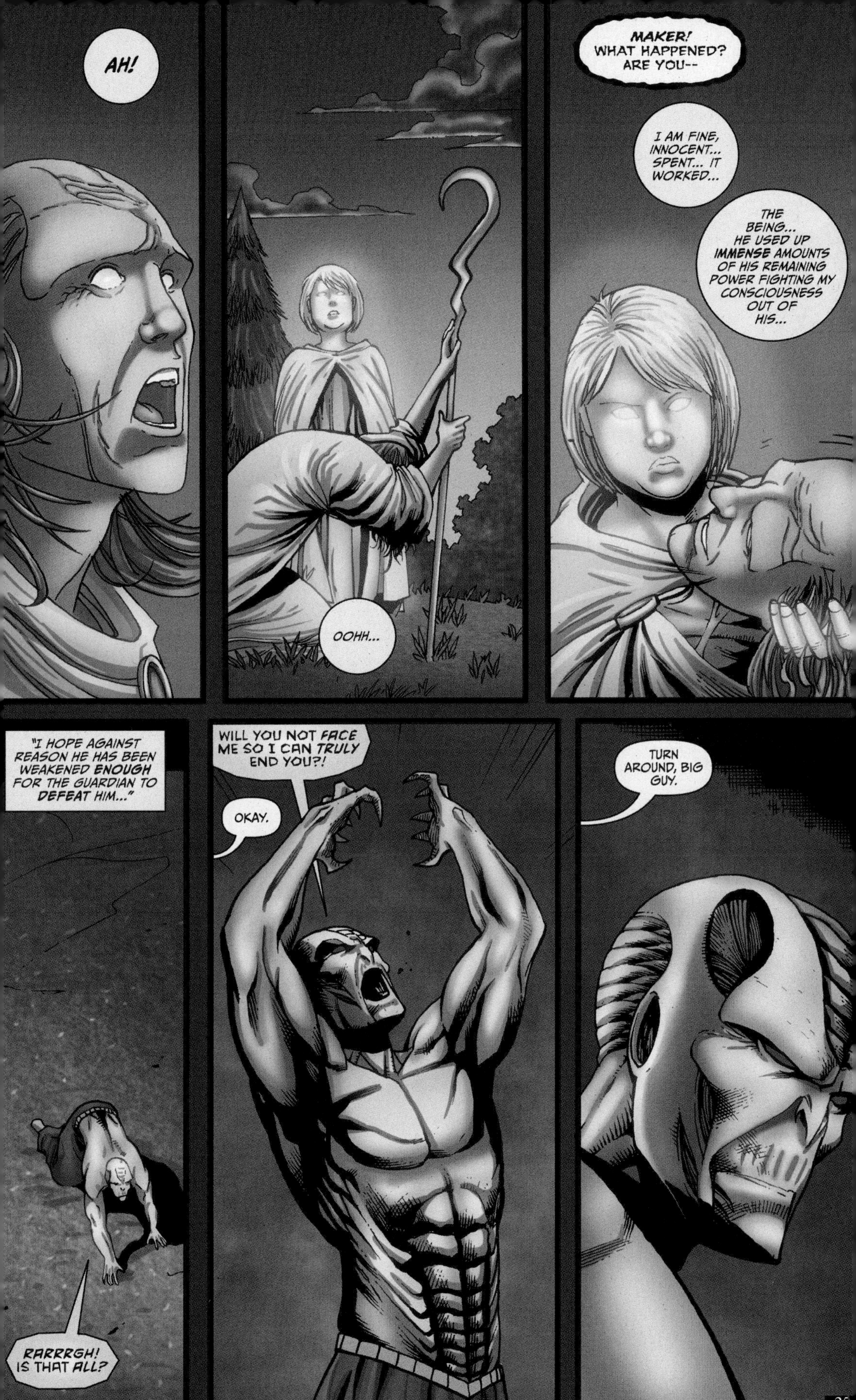
AH!
OOHH...
MAKER! WHAT HAPPENED? ARE YOU--
I AM FINE, INNOCENT... SPENT... IT WORKED...
THE BEING... HE USED UP IMMENSE AMOUNTS OF HIS REMAINING POWER FIGHTING MY CONSCIOUSNESS OUT OF HIS...
"I HOPE AGAINST REASON HE HAS BEEN WEAKENED ENOUGH FOR THE GUARDIAN TO DEFEAT HIM..."
RARRRGH! IS THAT ALL?
WILL YOU NOT FACE ME SO I CAN TRULY END YOU?!
OKAY.
TURN AROUND, BIG GUY.

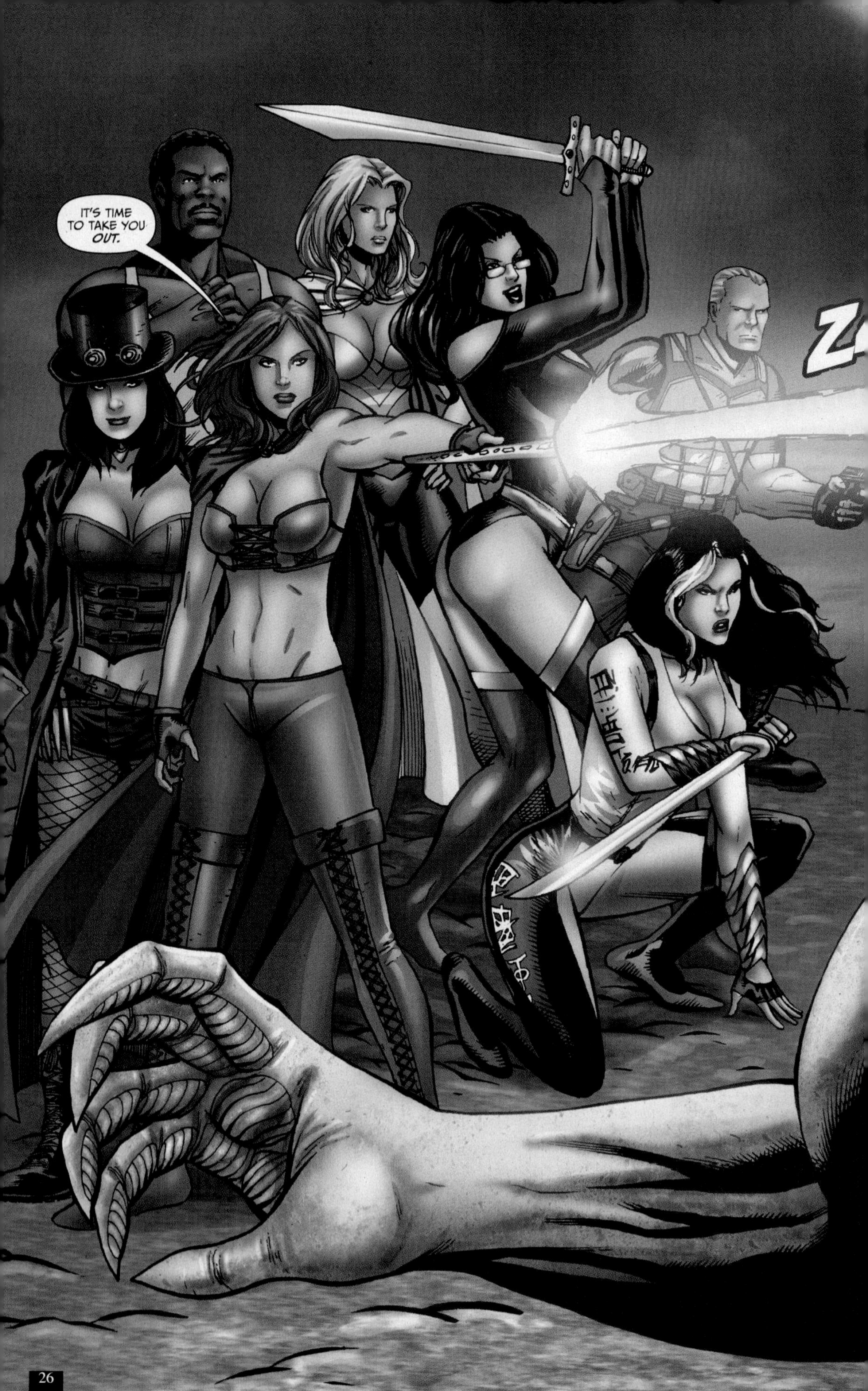
IT'S TIME TO TAKE YOU *OUT.*

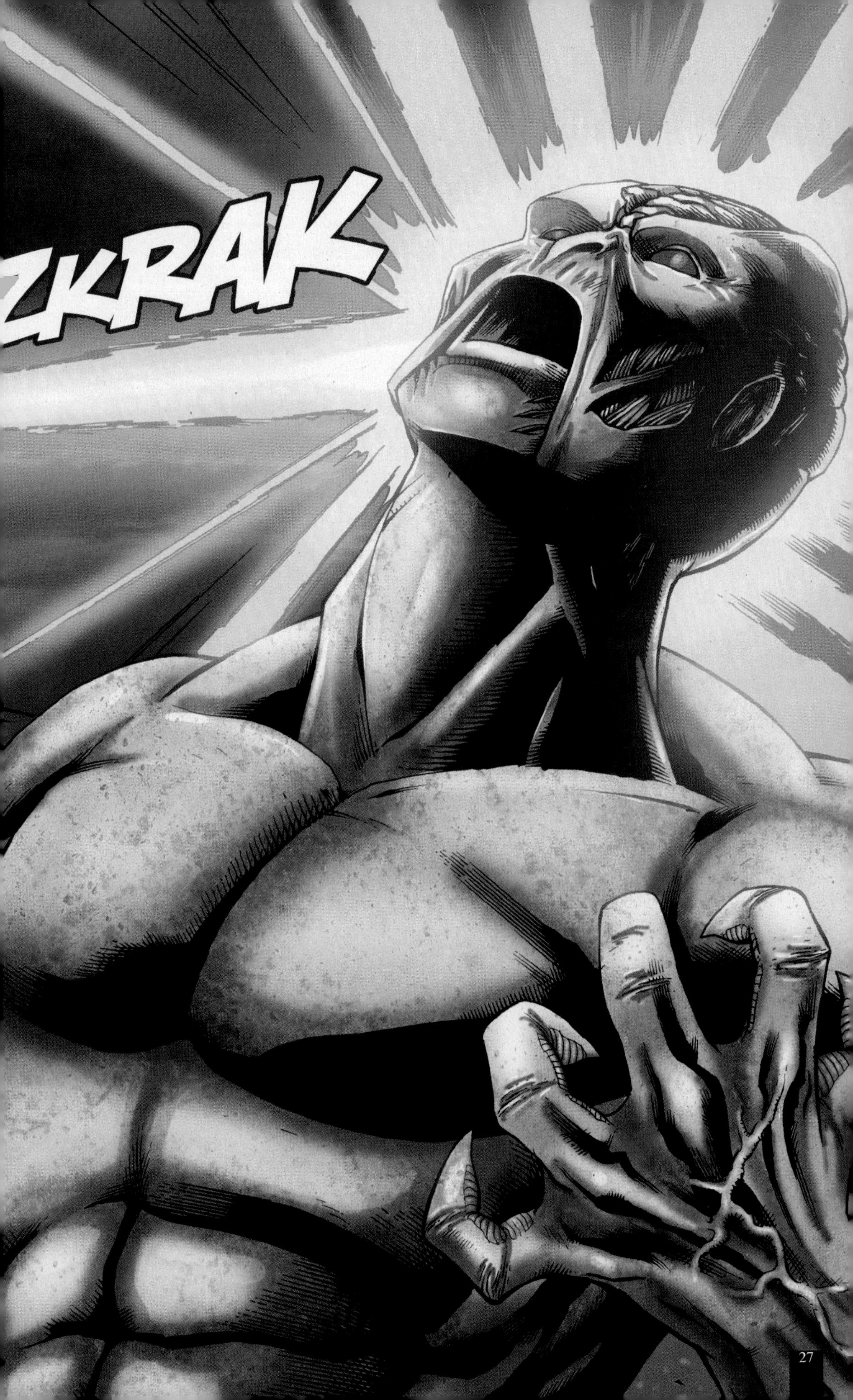
ZKRAK

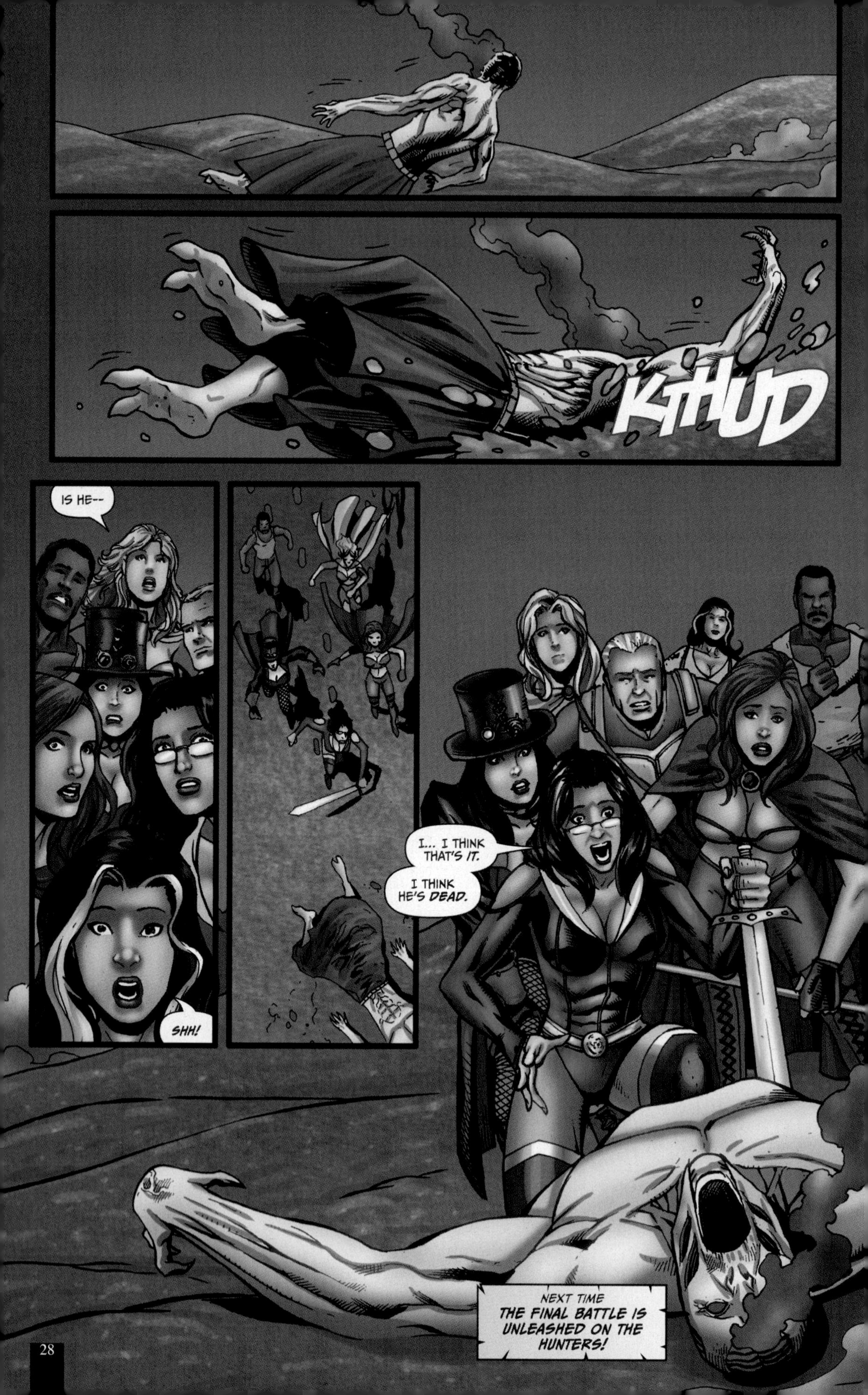
KTHUD
IS HE--
SHH!
I... I THINK THAT'S *IT.*
I THINK HE'S *DEAD.*
NEXT TIME
THE FINAL BATTLE IS UNLEASHED ON THE HUNTERS!

Grimm Fairy Tales

UNLEASHED

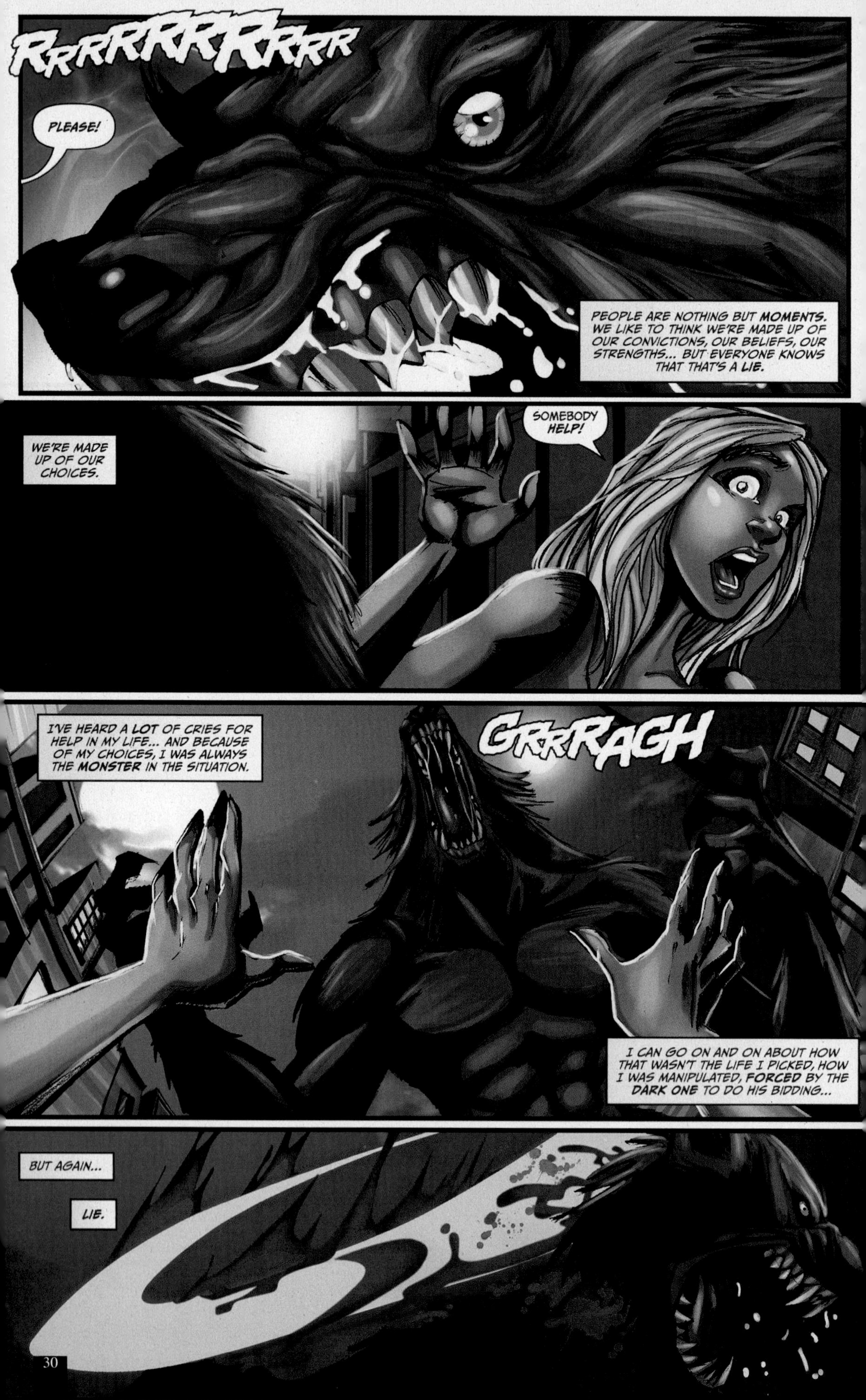
RRRRRRRRRRRR
PLEASE!
PEOPLE ARE NOTHING BUT MOMENTS. WE LIKE TO THINK WE'RE MADE UP OF OUR CONVICTIONS, OUR BELIEFS, OUR STRENGTHS... BUT EVERYONE KNOWS THAT THAT'S A LIE.
WE'RE MADE UP OF OUR CHOICES.
SOMEBODY HELP!
I'VE HEARD A LOT OF CRIES FOR HELP IN MY LIFE... AND BECAUSE OF MY CHOICES, I WAS ALWAYS THE MONSTER IN THE SITUATION.
GRRRAGH
I CAN GO ON AND ON ABOUT HOW THAT WASN'T THE LIFE I PICKED, HOW I WAS MANIPULATED, FORCED BY THE DARK ONE TO DO HIS BIDDING...
BUT AGAIN...
LIE.

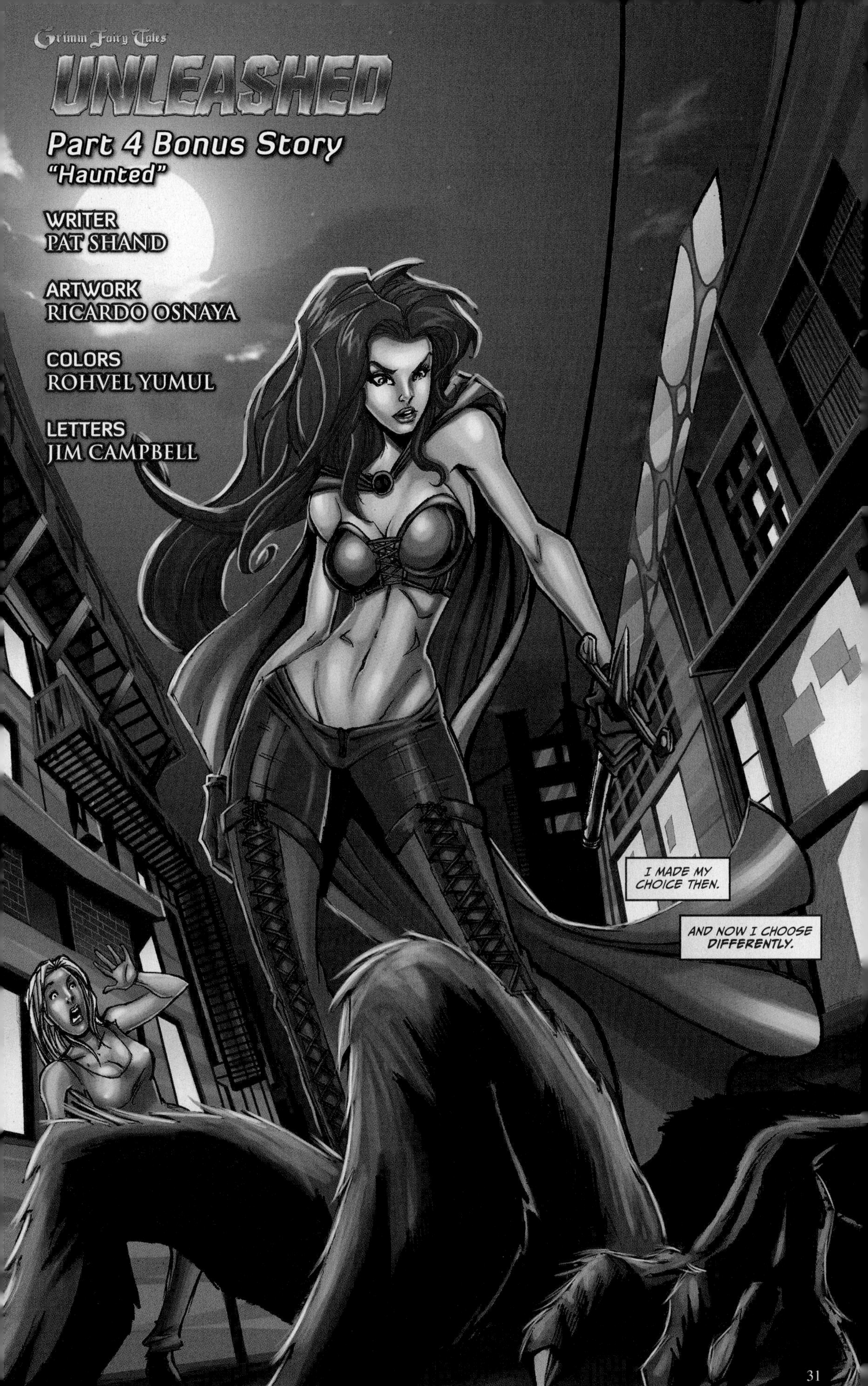
Grimm Fairy Tales
UNLEASHED
Part 4 Bonus Story
"Haunted"
WRITER
PAT SHAND
ARTWORK
RICARDO OSNAYA
COLORS
ROHVEL YUMUL
LETTERS
JIM CAMPBELL
I MADE MY CHOICE THEN.
AND NOW I CHOOSE DIFFERENTLY.

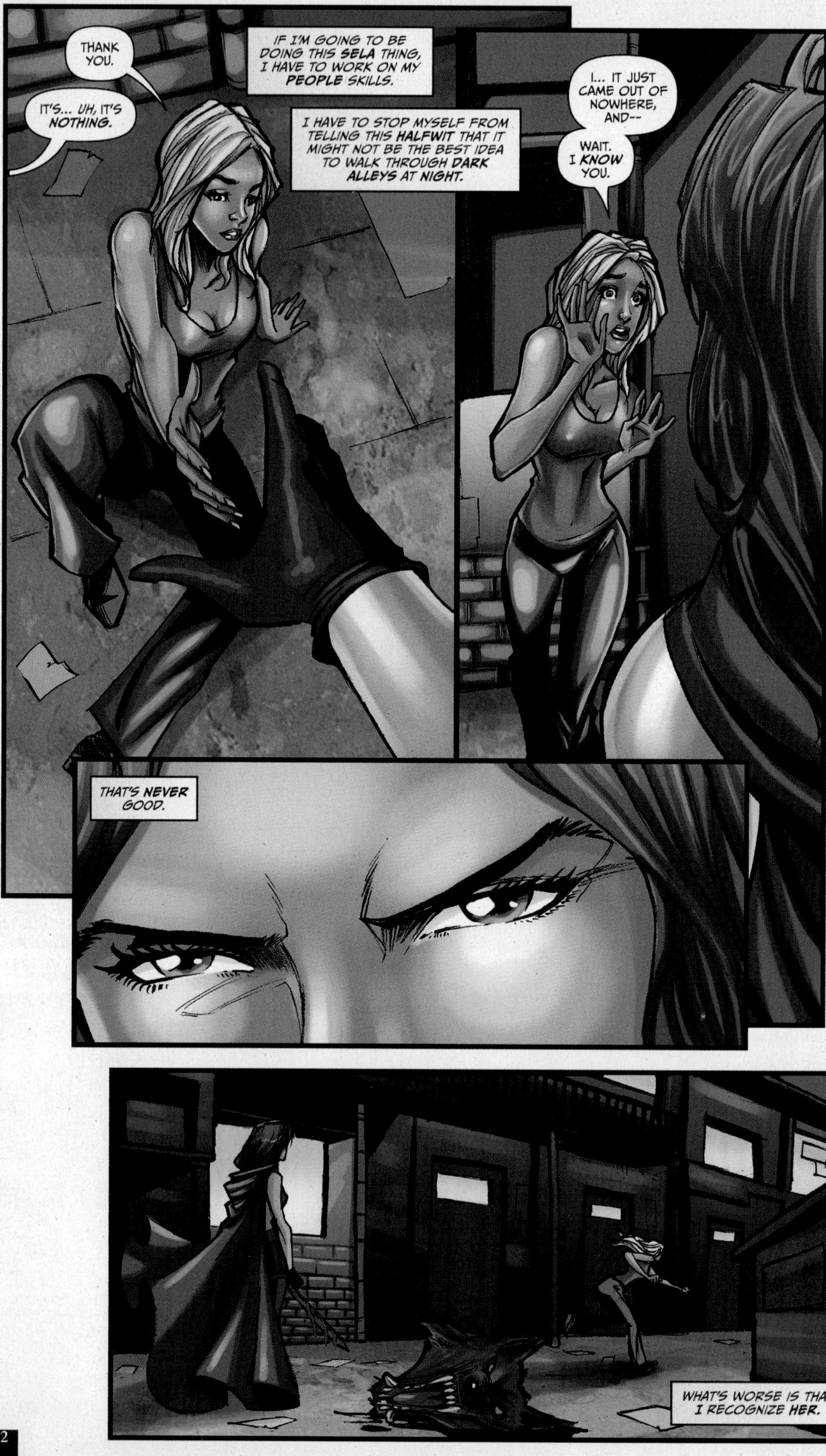

IF I'M GOING TO BE DOING THIS SELA THING, I HAVE TO WORK ON MY PEOPLE SKILLS.
THANK YOU.
IT'S... UH, IT'S NOTHING.
I HAVE TO STOP MYSELF FROM TELLING THIS HALFWIT THAT IT MIGHT NOT BE THE BEST IDEA TO WALK THROUGH DARK ALLEYS AT NIGHT.
I... IT JUST CAME OUT OF NOWHERE, AND--
WAIT. I KNOW YOU.
THAT'S NEVER GOOD.
WHAT'S WORSE IS THAT I RECOGNIZE HER.

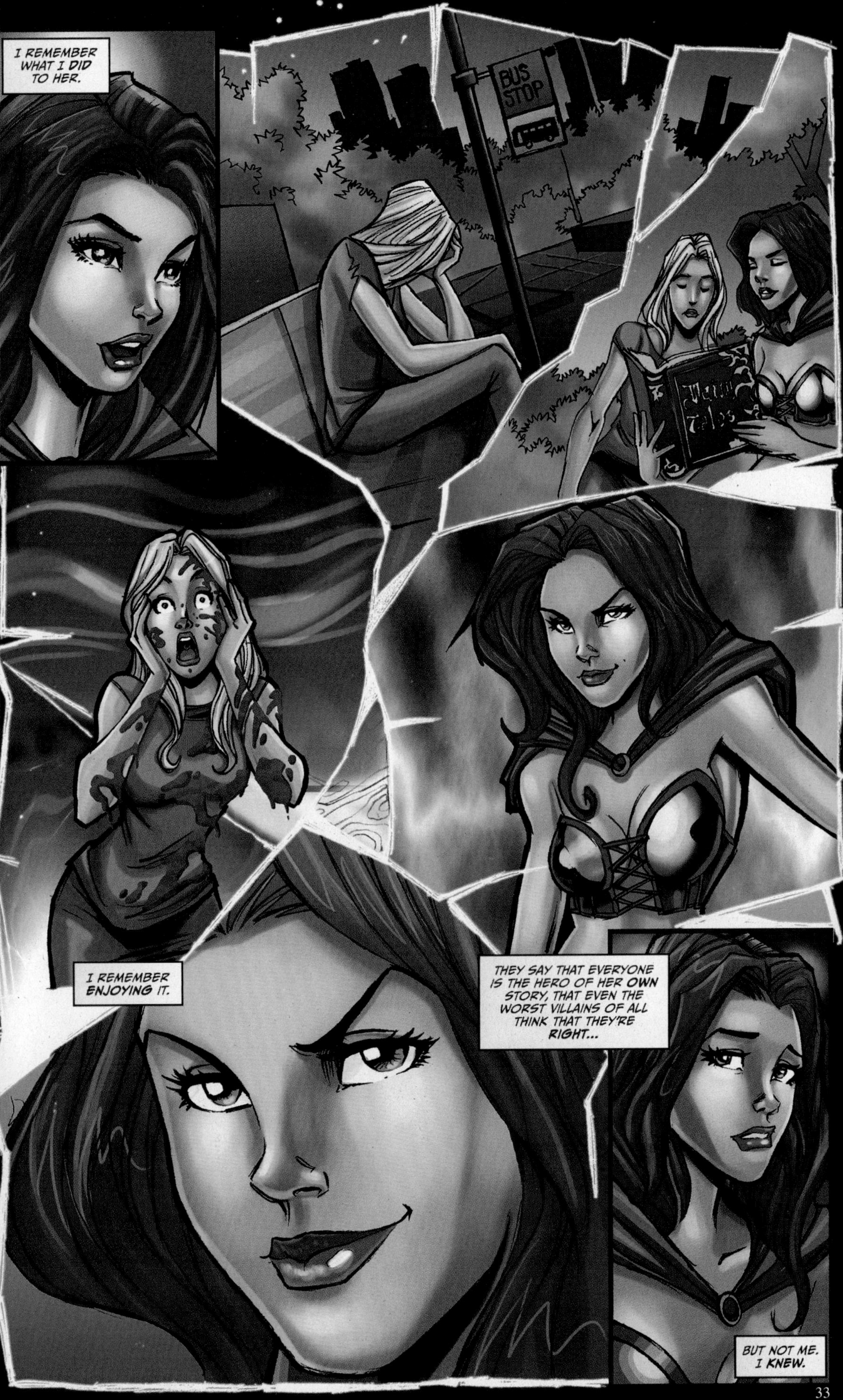
I REMEMBER WHAT I DID TO HER.
BUS STOP
I REMEMBER ENJOYING IT.
THEY SAY THAT EVERYONE IS THE HERO OF HER OWN STORY, THAT EVEN THE WORST VILLAINS OF ALL THINK THAT THEY'RE RIGHT...
BUT NOT ME. I KNEW.

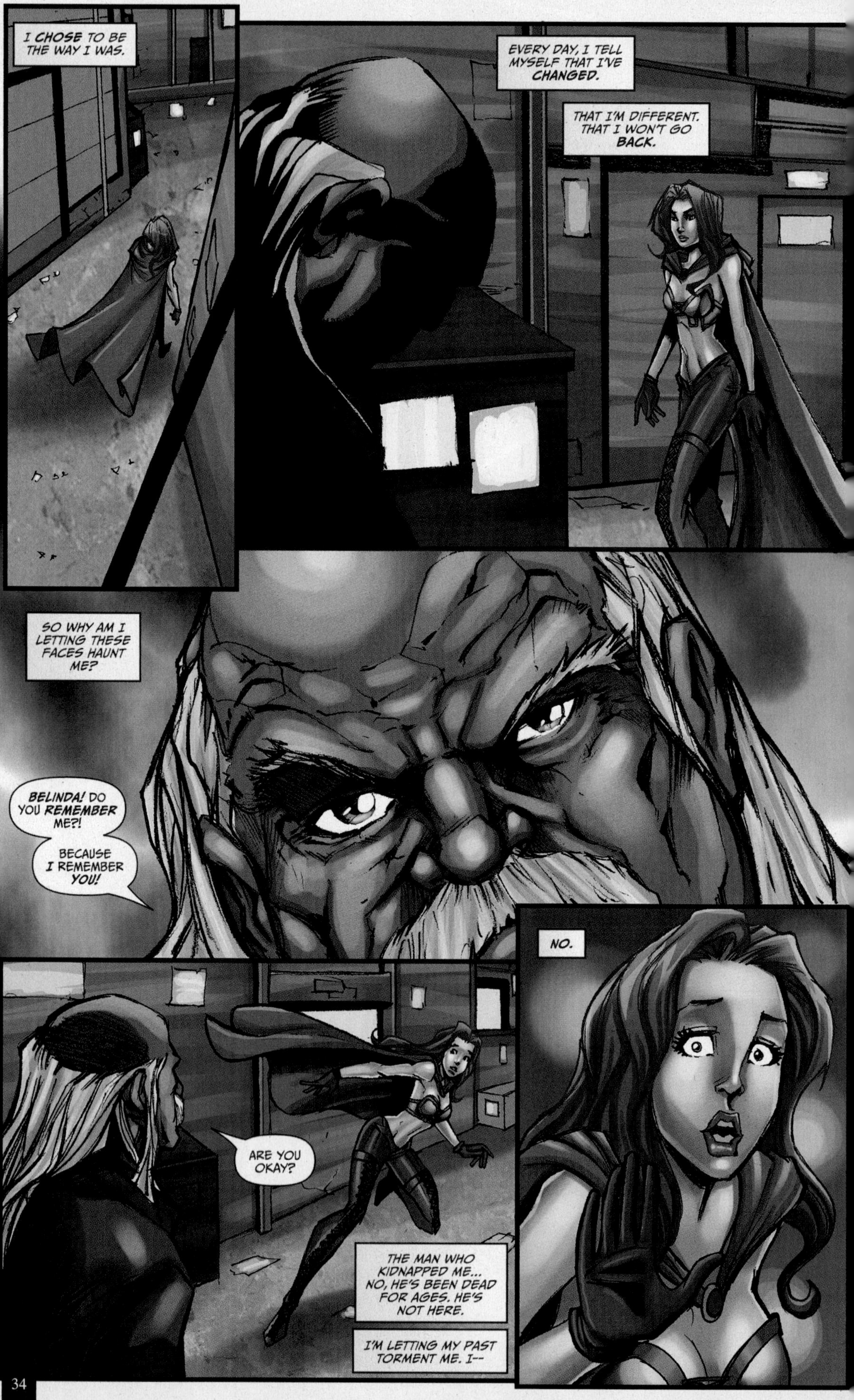
I CHOSE TO BE THE WAY I WAS.
EVERY DAY, I TELL MYSELF THAT I'VE CHANGED.
THAT I'M DIFFERENT. THAT I WON'T GO BACK.
SO WHY AM I LETTING THESE FACES HAUNT ME?
BELINDA! DO YOU REMEMBER ME?!
BECAUSE I REMEMBER YOU!
ARE YOU OKAY?
THE MAN WHO KIDNAPPED ME... NO, HE'S BEEN DEAD FOR AGES. HE'S NOT HERE.
I'M LETTING MY PAST TORMENT ME. I--
NO.

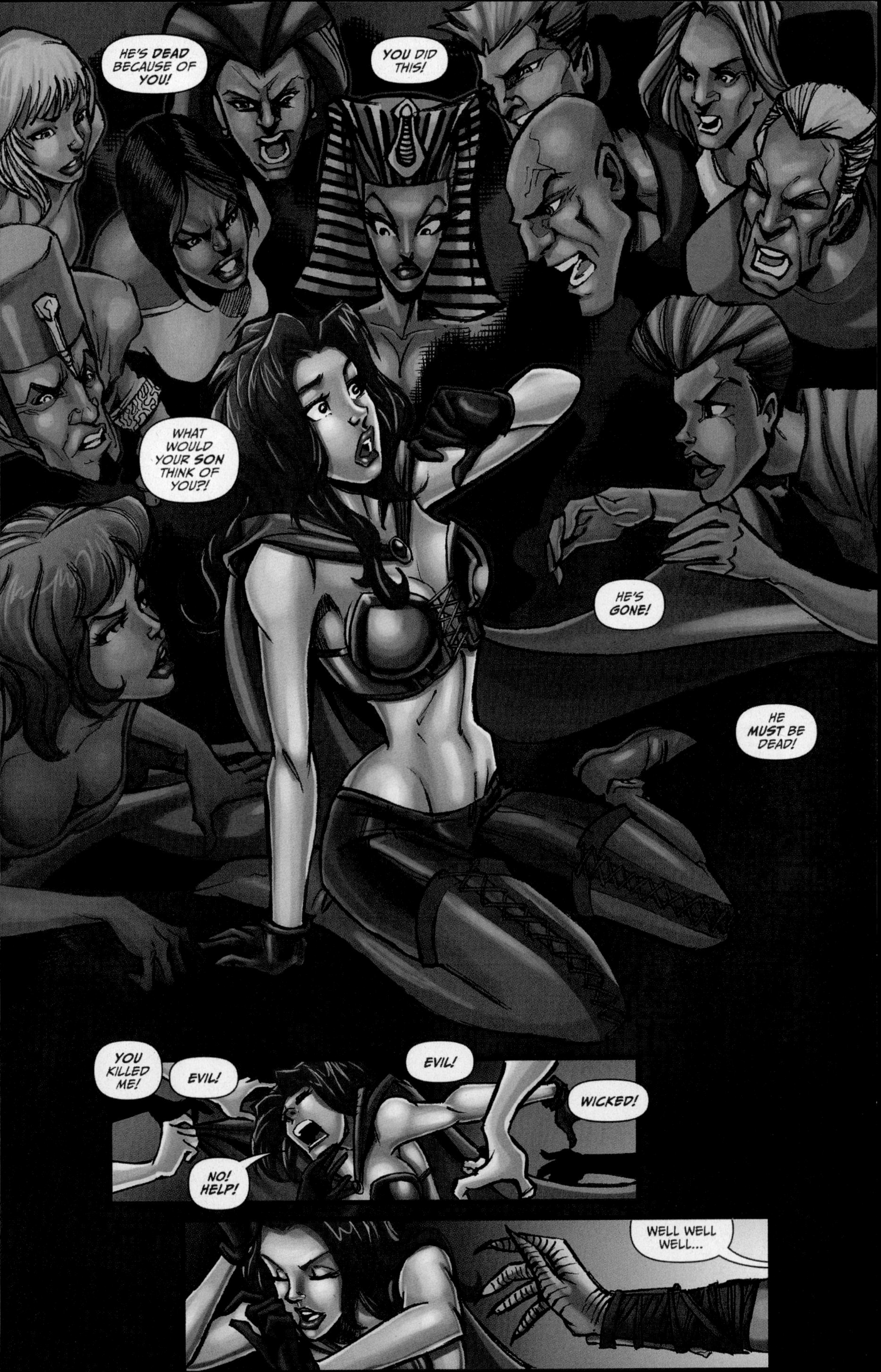
HE'S DEAD BECAUSE OF YOU!
YOU DID THIS!
WHAT WOULD YOUR SON THINK OF YOU?!
HE'S GONE!
HE MUST BE DEAD!
YOU KILLED ME!
EVIL!
EVIL!
WICKED!
NO! HELP!
WELL WELL WELL...

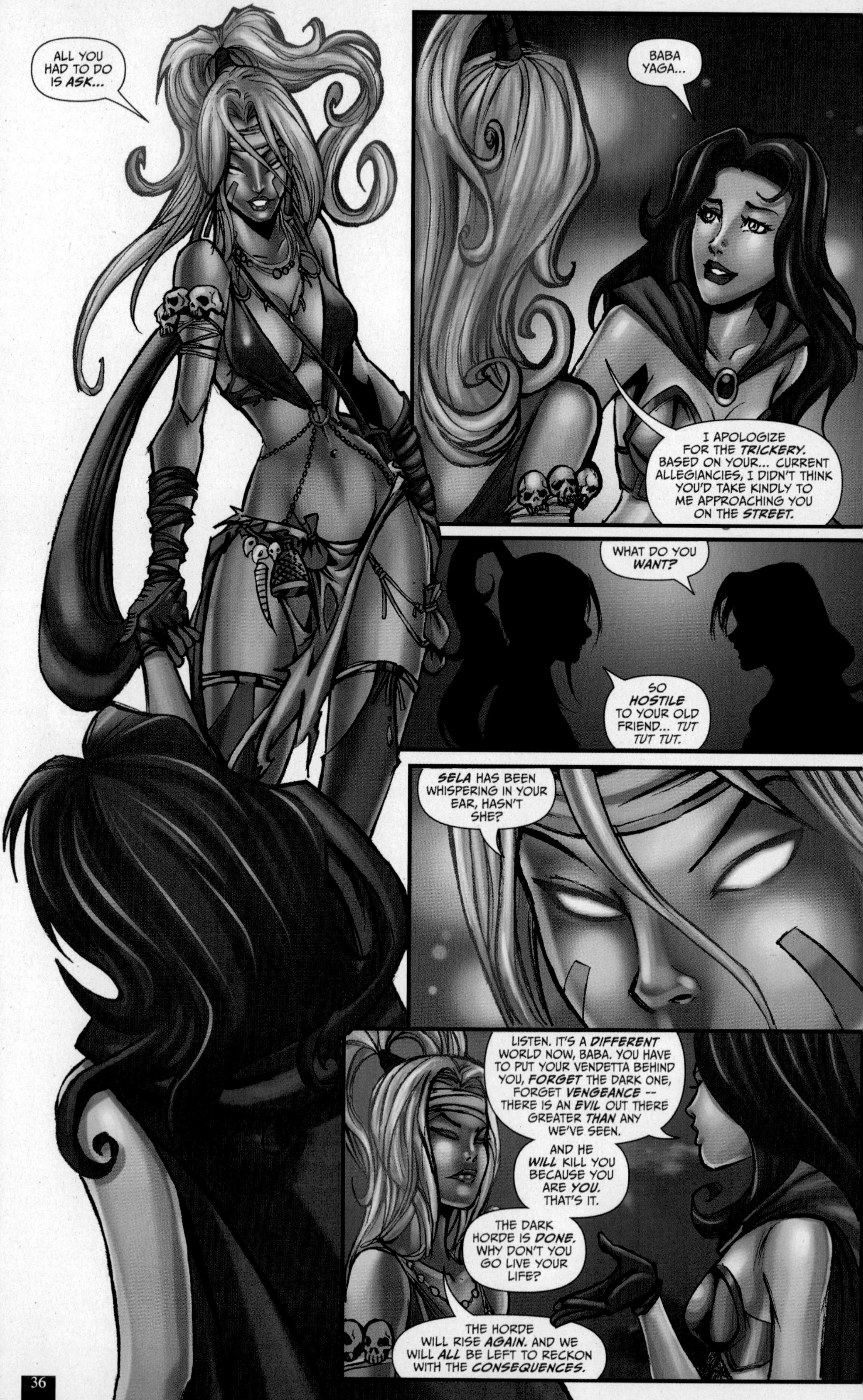
ALL YOU HAD TO DO IS ASK...
BABA YAGA...
I APOLOGIZE FOR THE TRICKERY. BASED ON YOUR... CURRENT ALLEGIANCIES, I DIDN'T THINK YOU'D TAKE KINDLY TO ME APPROACHING YOU ON THE STREET.
WHAT DO YOU WANT?
SO HOSTILE TO YOUR OLD FRIEND... TUT TUT TUT.
SELA HAS BEEN WHISPERING IN YOUR EAR, HASN'T SHE?
LISTEN. IT'S A DIFFERENT WORLD NOW, BABA. YOU HAVE TO PUT YOUR VENDETTA BEHIND YOU, FORGET THE DARK ONE, FORGET VENGEANCE -- THERE IS AN EVIL OUT THERE GREATER THAN ANY WE'VE SEEN.
AND HE WILL KILL YOU BECAUSE YOU ARE YOU. THAT'S IT.
THE DARK HORDE IS DONE. WHY DON'T YOU GO LIVE YOUR LIFE?
THE HORDE WILL RISE AGAIN. AND WE WILL ALL BE LEFT TO RECKON WITH THE CONSEQUENCES.

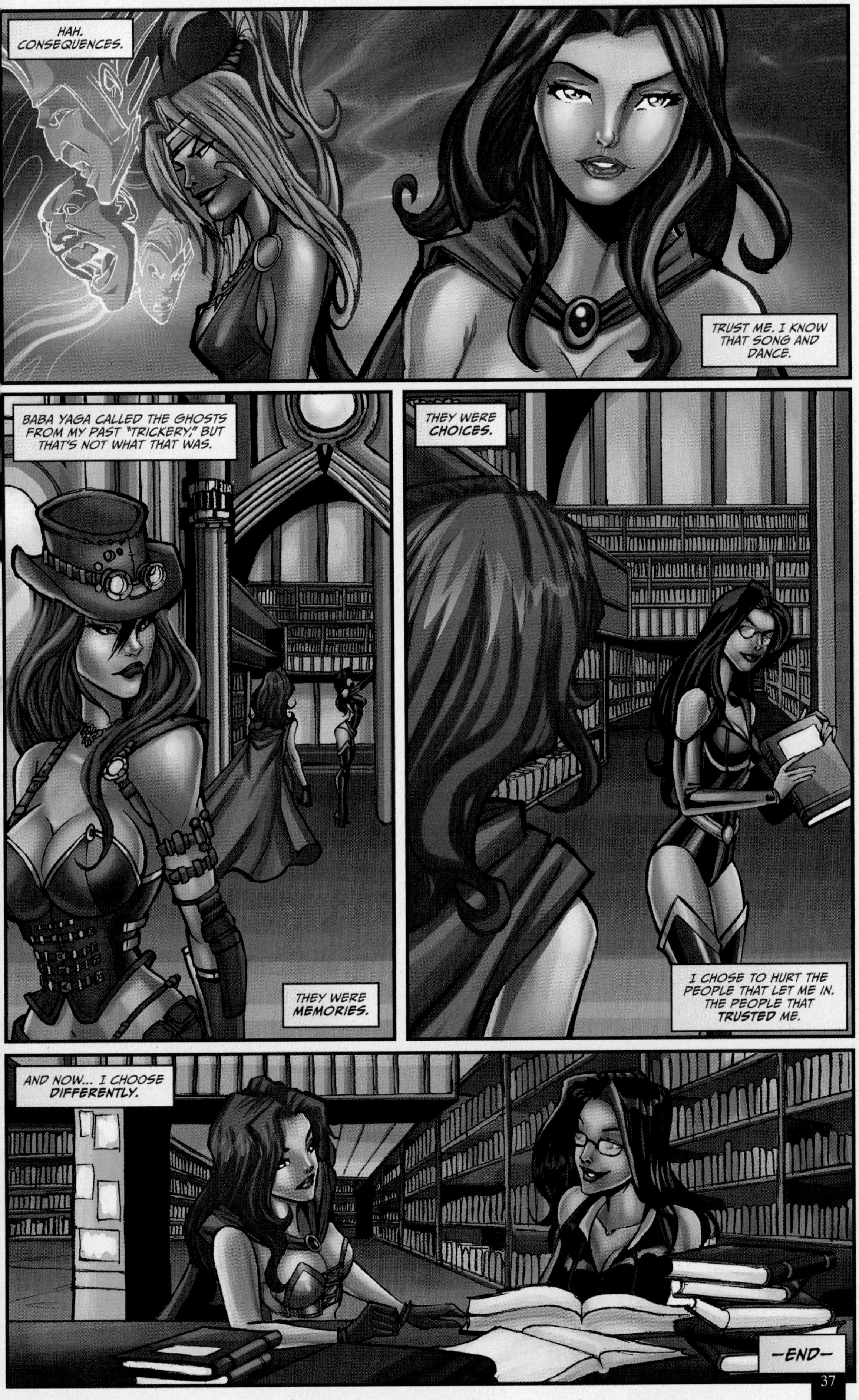

HAH. CONSEQUENCES.
TRUST ME. I KNOW THAT SONG AND DANCE.
BABA YAGA CALLED THE GHOSTS FROM MY PAST "TRICKERY," BUT THAT'S NOT WHAT THAT WAS.
THEY WERE MEMORIES.
THEY WERE CHOICES.
I CHOSE TO HURT THE PEOPLE THAT LET ME IN. THE PEOPLE THAT TRUSTED ME.
AND NOW... I CHOOSE DIFFERENTLY.
—END—

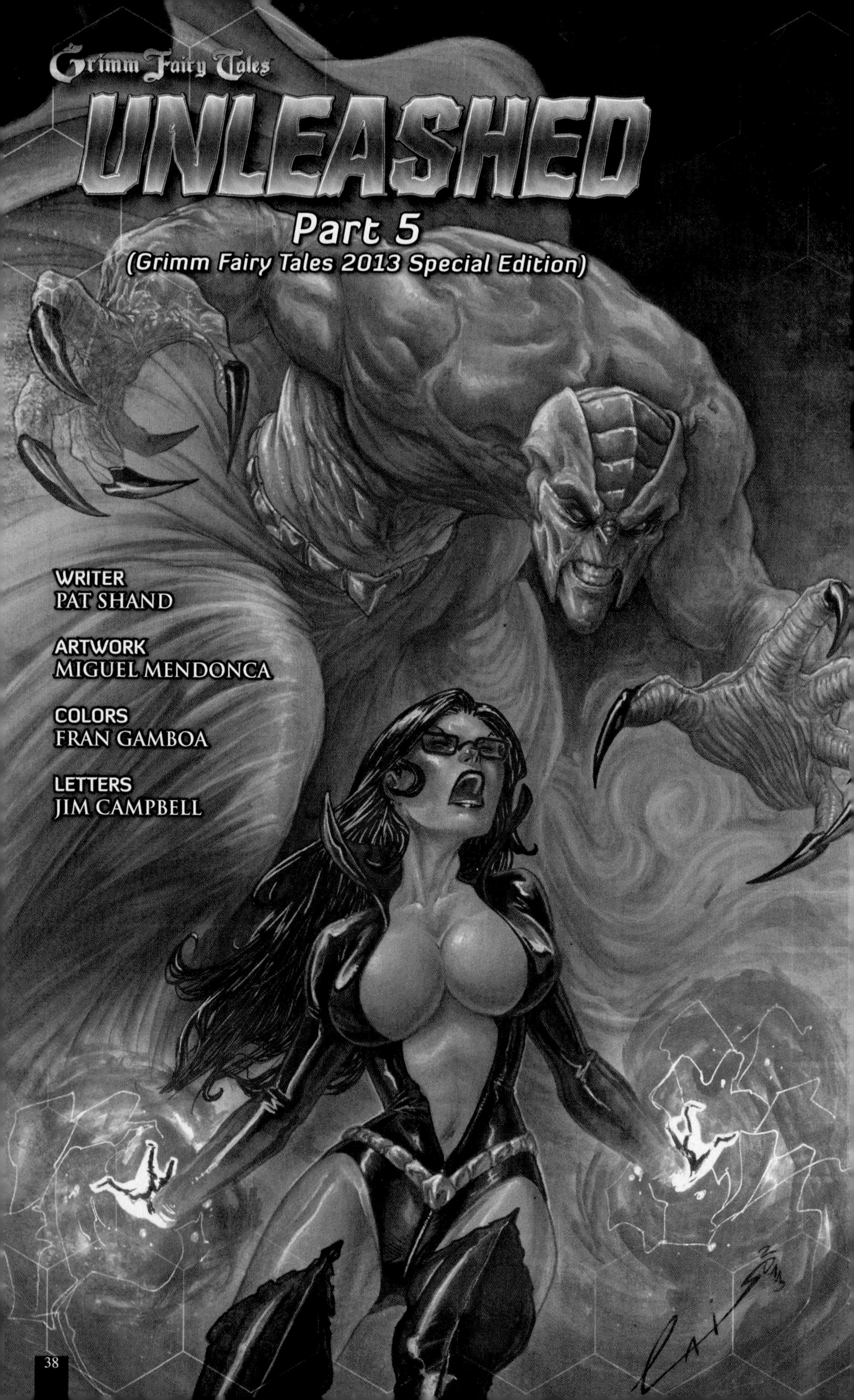
Grimm Fairy Tales
UNLEASHED
Part 5
(Grimm Fairy Tales 2013 Special Edition)
WRITER
PAT SHAND
ARTWORK
MIGUEL MENDONCA
COLORS
FRAN GAMBOA
LETTERS
JIM CAMPBELL

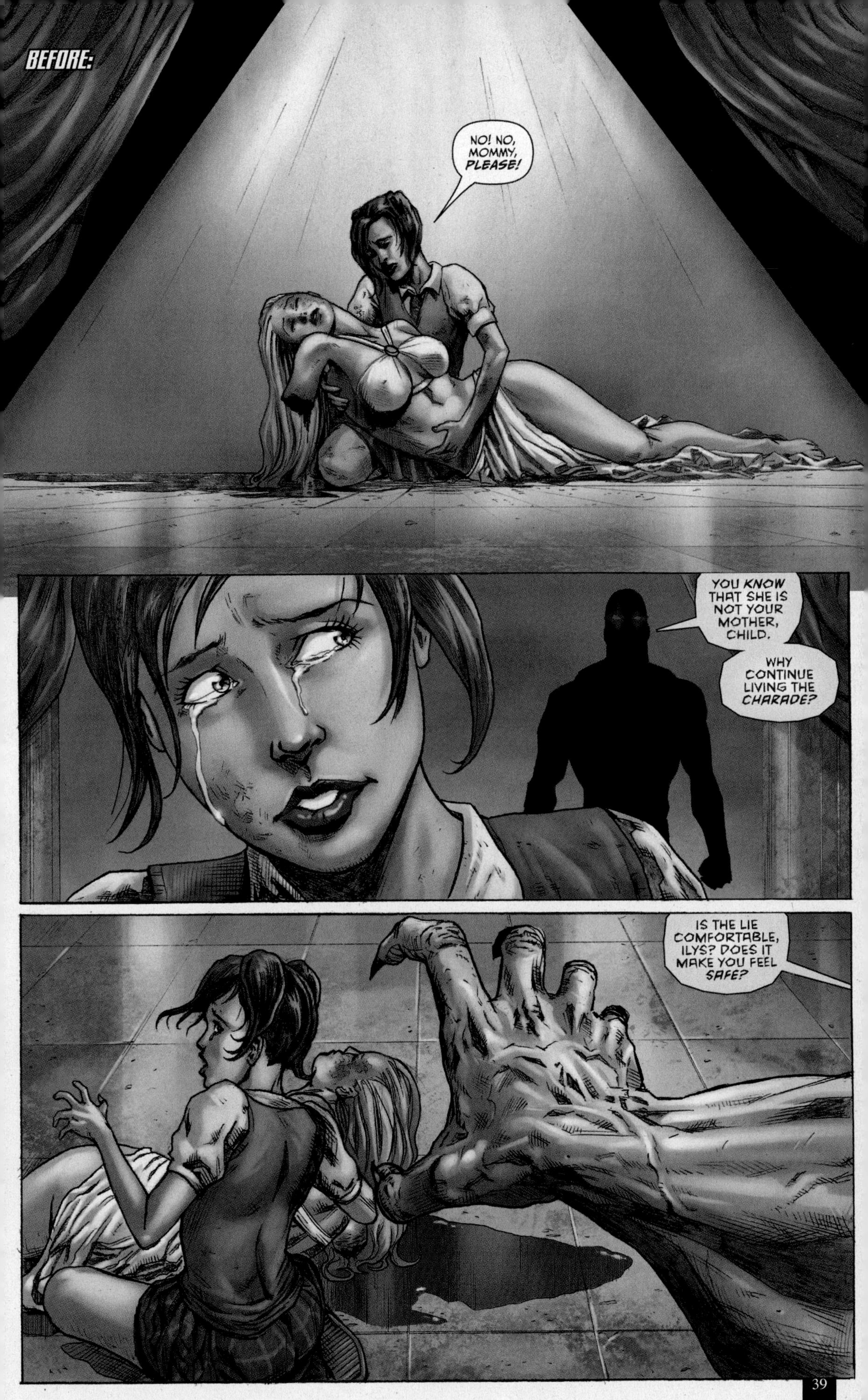
BEFORE:
NO! NO, MOMMY, PLEASE!
YOU KNOW THAT SHE IS NOT YOUR MOTHER, CHILD.
WHY CONTINUE LIVING THE CHARADE?
IS THE LIE COMFORTABLE, ILYS? DOES IT MAKE YOU FEEL SAFE?

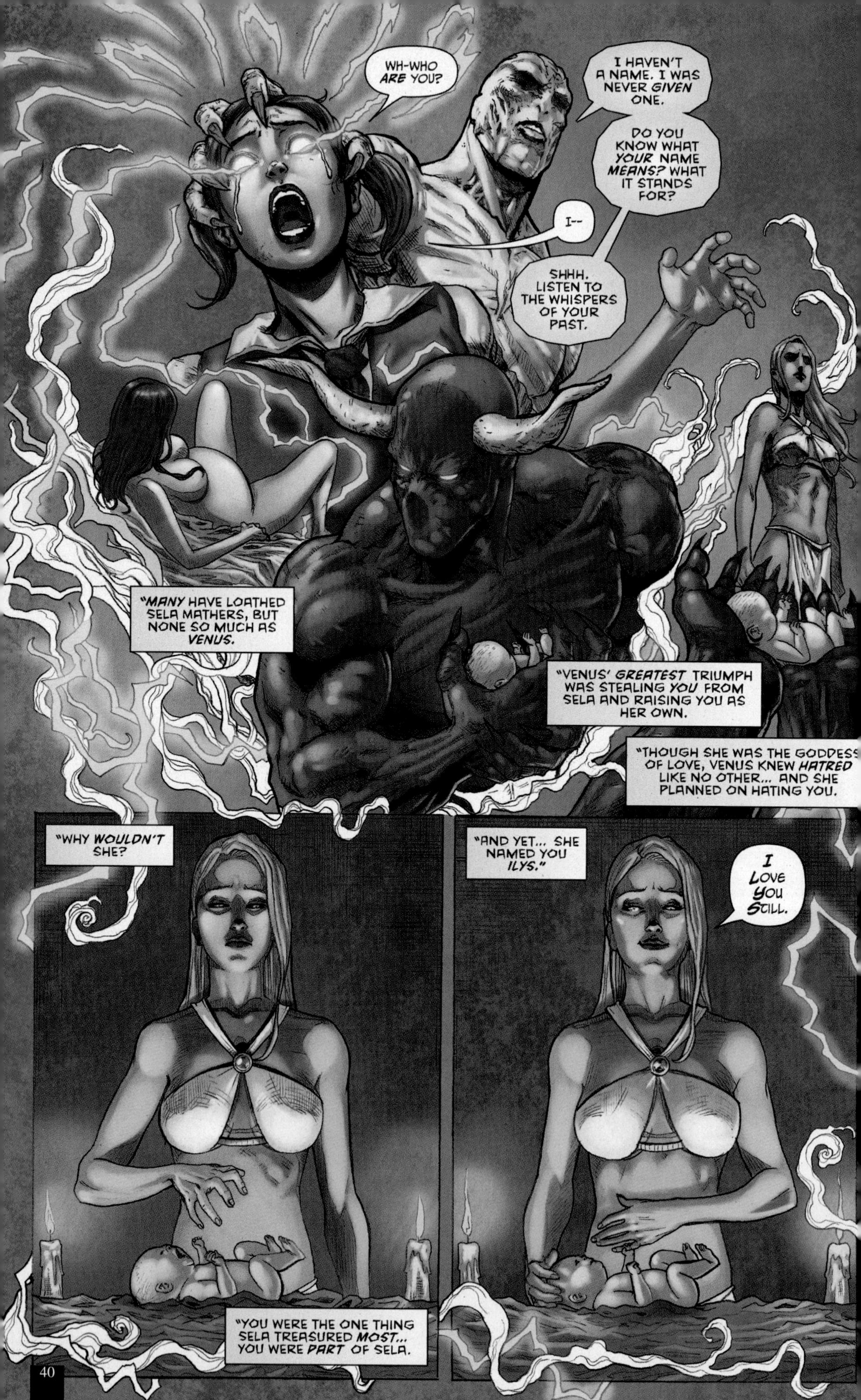
WH-WHO ARE YOU?
I HAVEN'T A NAME. I WAS NEVER GIVEN ONE.
DO YOU KNOW WHAT YOUR NAME MEANS? WHAT IT STANDS FOR?
I--
SHHH. LISTEN TO THE WHISPERS OF YOUR PAST.
"MANY HAVE LOATHED SELA MATHERS, BUT NONE SO MUCH AS VENUS.
"VENUS' GREATEST TRIUMPH WAS STEALING YOU FROM SELA AND RAISING YOU AS HER OWN.
"THOUGH SHE WAS THE GODDESS OF LOVE, VENUS KNEW HATRED LIKE NO OTHER... AND SHE PLANNED ON HATING YOU.
"WHY WOULDN'T SHE?
"YOU WERE THE ONE THING SELA TREASURED MOST... YOU WERE PART OF SELA.
"AND YET... SHE NAMED YOU ILYS."
I LOVE YOU STILL.

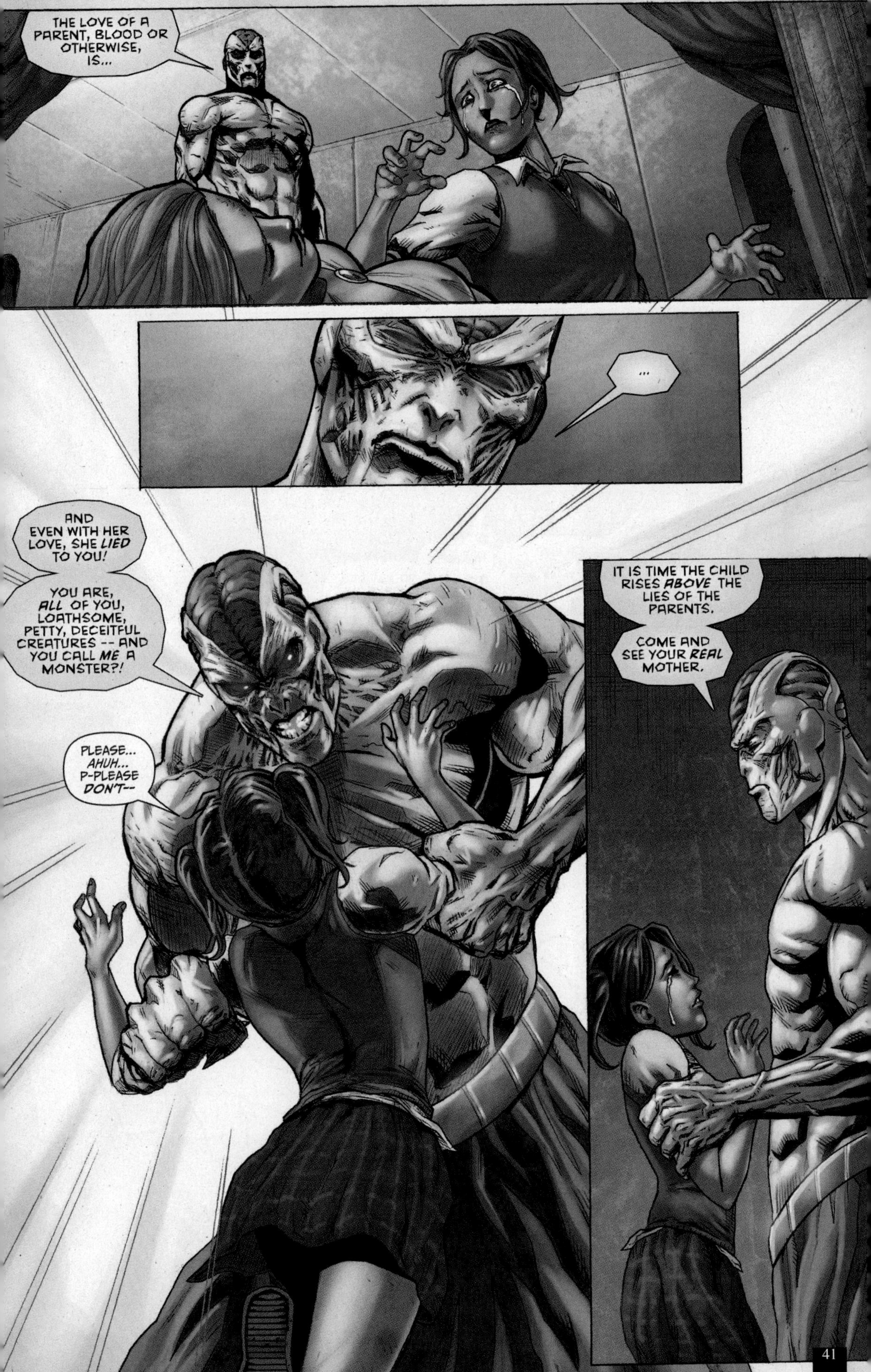
THE LOVE OF A PARENT, BLOOD OR OTHERWISE, IS...
...
AND EVEN WITH HER LOVE, SHE *LIED* TO YOU!
YOU ARE, *ALL* OF YOU, LOATHSOME, PETTY, DECEITFUL CREATURES -- AND YOU CALL *ME* A MONSTER?!
PLEASE... *AHUH...* P-PLEASE *DON'T*--
IT IS TIME THE CHILD RISES *ABOVE* THE LIES OF THE PARENTS.
COME AND SEE YOUR *REAL* MOTHER.

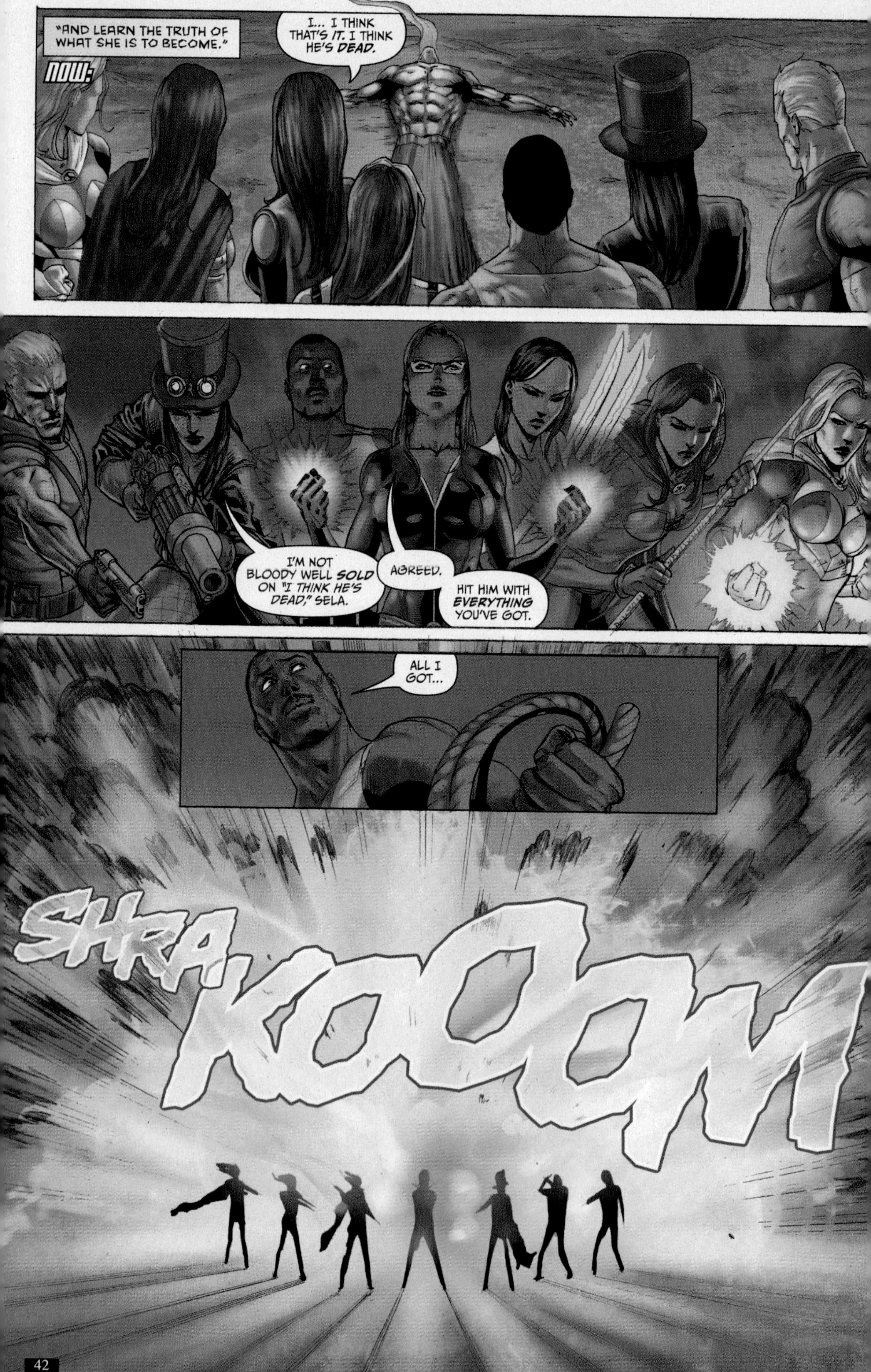

"AND LEARN THE TRUTH OF WHAT SHE IS TO BECOME."
NOW:
I... I THINK THAT'S IT. I THINK HE'S DEAD.
I'M NOT BLOODY WELL SOLD ON "I THINK HE'S DEAD," SELA.
AGREED.
HIT HIM WITH EVERYTHING YOU'VE GOT.
ALL I GOT...
SHRA KOOOM

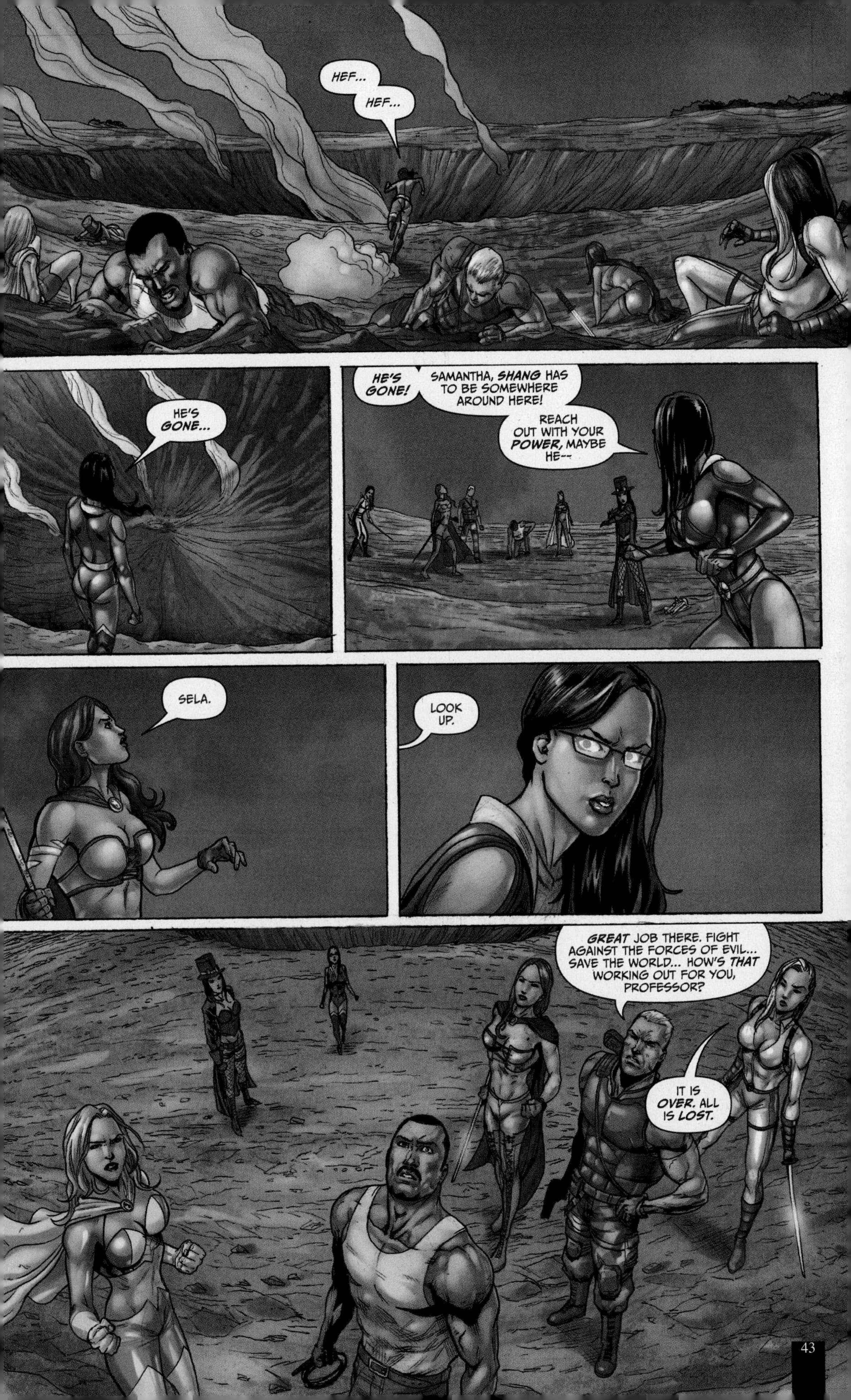
HEF... HEF...
HE'S GONE...
HE'S GONE!
SAMANTHA, SHANG HAS TO BE SOMEWHERE AROUND HERE!
REACH OUT WITH YOUR POWER, MAYBE HE--
SELA.
LOOK UP.
GREAT JOB THERE. FIGHT AGAINST THE FORCES OF EVIL... SAVE THE WORLD... HOW'S THAT WORKING OUT FOR YOU, PROFESSOR?
IT IS OVER. ALL IS LOST.

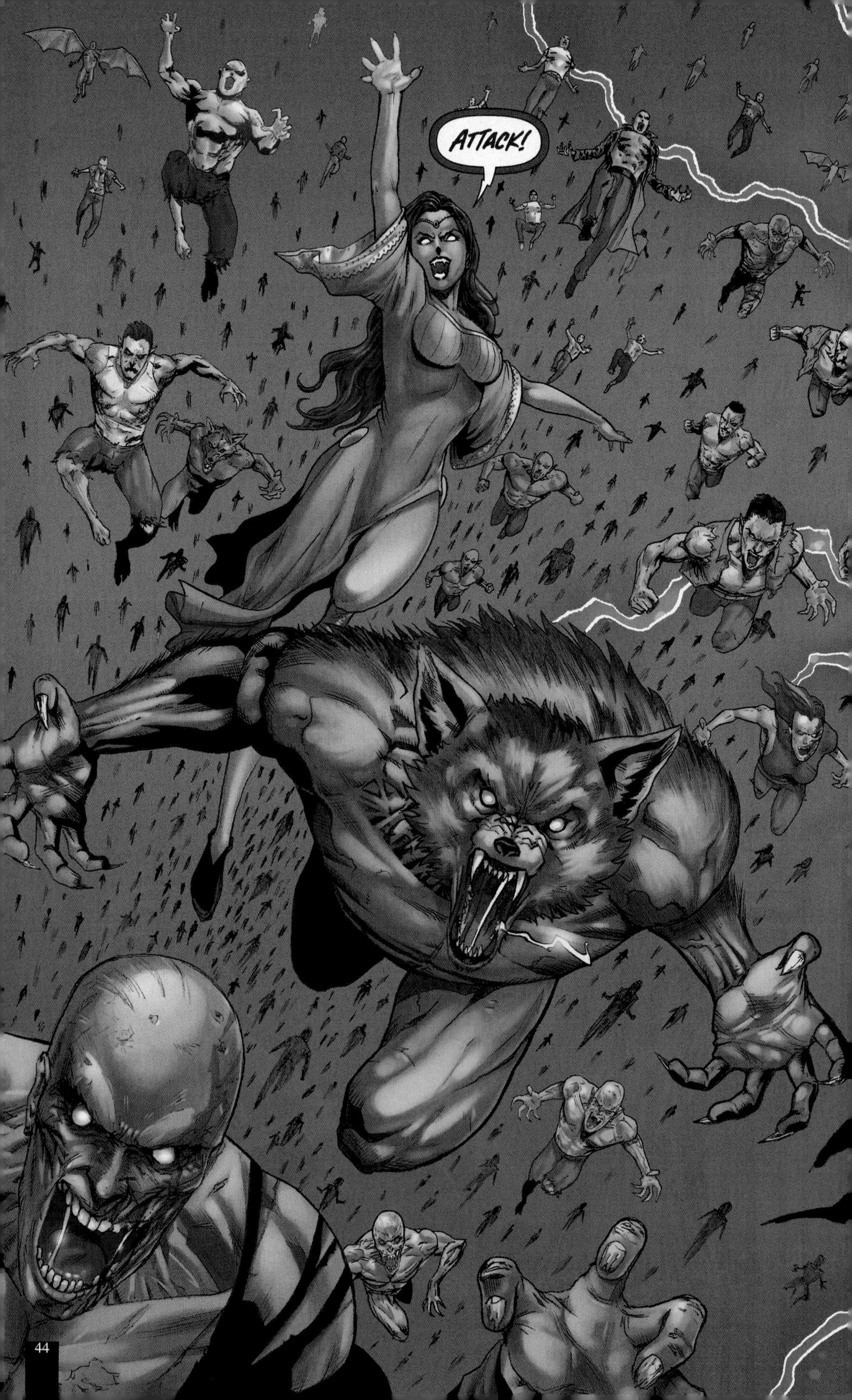
ATTACK!

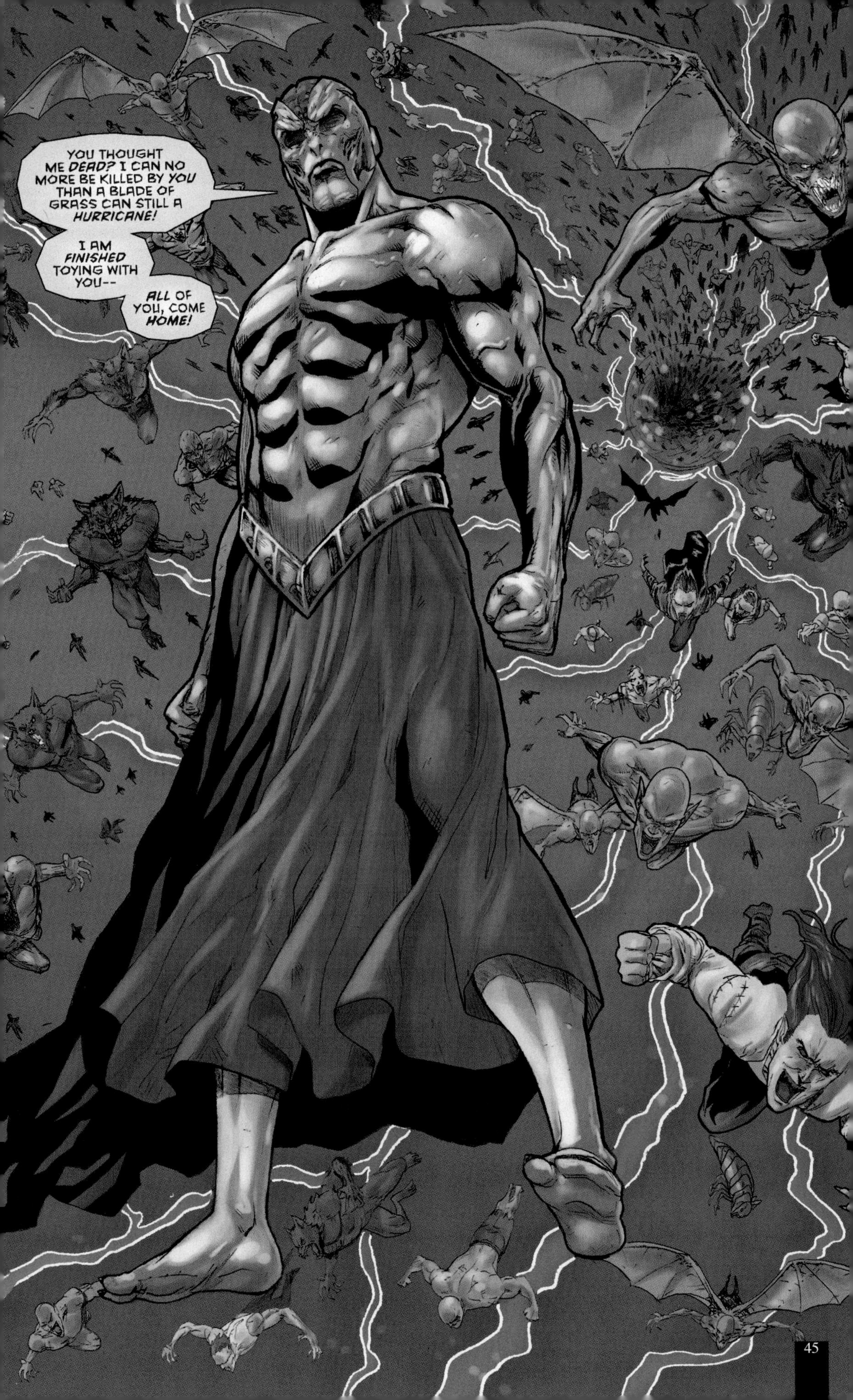
YOU THOUGHT ME DEAD? I CAN NO MORE BE KILLED BY YOU THAN A BLADE OF GRASS CAN STILL A HURRICANE!
I AM FINISHED TOYING WITH YOU--
ALL OF YOU, COME HOME!

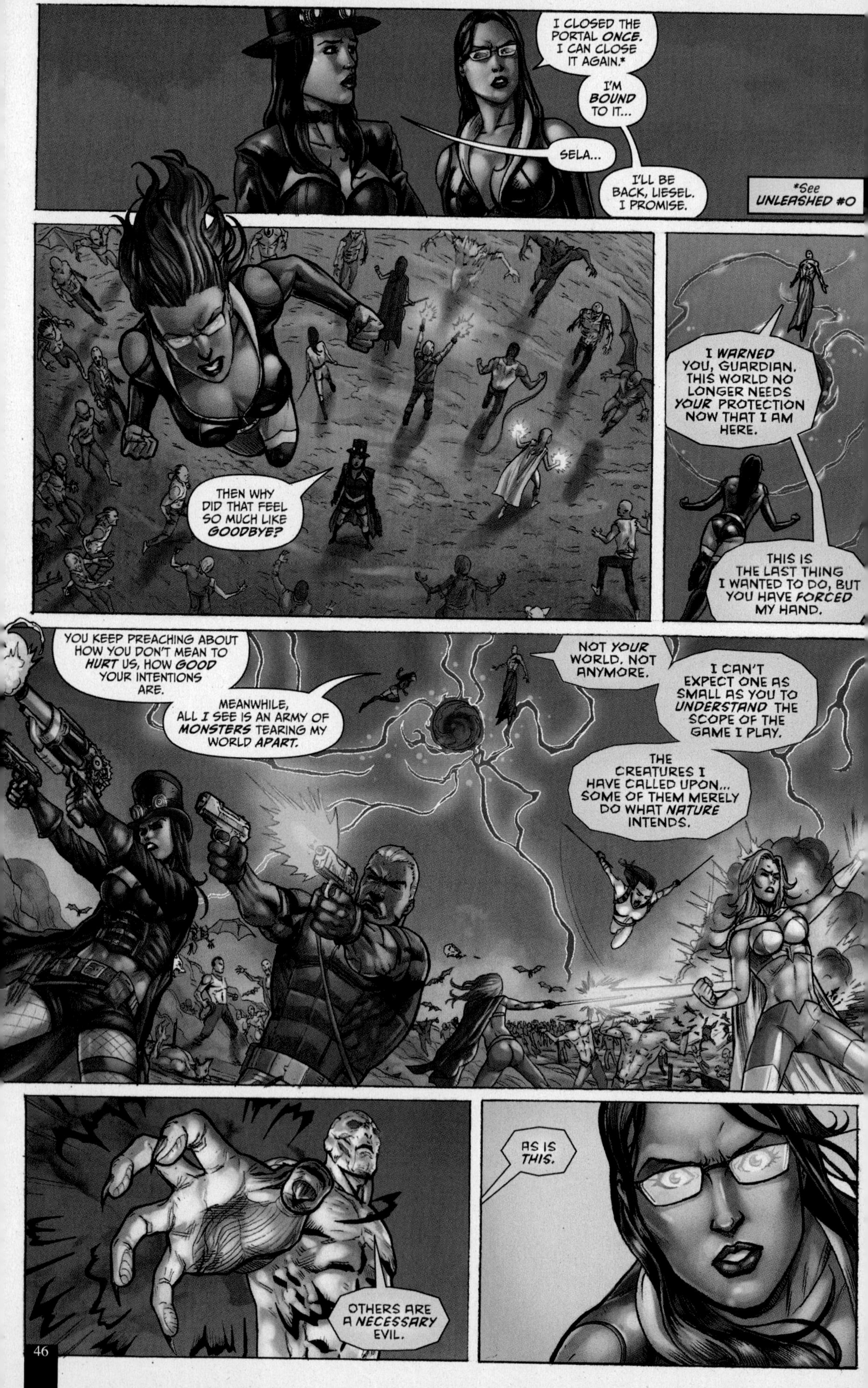
I CLOSED THE PORTAL ONCE. I CAN CLOSE IT AGAIN.*
I'M BOUND TO IT...
SELA...
I'LL BE BACK, LIESEL. I PROMISE.
*See UNLEASHED #0
THEN WHY DID THAT FEEL SO MUCH LIKE GOODBYE?
I WARNED YOU, GUARDIAN. THIS WORLD NO LONGER NEEDS YOUR PROTECTION NOW THAT I AM HERE.
THIS IS THE LAST THING I WANTED TO DO, BUT YOU HAVE FORCED MY HAND.
YOU KEEP PREACHING ABOUT HOW YOU DON'T MEAN TO HURT US, HOW GOOD YOUR INTENTIONS ARE.
MEANWHILE, ALL I SEE IS AN ARMY OF MONSTERS TEARING MY WORLD APART.
NOT YOUR WORLD. NOT ANYMORE.
I CAN'T EXPECT ONE AS SMALL AS YOU TO UNDERSTAND THE SCOPE OF THE GAME I PLAY.
THE CREATURES I HAVE CALLED UPON... SOME OF THEM MERELY DO WHAT NATURE INTENDS.
OTHERS ARE A NECESSARY EVIL.
AS IS THIS.

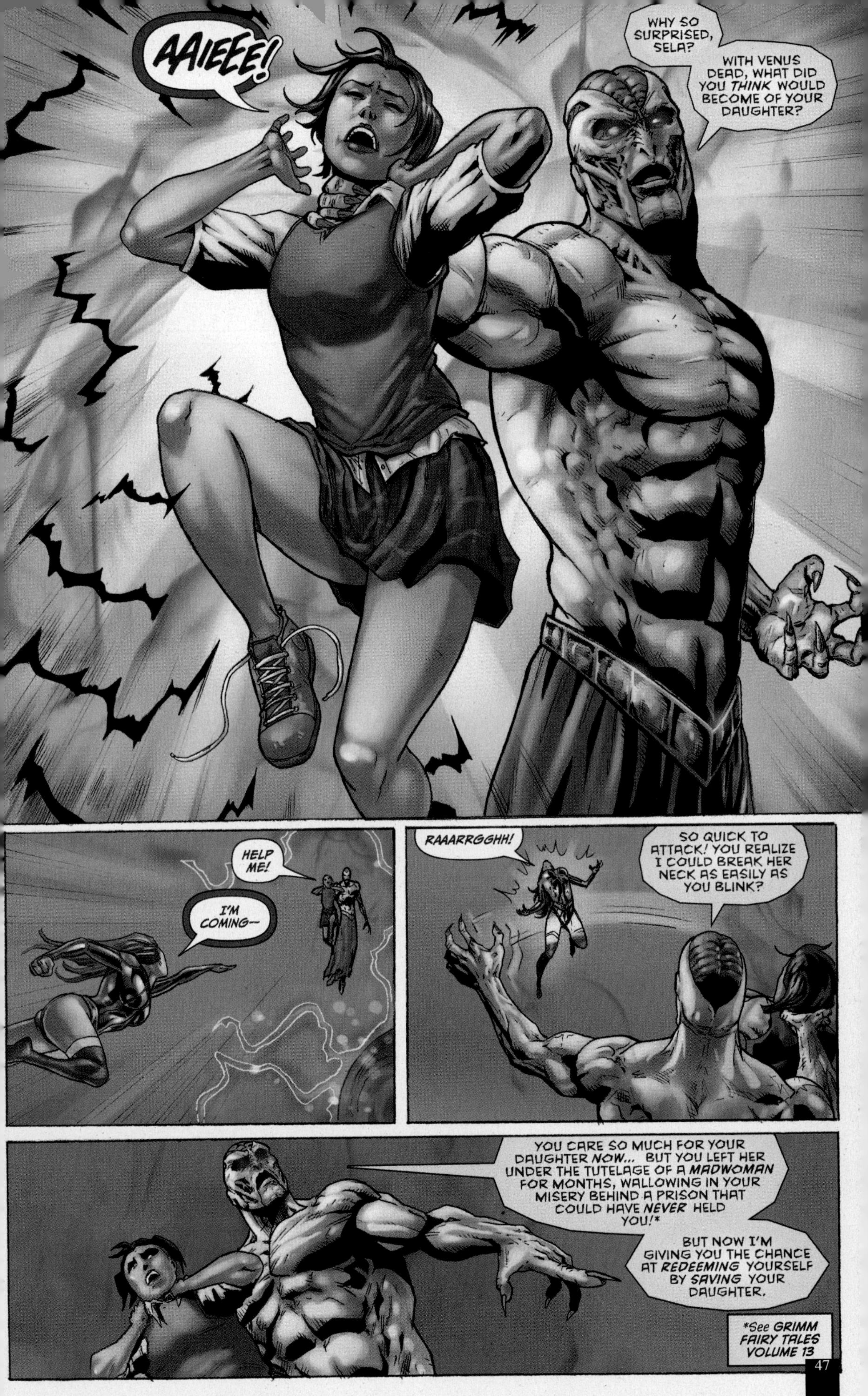
AAIEEE!
WHY SO SURPRISED, SELA?
WITH VENUS DEAD, WHAT DID YOU THINK WOULD BECOME OF YOUR DAUGHTER?
HELP ME!
I'M COMING--
RAAARRGGHH!
SO QUICK TO ATTACK! YOU REALIZE I COULD BREAK HER NECK AS EASILY AS YOU BLINK?
YOU CARE SO MUCH FOR YOUR DAUGHTER NOW... BUT YOU LEFT HER UNDER THE TUTELAGE OF A MADWOMAN FOR MONTHS, WALLOWING IN YOUR MISERY BEHIND A PRISON THAT COULD HAVE NEVER HELD YOU!*
BUT NOW I'M GIVING YOU THE CHANCE AT REDEEMING YOURSELF BY SAVING YOUR DAUGHTER.
*See GRIMM FAIRY TALES VOLUME 13

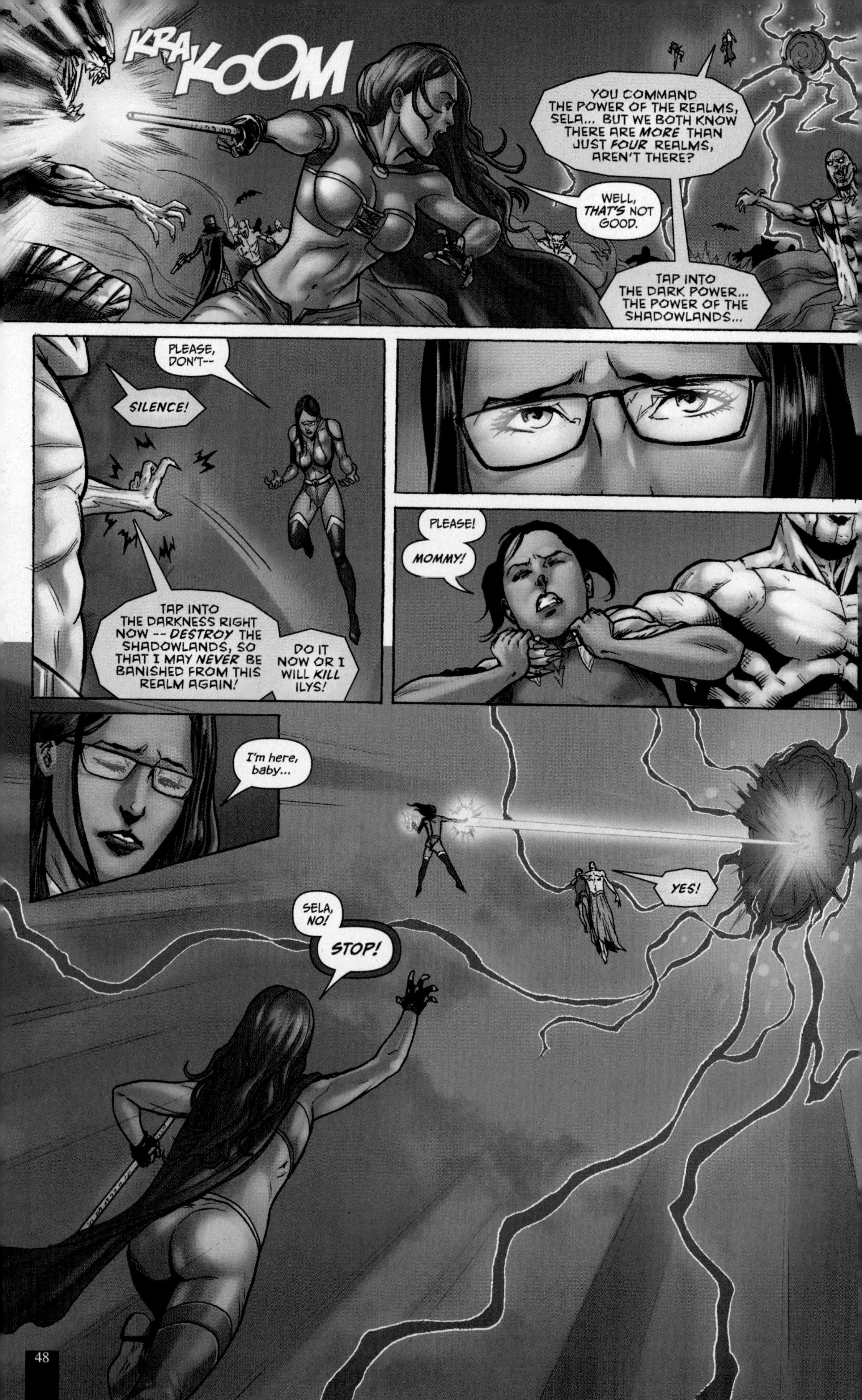
KRAKOOM
YOU COMMAND THE POWER OF THE REALMS, SELA... BUT WE BOTH KNOW THERE ARE MORE THAN JUST FOUR REALMS, AREN'T THERE?
WELL, THAT'S NOT GOOD.
TAP INTO THE DARK POWER... THE POWER OF THE SHADOWLANDS...
PLEASE, DON'T--
SILENCE!
TAP INTO THE DARKNESS RIGHT NOW -- DESTROY THE SHADOWLANDS, SO THAT I MAY NEVER BE BANISHED FROM THIS REALM AGAIN!
DO IT NOW OR I WILL KILL ILYS!
PLEASE!
MOMMY!
I'm here, baby...
YES!
SELA, NO!
STOP!

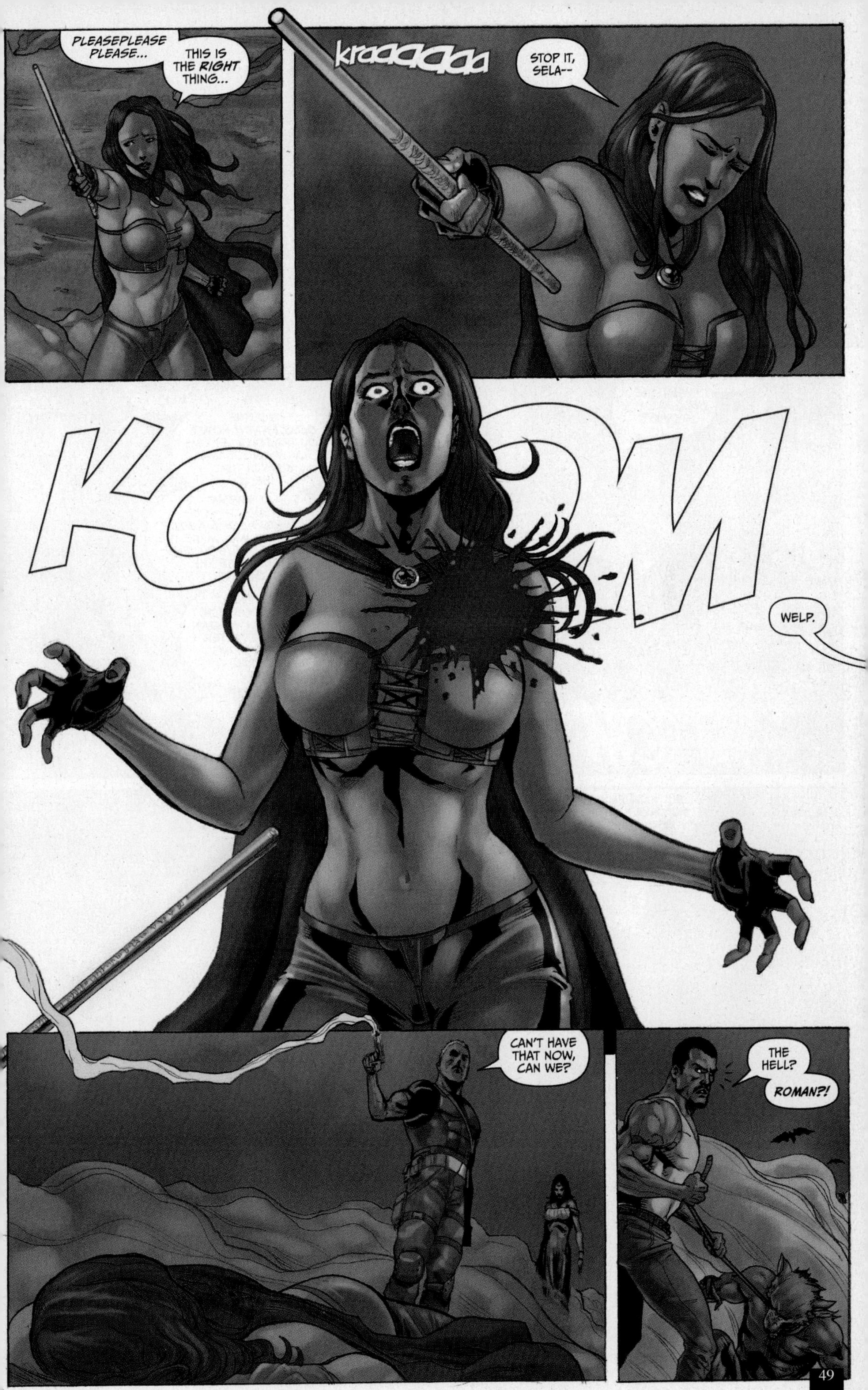
PLEASEPLEASE PLEASE...
THIS IS THE *RIGHT* THING...
kraaaaaa
STOP IT, SELA--
WELP.
CAN'T HAVE THAT NOW, CAN WE?
THE HELL?
ROMAN?!

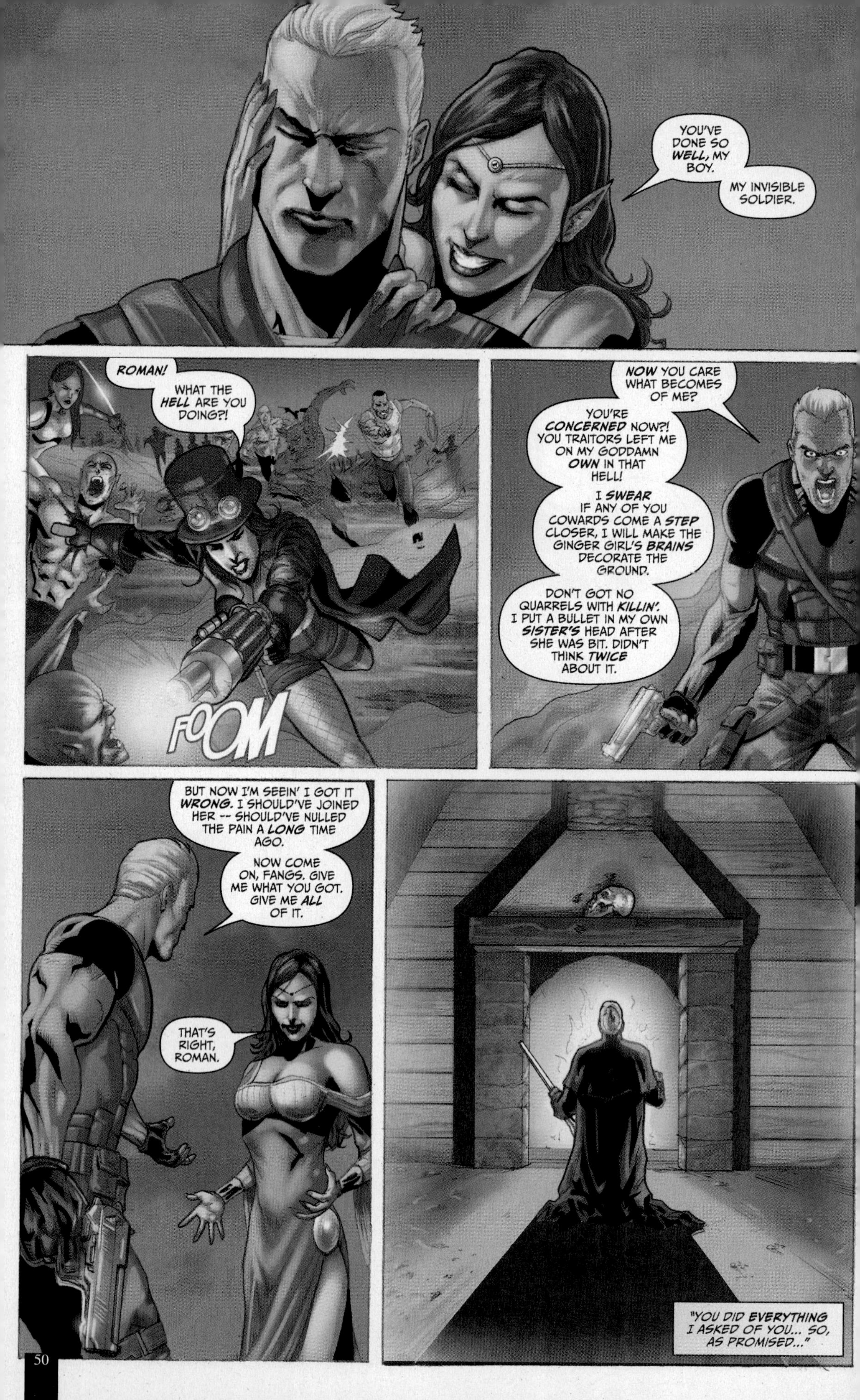

YOU'VE DONE SO WELL, MY BOY.
MY INVISIBLE SOLDIER.
ROMAN!
WHAT THE HELL ARE YOU DOING?!
FOOM
NOW YOU CARE WHAT BECOMES OF ME?
YOU'RE CONCERNED NOW?! YOU TRAITORS LEFT ME ON MY GODDAMN OWN IN THAT HELL!
I SWEAR IF ANY OF YOU COWARDS COME A STEP CLOSER, I WILL MAKE THE GINGER GIRL'S BRAINS DECORATE THE GROUND.
DON'T GOT NO QUARRELS WITH KILLIN'. I PUT A BULLET IN MY OWN SISTER'S HEAD AFTER SHE WAS BIT. DIDN'T THINK TWICE ABOUT IT.
BUT NOW I'M SEEIN' I GOT IT WRONG. I SHOULD'VE JOINED HER -- SHOULD'VE NULLED THE PAIN A LONG TIME AGO.
NOW COME ON, FANGS. GIVE ME WHAT YOU GOT. GIVE ME ALL OF IT.
THAT'S RIGHT, ROMAN.
"YOU DID EVERYTHING I ASKED OF YOU... SO, AS PROMISED..."

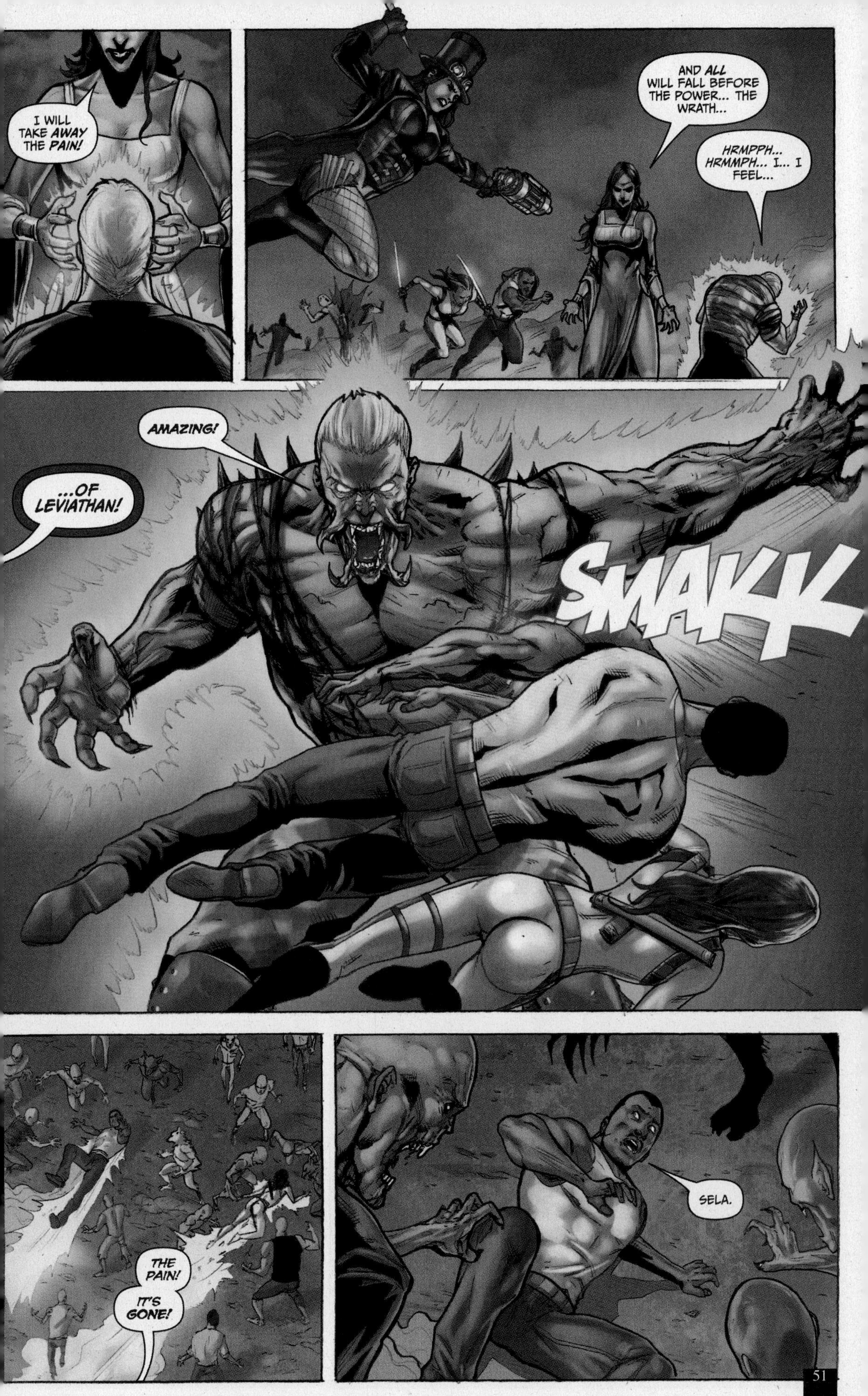
I WILL TAKE AWAY THE PAIN!
AND ALL WILL FALL BEFORE THE POWER... THE WRATH...
HRMPPH... HRMMPH... I... I FEEL...
AMAZING!
...OF LEVIATHAN!
SMAKK
THE PAIN!
IT'S GONE!
SELA.

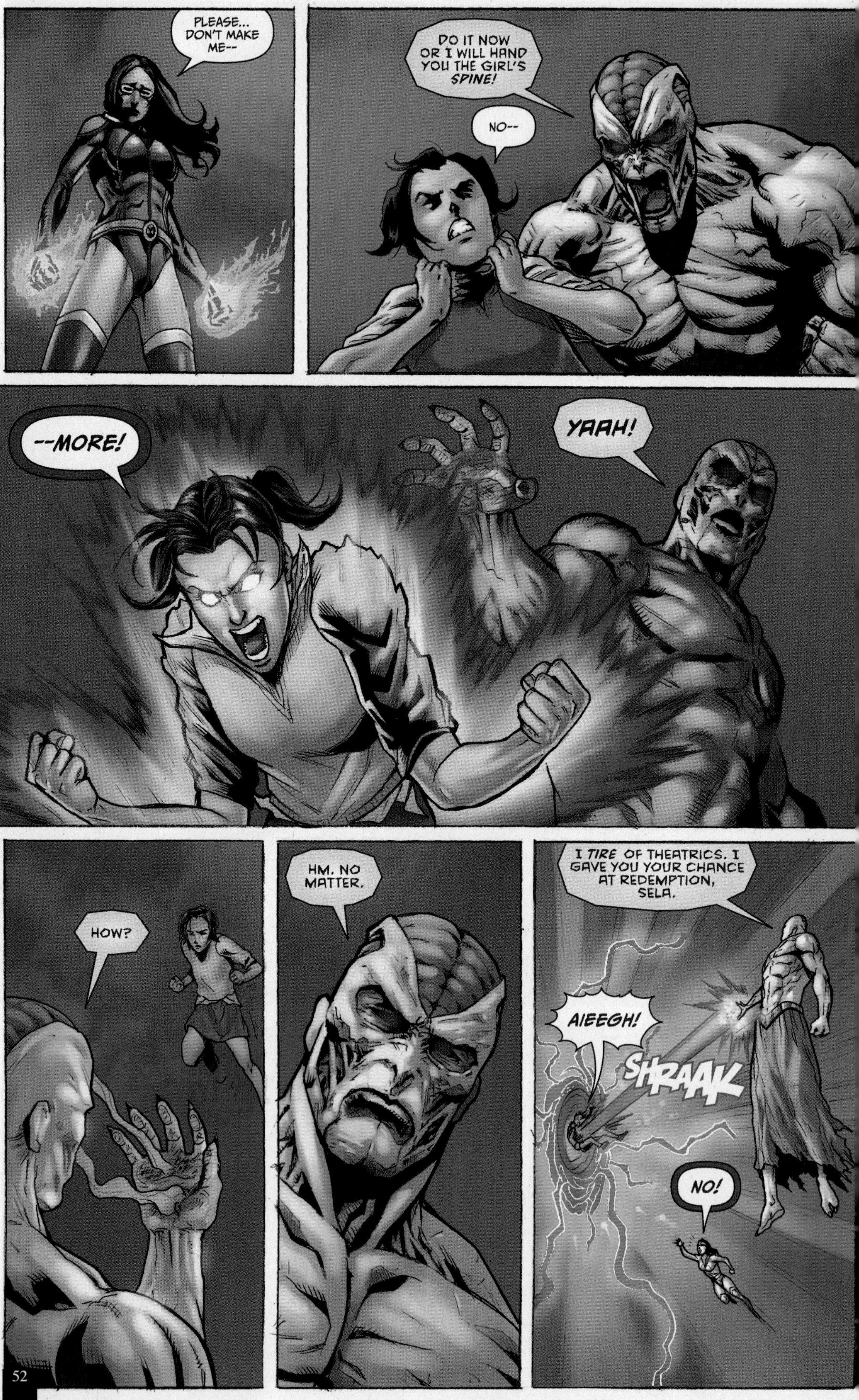
PLEASE... DON'T MAKE ME--
DO IT NOW OR I WILL HAND YOU THE GIRL'S SPINE!
NO--
--MORE!
YAAH!
HOW?
HM. NO MATTER.
I TIRE OF THEATRICS. I GAVE YOU YOUR CHANCE AT REDEMPTION, SELA.
AIEEGH!
SHRAAK
NO!

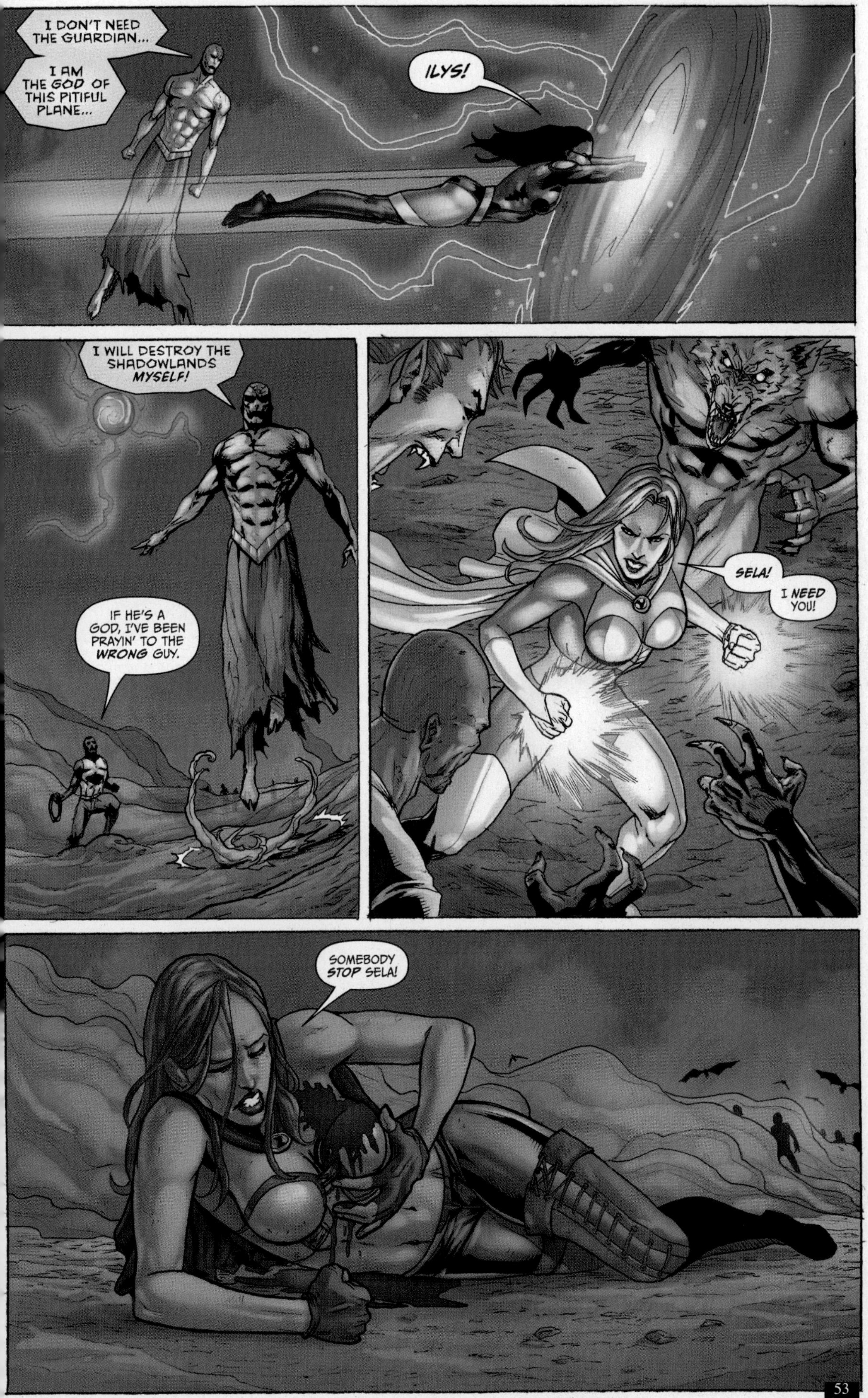
I DON'T NEED THE GUARDIAN...
I AM THE GOD OF THIS PITIFUL PLANE...
ILYS!
I WILL DESTROY THE SHADOWLANDS MYSELF!
IF HE'S A GOD, I'VE BEEN PRAYIN' TO THE WRONG GUY.
SELA!
I NEED YOU!
SOMEBODY STOP SELA!

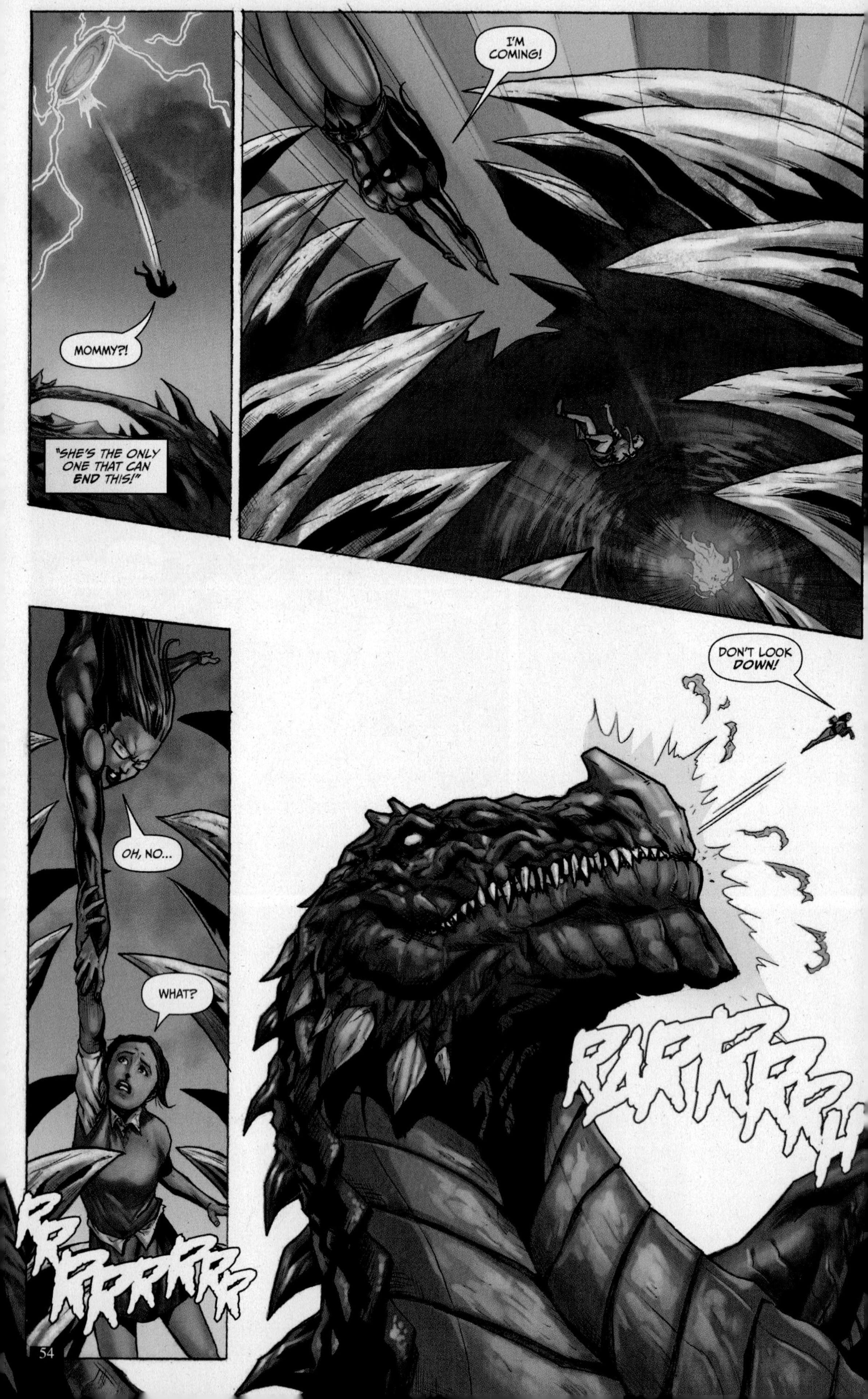
MOMMY?!
"SHE'S THE ONLY ONE THAT CAN END THIS!"
I'M COMING!
OH, NO...
WHAT?
DON'T LOOK DOWN!
RAAARRRRRH
RRRRRRRRR

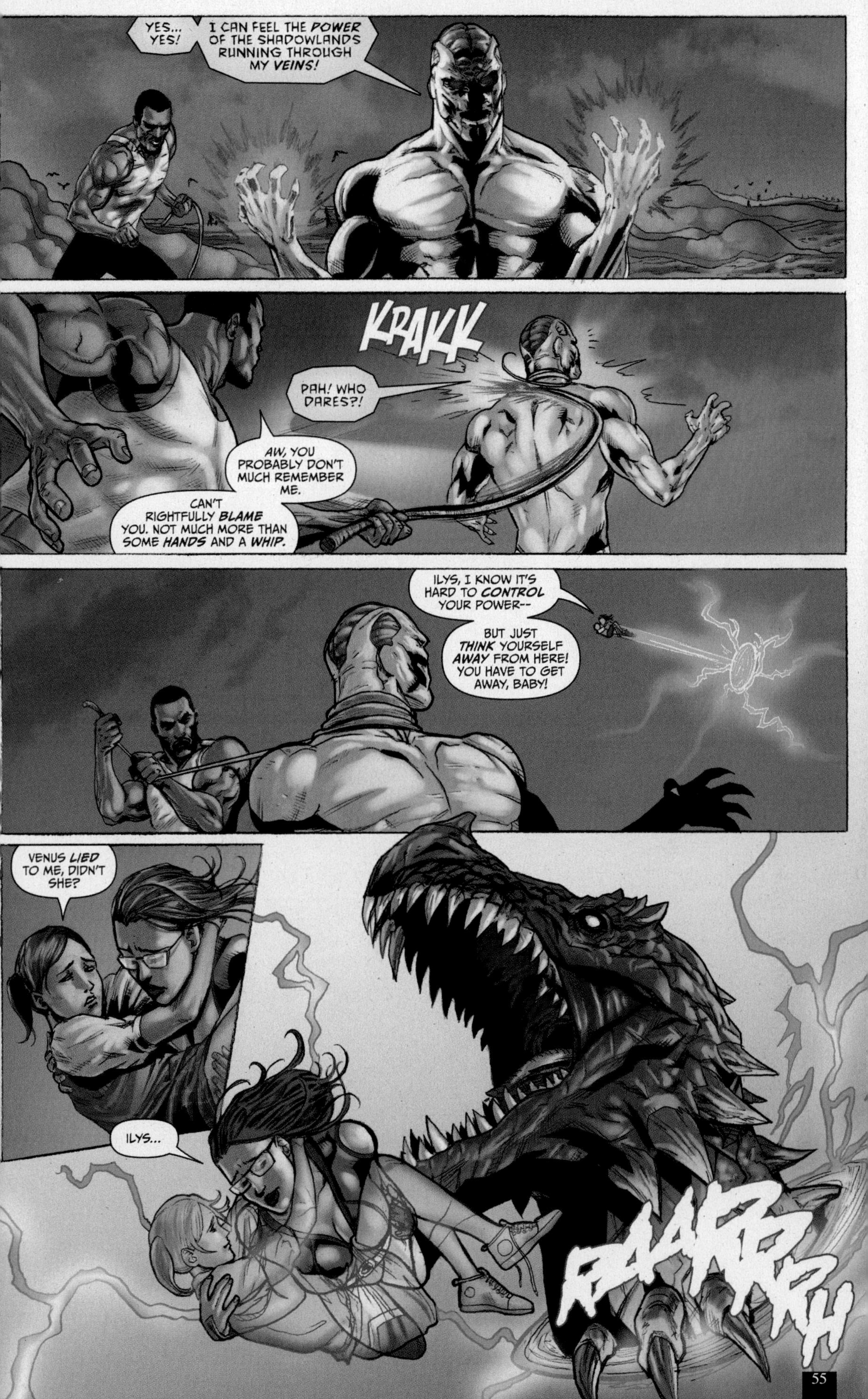
YES... YES!
I CAN FEEL THE POWER OF THE SHADOWLANDS RUNNING THROUGH MY VEINS!
KRAKK
PAH! WHO DARES?!
AW, YOU PROBABLY DON'T MUCH REMEMBER ME.
CAN'T RIGHTFULLY BLAME YOU. NOT MUCH MORE THAN SOME HANDS AND A WHIP.
ILYS, I KNOW IT'S HARD TO CONTROL YOUR POWER--
BUT JUST THINK YOURSELF AWAY FROM HERE! YOU HAVE TO GET AWAY, BABY!
VENUS LIED TO ME, DIDN'T SHE?
ILYS...

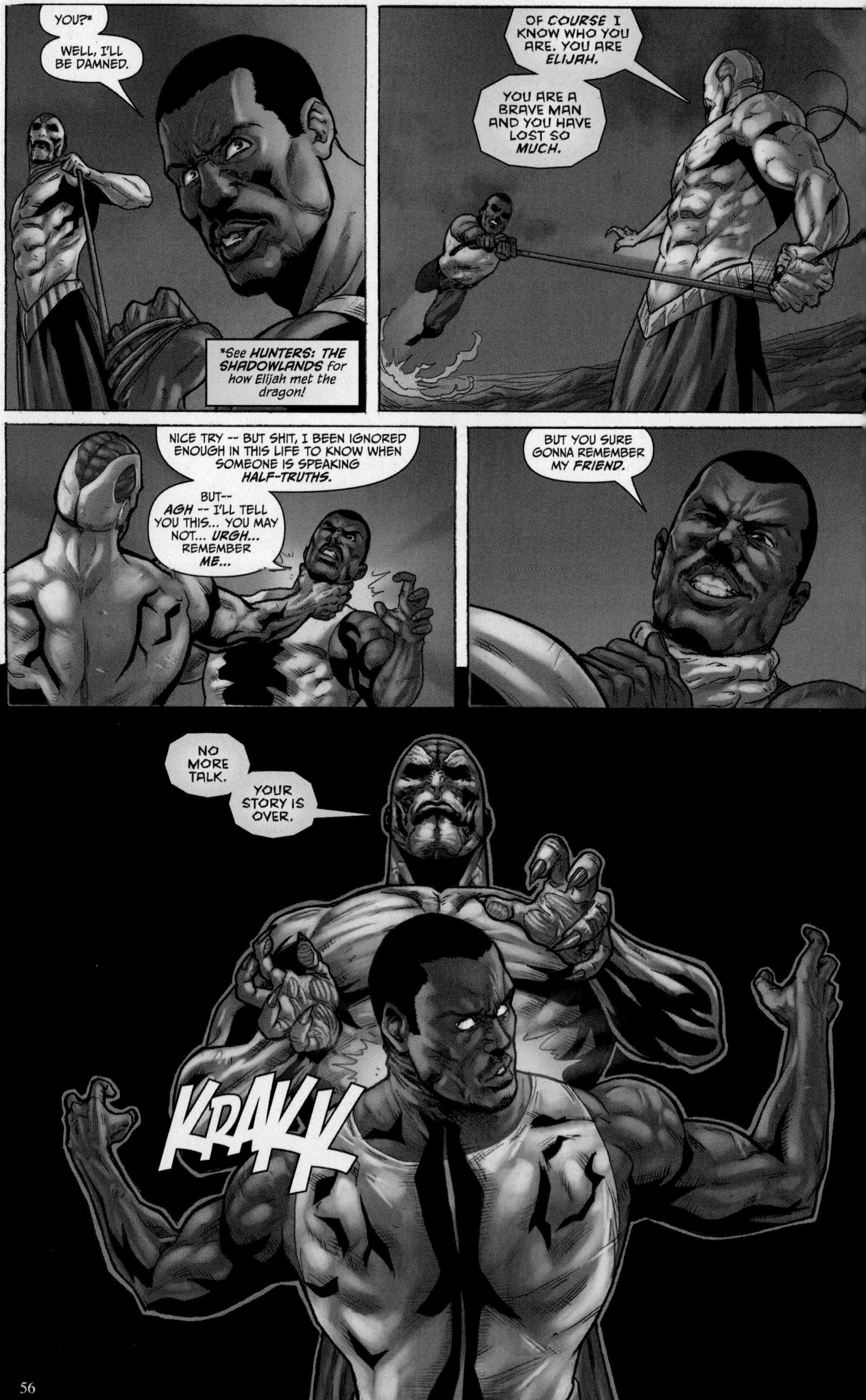
YOU?*
WELL, I'LL BE DAMNED.
*See HUNTERS: THE SHADOWLANDS for how Elijah met the dragon!
OF COURSE I KNOW WHO YOU ARE. YOU ARE ELIJAH.
YOU ARE A BRAVE MAN AND YOU HAVE LOST SO MUCH.
NICE TRY -- BUT SHIT, I BEEN IGNORED ENOUGH IN THIS LIFE TO KNOW WHEN SOMEONE IS SPEAKING HALF-TRUTHS.
BUT-- AGH -- I'LL TELL YOU THIS... YOU MAY NOT... URGH... REMEMBER ME...
BUT YOU SURE GONNA REMEMBER MY FRIEND.
NO MORE TALK.
YOUR STORY IS OVER.
KRAKK

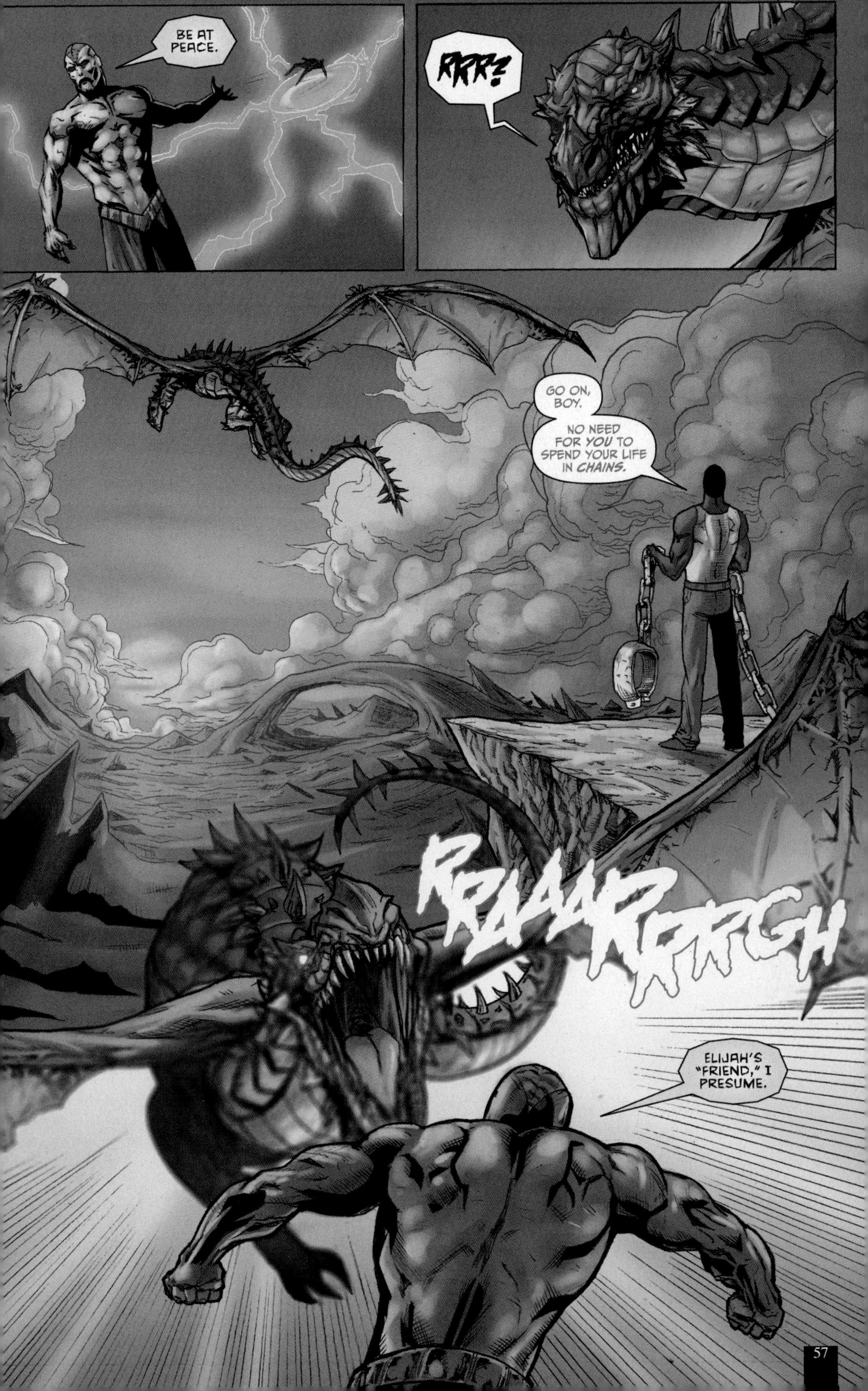
BE AT PEACE.
RRRR?
GO ON, BOY.
NO NEED FOR *YOU* TO SPEND YOUR LIFE IN *CHAINS*.
RRAAARRRRGH
ELIJAH'S "FRIEND," I PRESUME.

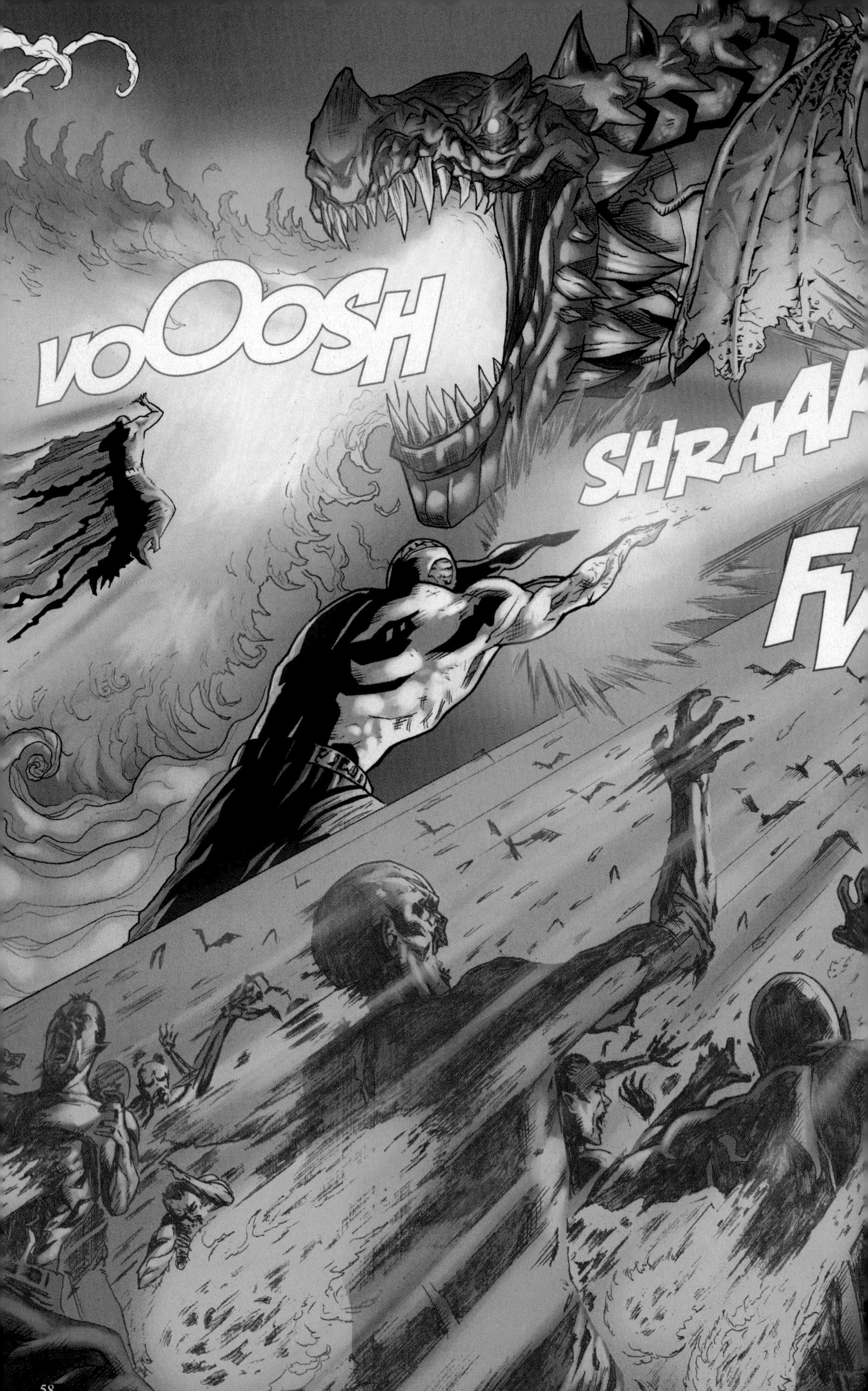
VOOOSH
SHRAA
FW

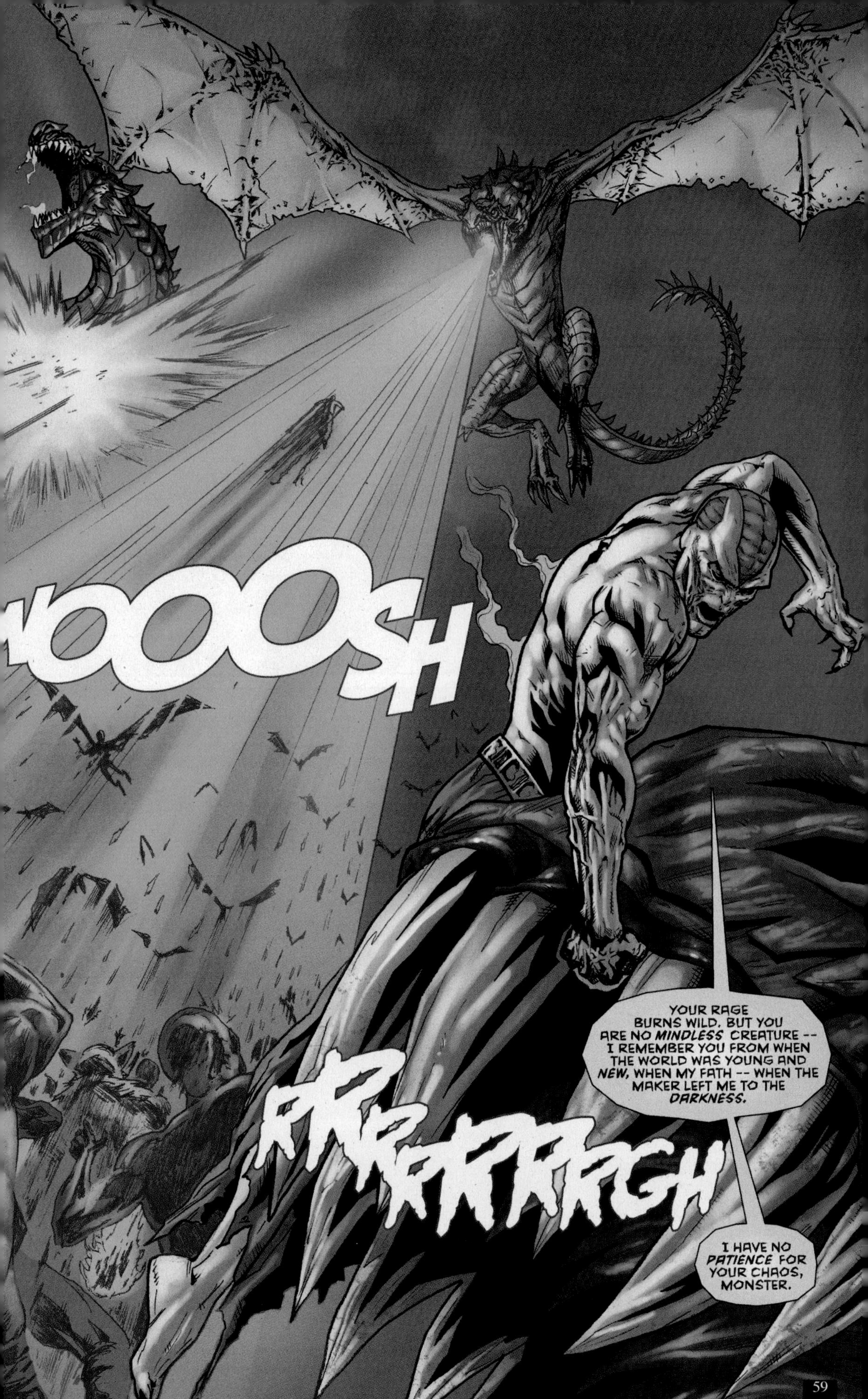
WHOOOSH
YOUR RAGE BURNS WILD, BUT YOU ARE NO MINDLESS CREATURE -- I REMEMBER YOU FROM WHEN THE WORLD WAS YOUNG AND NEW, WHEN MY FATH -- WHEN THE MAKER LEFT ME TO THE DARKNESS.
RRRRRRRGH
I HAVE NO PATIENCE FOR YOUR CHAOS, MONSTER.

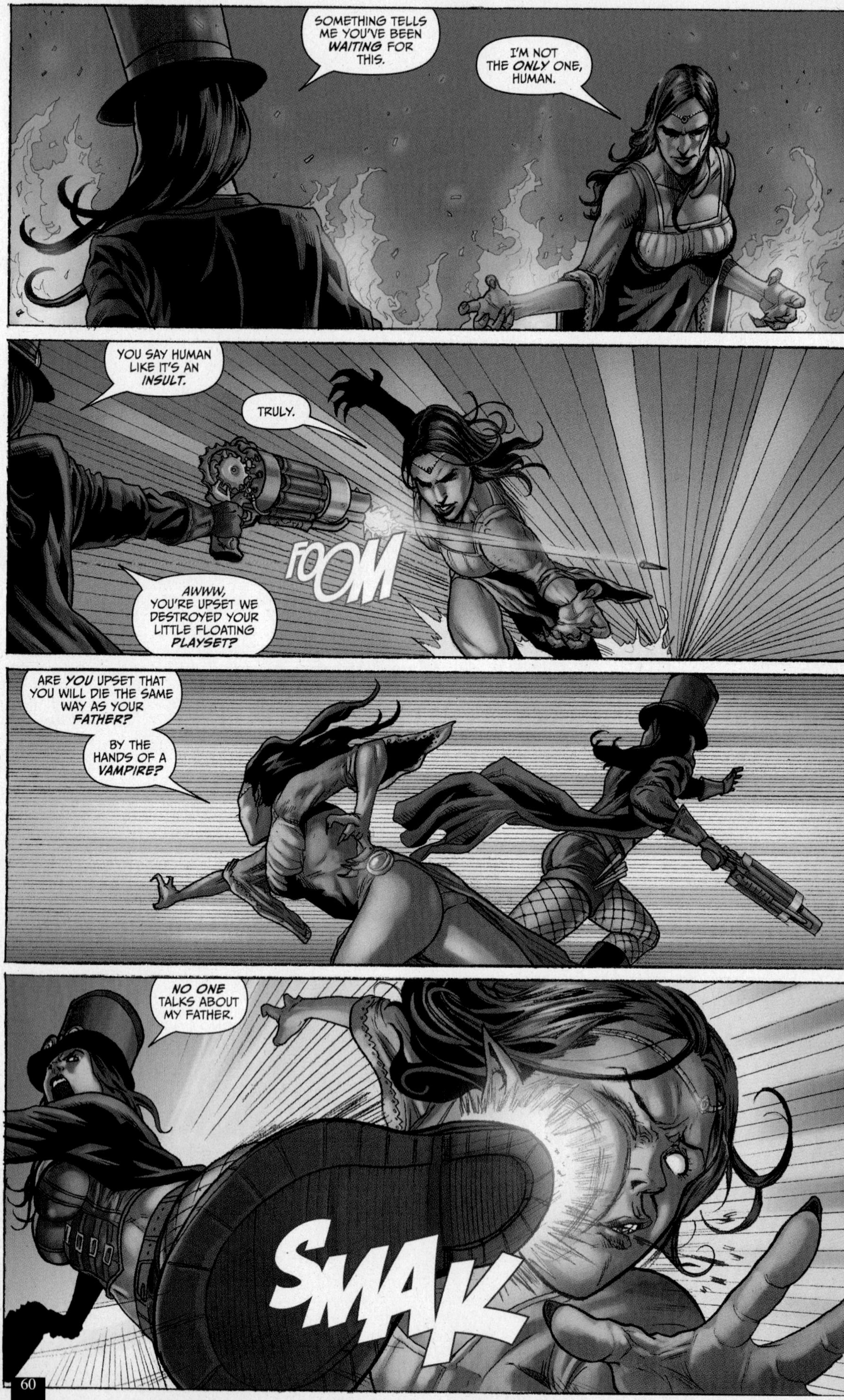
SOMETHING TELLS ME YOU'VE BEEN *WAITING* FOR THIS.
I'M NOT THE *ONLY* ONE, HUMAN.
YOU SAY HUMAN LIKE IT'S AN *INSULT.*
TRULY.
FOOM
AWWW, YOU'RE UPSET WE DESTROYED YOUR LITTLE FLOATING *PLAYSET?*
ARE *YOU* UPSET THAT YOU WILL DIE THE SAME WAY AS YOUR *FATHER?*
BY THE HANDS OF A *VAMPIRE?*
NO ONE TALKS ABOUT MY FATHER.
SMAK

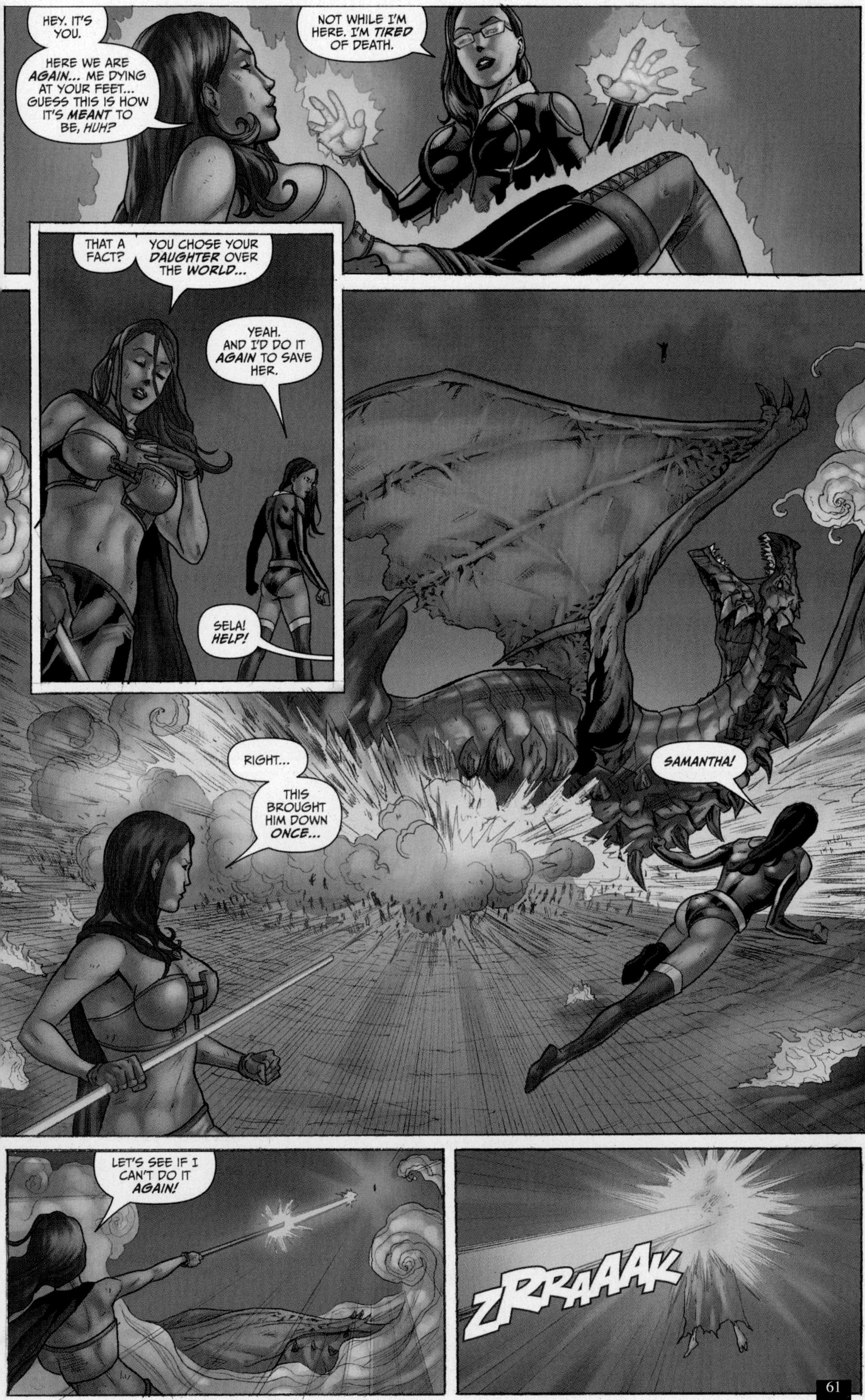

HEY. IT'S YOU.
HERE WE ARE AGAIN... ME DYING AT YOUR FEET... GUESS THIS IS HOW IT'S MEANT TO BE, HUH?
NOT WHILE I'M HERE. I'M TIRED OF DEATH.
THAT A FACT?
YOU CHOSE YOUR DAUGHTER OVER THE WORLD...
YEAH. AND I'D DO IT AGAIN TO SAVE HER.
SELA! HELP!
RIGHT...
THIS BROUGHT HIM DOWN ONCE...
SAMANTHA!
LET'S SEE IF I CAN'T DO IT AGAIN!
ZRRAAAK

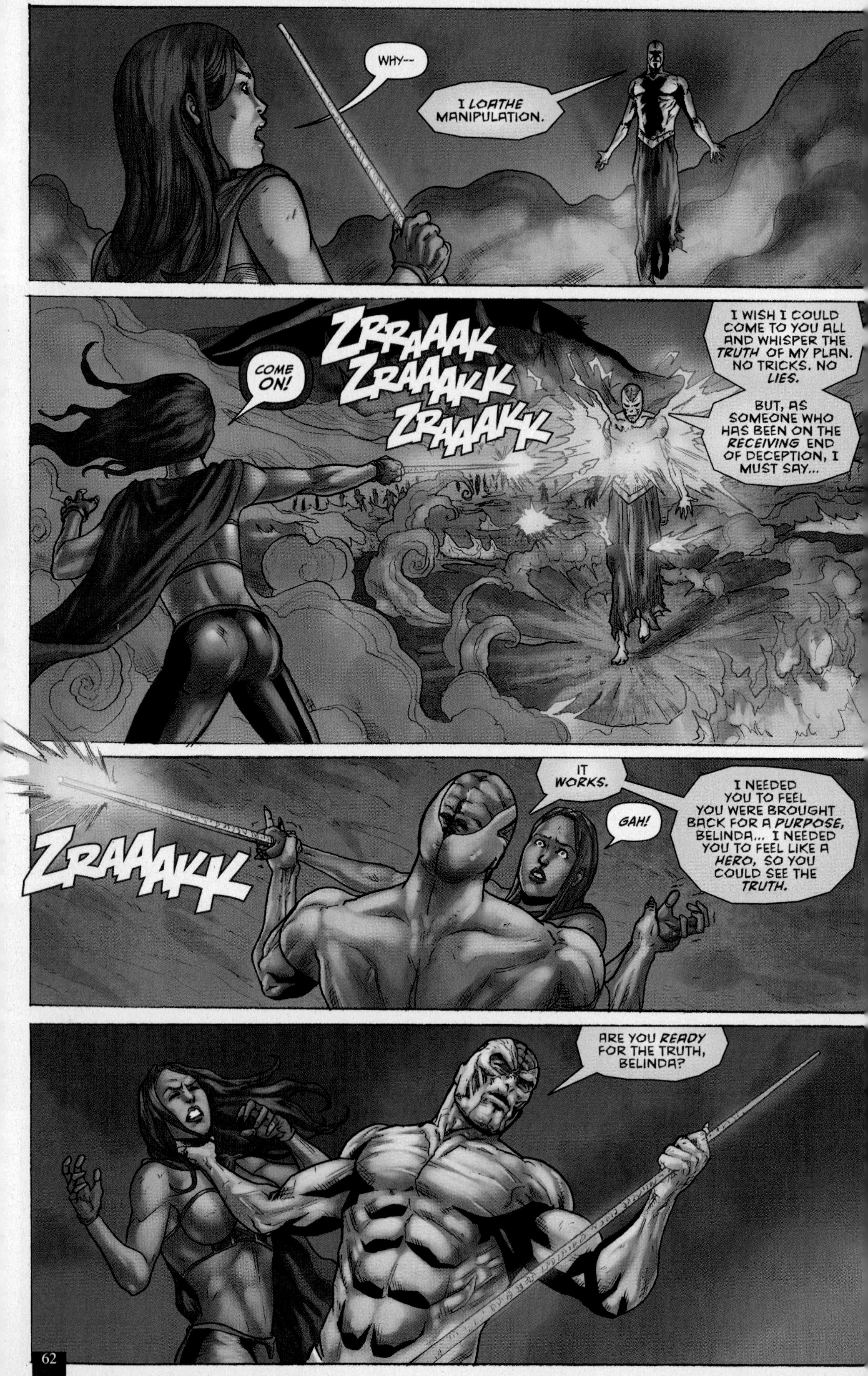
WHY--
I LOATHE MANIPULATION.
ZRRAAAK ZRAAAKK ZRAAAKK
COME ON!
I WISH I COULD COME TO YOU ALL AND WHISPER THE TRUTH OF MY PLAN. NO TRICKS. NO LIES.
BUT, AS SOMEONE WHO HAS BEEN ON THE RECEIVING END OF DECEPTION, I MUST SAY...
ZRAAAKK
IT WORKS.
GAH!
I NEEDED YOU TO FEEL YOU WERE BROUGHT BACK FOR A PURPOSE, BELINDA... I NEEDED YOU TO FEEL LIKE A HERO, SO YOU COULD SEE THE TRUTH.
ARE YOU READY FOR THE TRUTH, BELINDA?

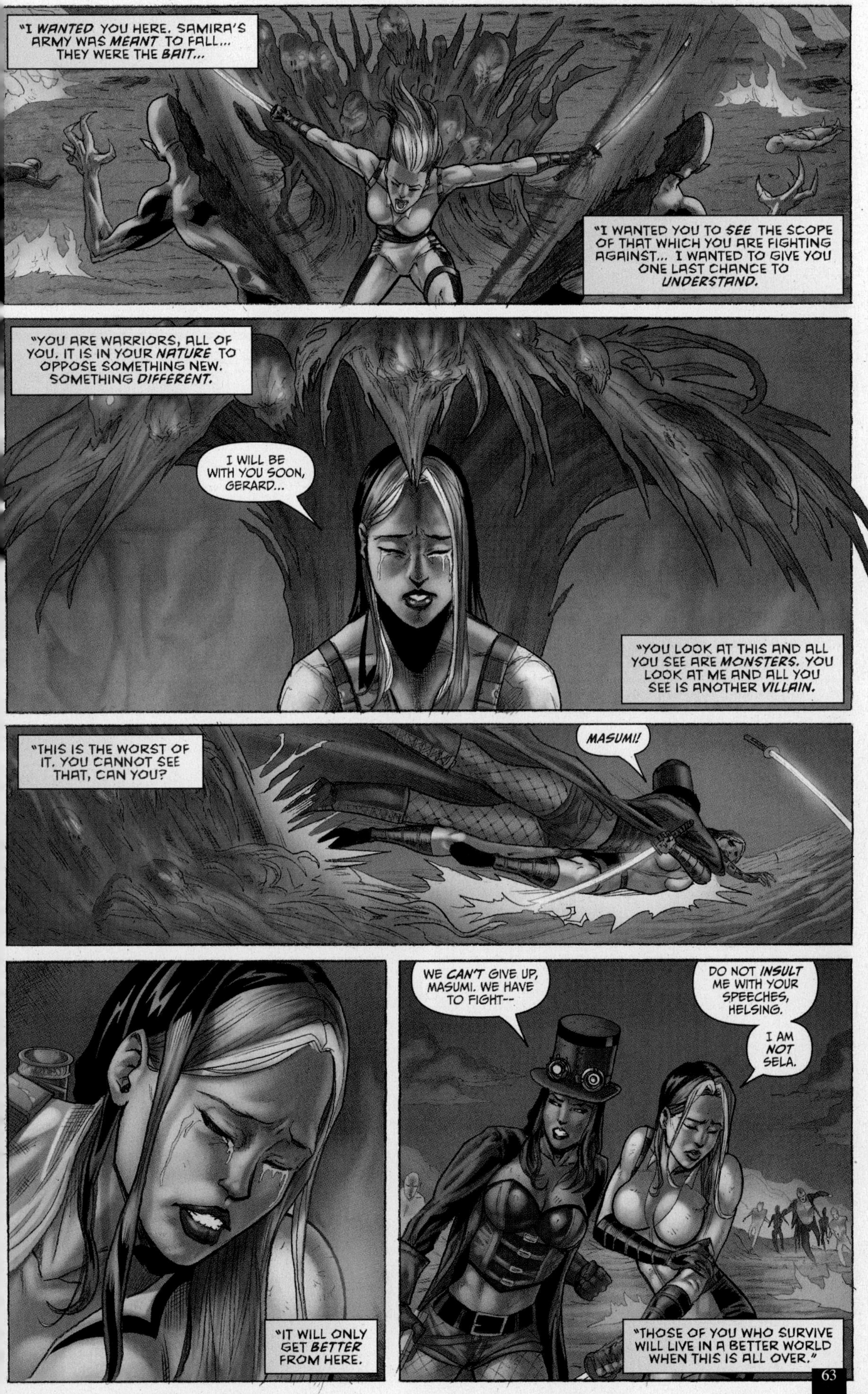
"I WANTED YOU HERE. SAMIRA'S ARMY WAS MEANT TO FALL... THEY WERE THE BAIT...
"I WANTED YOU TO SEE THE SCOPE OF THAT WHICH YOU ARE FIGHTING AGAINST... I WANTED TO GIVE YOU ONE LAST CHANCE TO UNDERSTAND.
"YOU ARE WARRIORS, ALL OF YOU. IT IS IN YOUR NATURE TO OPPOSE SOMETHING NEW. SOMETHING DIFFERENT.
I WILL BE WITH YOU SOON, GERARD...
"YOU LOOK AT THIS AND ALL YOU SEE ARE MONSTERS. YOU LOOK AT ME AND ALL YOU SEE IS ANOTHER VILLAIN.
"THIS IS THE WORST OF IT. YOU CANNOT SEE THAT, CAN YOU?
MASUMI!
"IT WILL ONLY GET BETTER FROM HERE.
WE CAN'T GIVE UP, MASUMI. WE HAVE TO FIGHT--
DO NOT INSULT ME WITH YOUR SPEECHES, HELSING.
I AM NOT SELA.
"THOSE OF YOU WHO SURVIVE WILL LIVE IN A BETTER WORLD WHEN THIS IS ALL OVER."

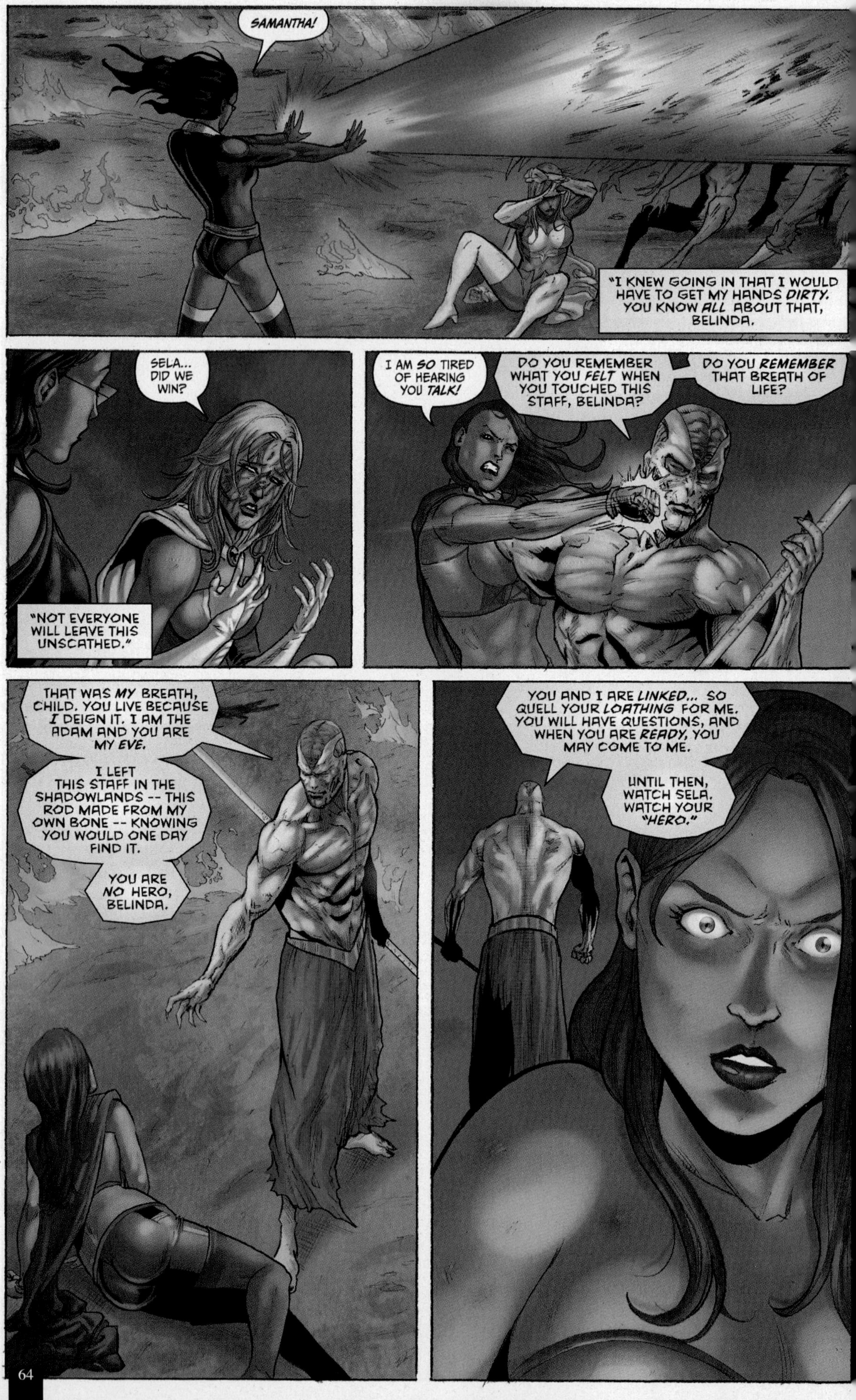

SAMANTHA!
"I KNEW GOING IN THAT I WOULD HAVE TO GET MY HANDS DIRTY. YOU KNOW ALL ABOUT THAT, BELINDA.
SELA... DID WE WIN?
"NOT EVERYONE WILL LEAVE THIS UNSCATHED."
I AM SO TIRED OF HEARING YOU TALK!
DO YOU REMEMBER WHAT YOU FELT WHEN YOU TOUCHED THIS STAFF, BELINDA?
DO YOU REMEMBER THAT BREATH OF LIFE?
THAT WAS MY BREATH, CHILD. YOU LIVE BECAUSE I DEIGN IT. I AM THE ADAM AND YOU ARE MY EVE.
I LEFT THIS STAFF IN THE SHADOWLANDS -- THIS ROD MADE FROM MY OWN BONE -- KNOWING YOU WOULD ONE DAY FIND IT.
YOU ARE NO HERO, BELINDA.
YOU AND I ARE LINKED... SO QUELL YOUR LOATHING FOR ME. YOU WILL HAVE QUESTIONS, AND WHEN YOU ARE READY, YOU MAY COME TO ME.
UNTIL THEN, WATCH SELA. WATCH YOUR "HERO."

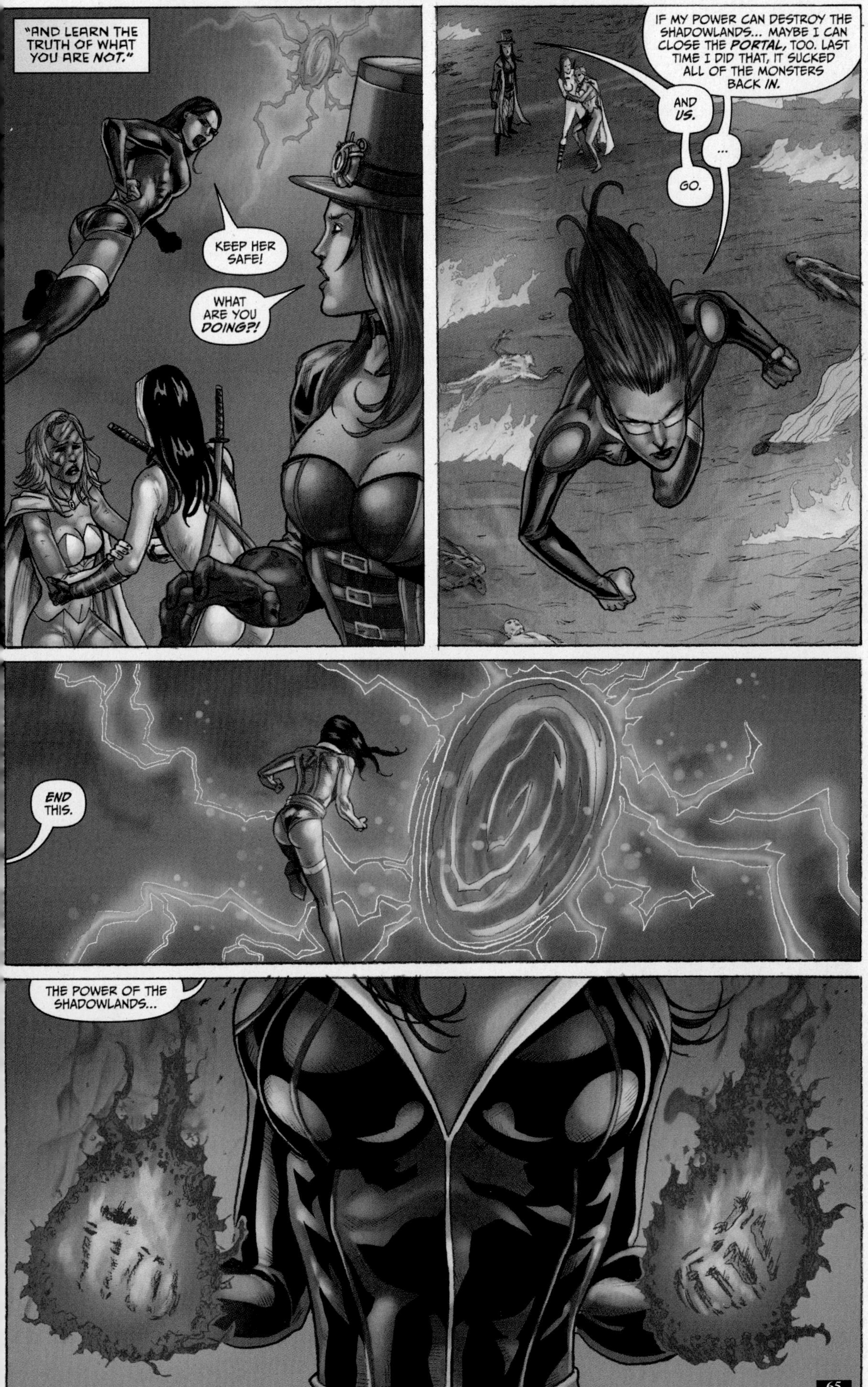
"AND LEARN THE TRUTH OF WHAT YOU ARE *NOT.*"
KEEP HER SAFE!
WHAT ARE YOU *DOING?!*
IF MY POWER CAN DESTROY THE SHADOWLANDS... MAYBE I CAN CLOSE THE *PORTAL,* TOO. LAST TIME I DID THAT, IT SUCKED ALL OF THE MONSTERS BACK *IN.*
AND *US.*
...
GO.
END THIS.
THE POWER OF THE SHADOWLANDS...

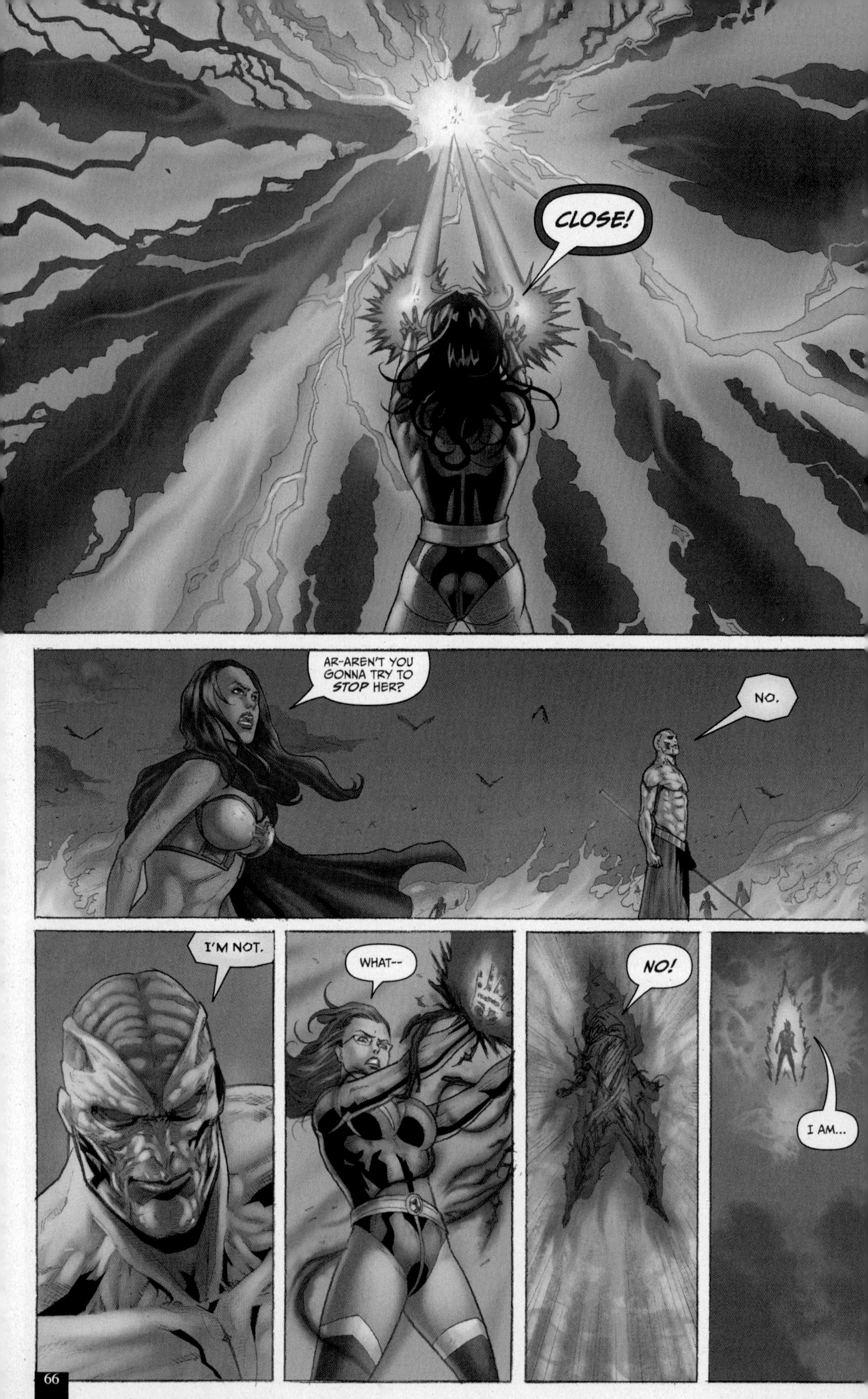
CLOSE!
AR-AREN'T YOU GONNA TRY TO STOP HER?
NO.
I'M NOT.
WHAT--
NO!
I AM...

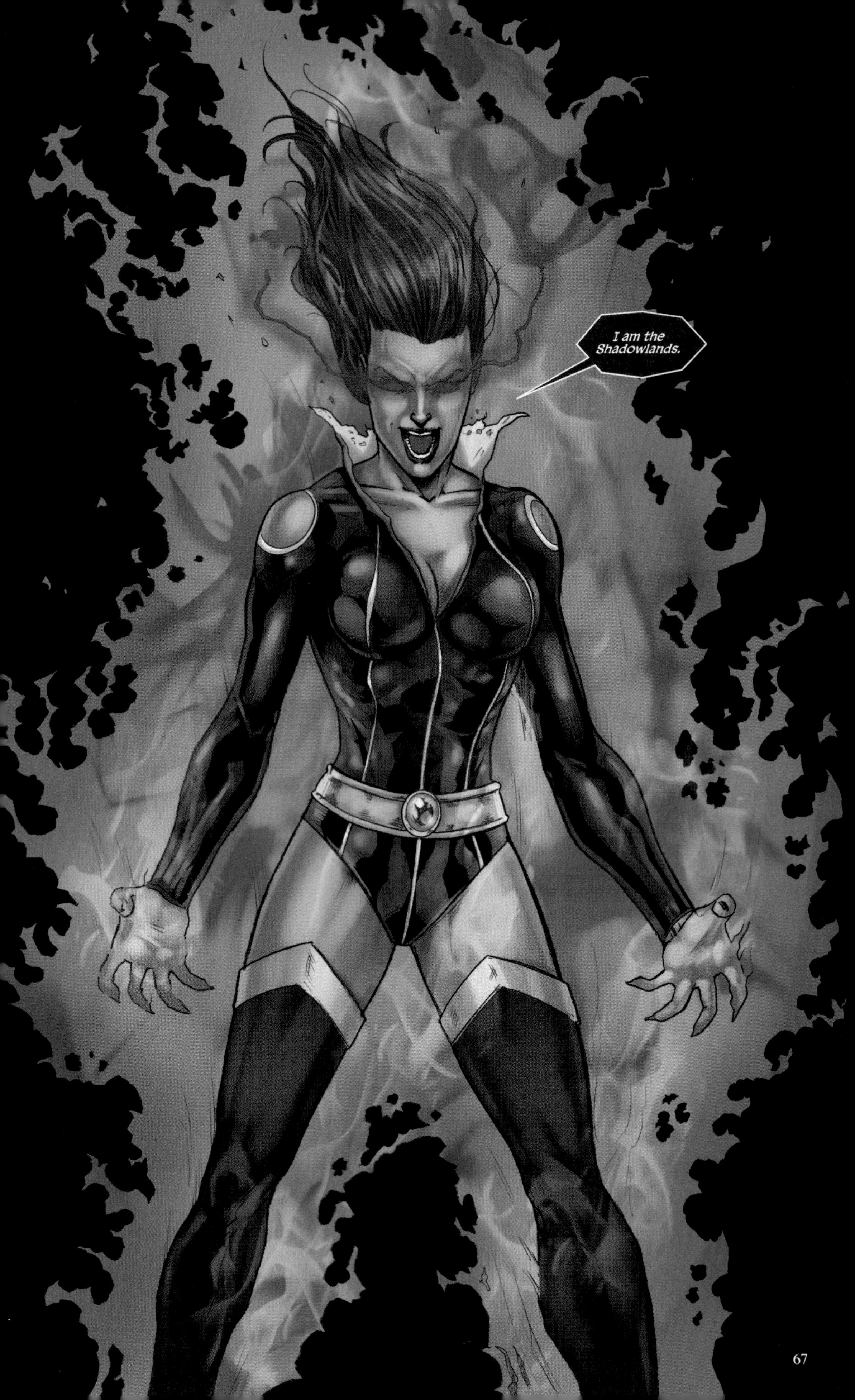
I am the Shadowlands.

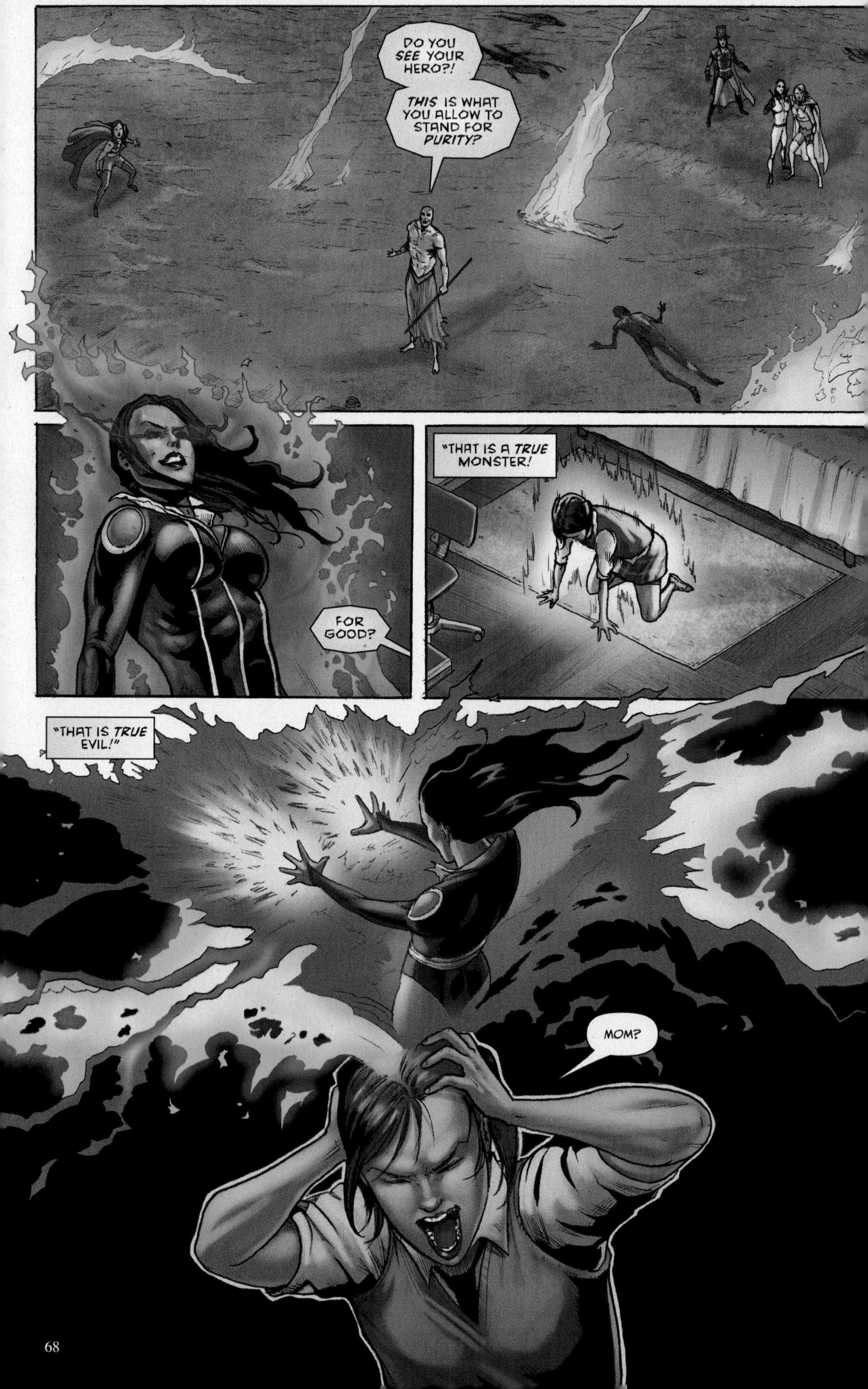
DO YOU SEE YOUR HERO?!
THIS IS WHAT YOU ALLOW TO STAND FOR PURITY?
FOR GOOD?
"THAT IS A TRUE MONSTER!
"THAT IS TRUE EVIL!"
MOM?

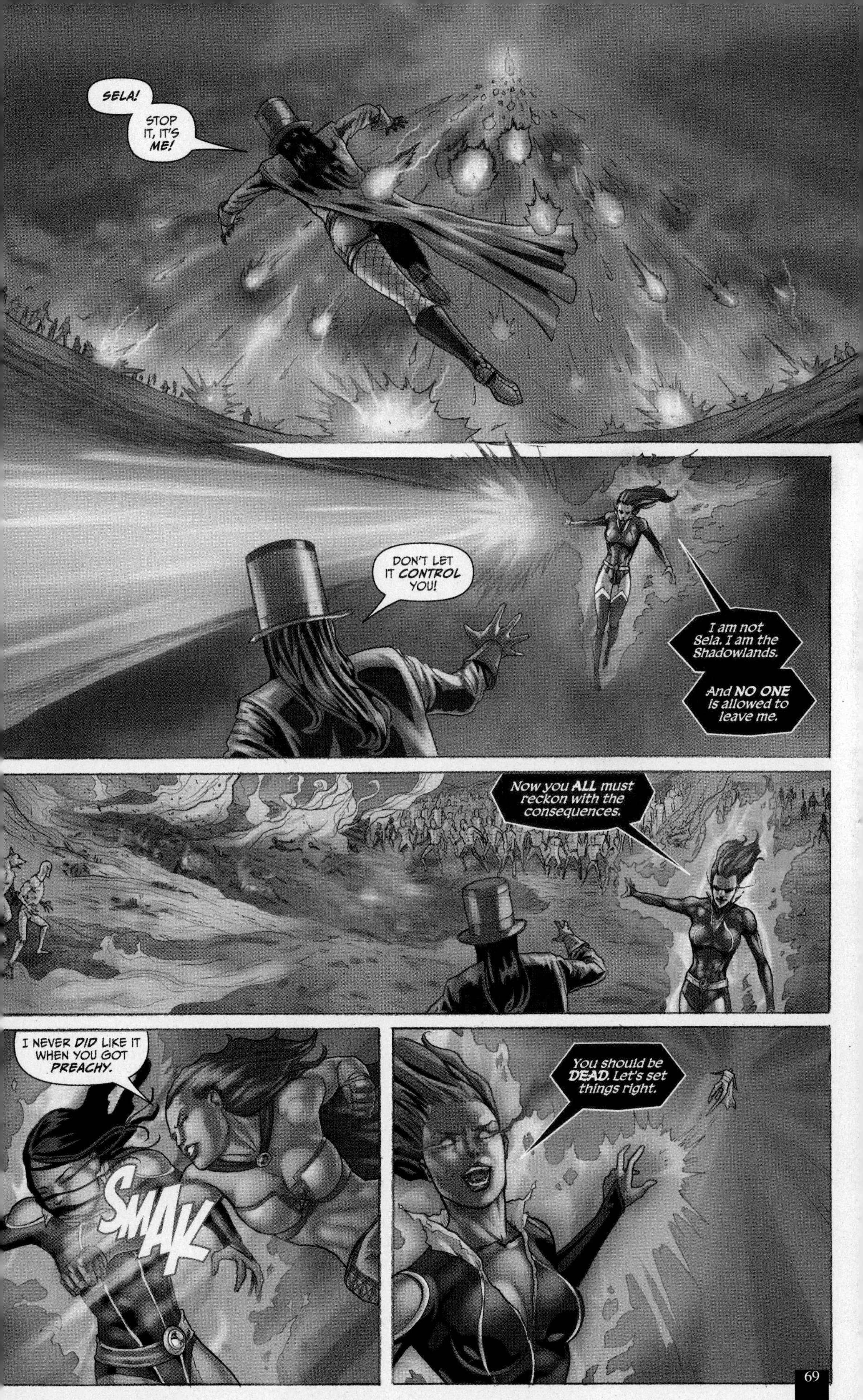
SELA!
STOP IT, IT'S ME!
DON'T LET IT CONTROL YOU!
I am not Sela. I am the Shadowlands.
And NO ONE is allowed to leave me.
Now you ALL must reckon with the consequences.
I NEVER DID LIKE IT WHEN YOU GOT PREACHY.
SMAK
You should be DEAD. Let's set things right.

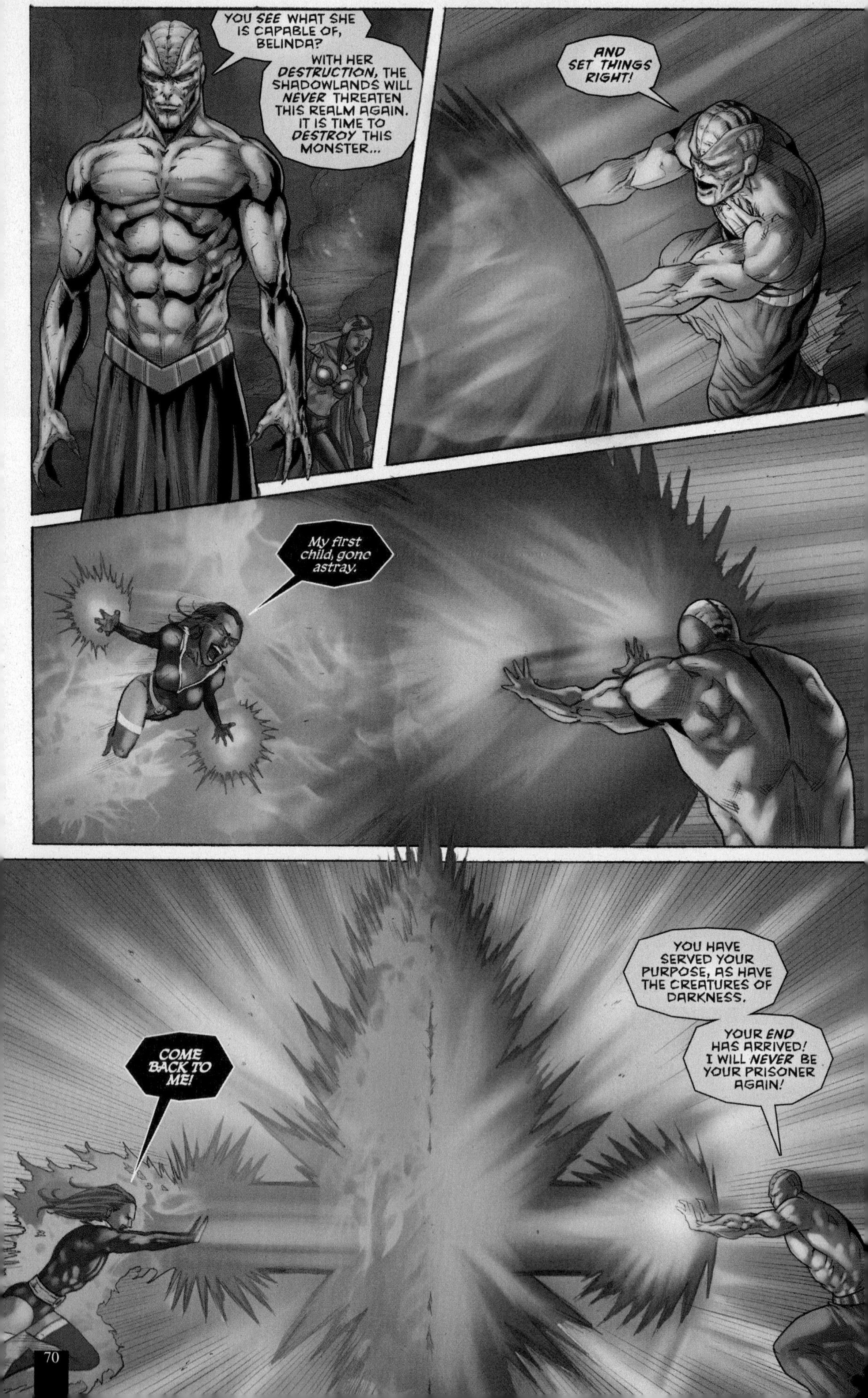
YOU SEE WHAT SHE IS CAPABLE OF, BELINDA?
WITH HER DESTRUCTION, THE SHADOWLANDS WILL NEVER THREATEN THIS REALM AGAIN. IT IS TIME TO DESTROY THIS MONSTER...
AND SET THINGS RIGHT!
My first child, gone astray.
YOU HAVE SERVED YOUR PURPOSE, AS HAVE THE CREATURES OF DARKNESS.
YOUR END HAS ARRIVED! I WILL NEVER BE YOUR PRISONER AGAIN!
COME BACK TO ME!

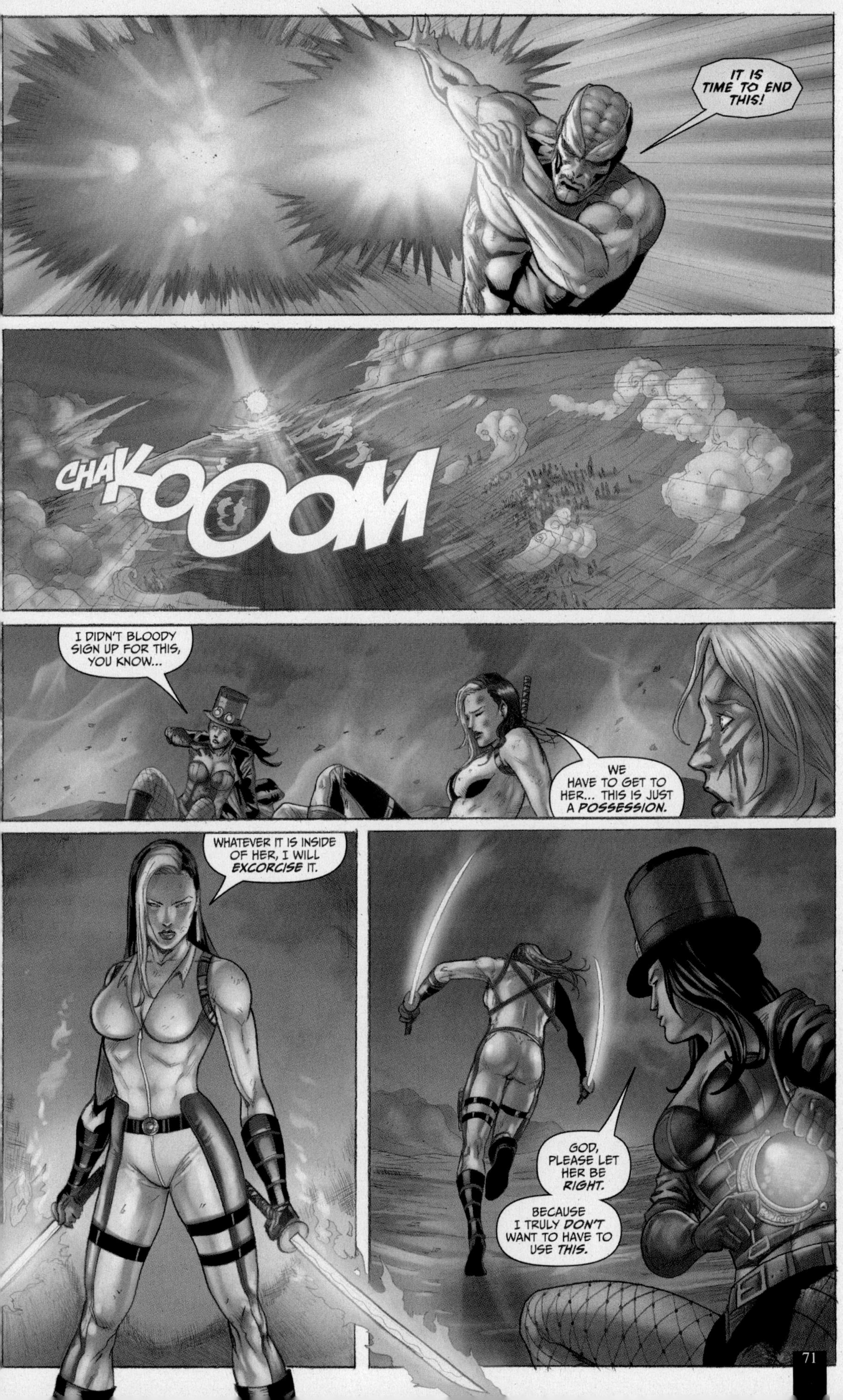
IT IS TIME TO END THIS!
CHAKOOOM
I DIDN'T BLOODY SIGN UP FOR THIS, YOU KNOW...
WE HAVE TO GET TO HER... THIS IS JUST A *POSSESSION.*
WHATEVER IT IS INSIDE OF HER, I WILL *EXCORCISE* IT.
GOD, PLEASE LET HER BE *RIGHT.*
BECAUSE I TRULY *DON'T* WANT TO HAVE TO USE *THIS.*

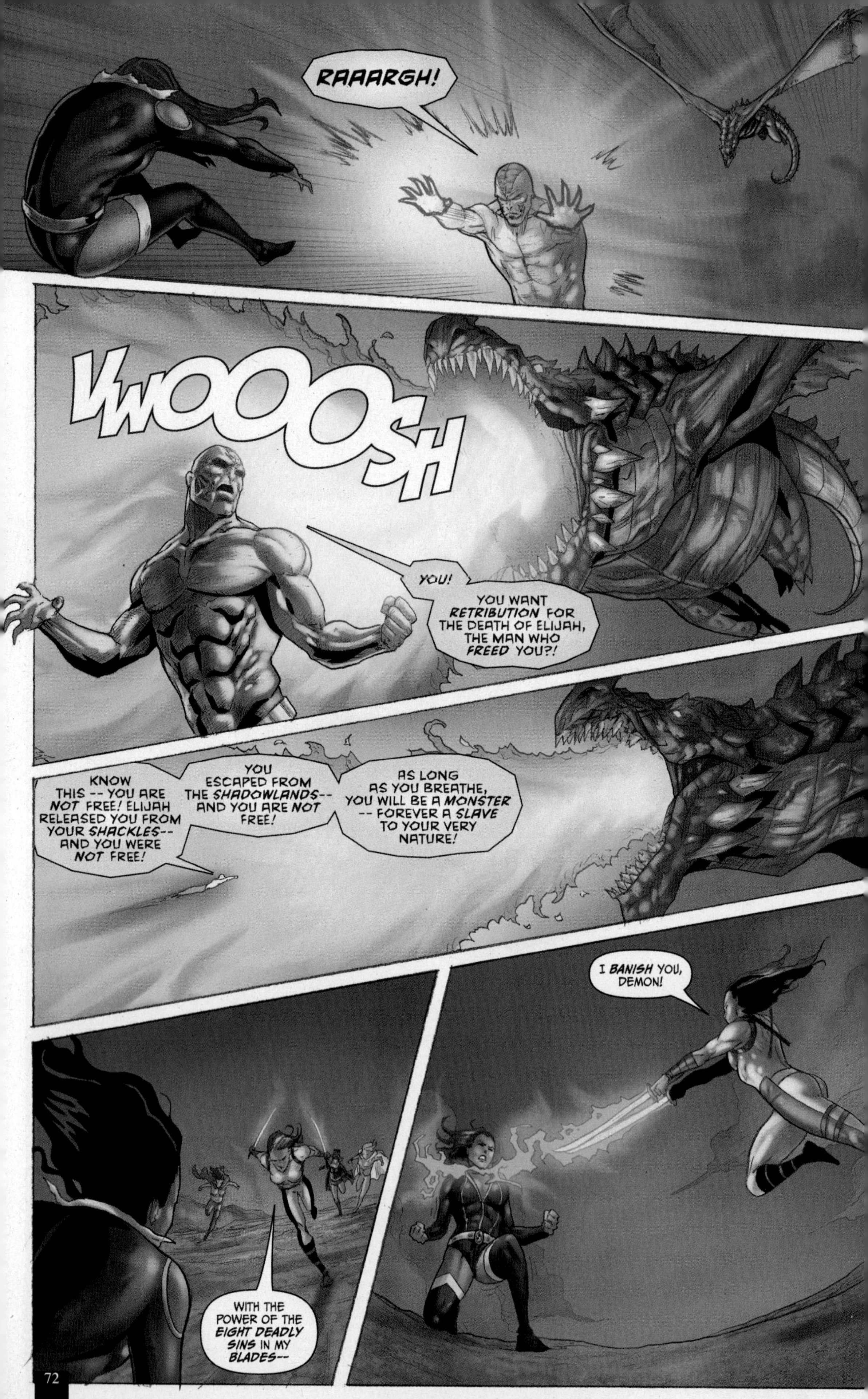
RAAARGH!
VWOOOSH
YOU!
YOU WANT RETRIBUTION FOR THE DEATH OF ELIJAH, THE MAN WHO FREED YOU?!
KNOW THIS -- YOU ARE NOT FREE! ELIJAH RELEASED YOU FROM YOUR SHACKLES-- AND YOU WERE NOT FREE!
YOU ESCAPED FROM THE SHADOWLANDS-- AND YOU ARE NOT FREE!
AS LONG AS YOU BREATHE, YOU WILL BE A MONSTER -- FOREVER A SLAVE TO YOUR VERY NATURE!
WITH THE POWER OF THE EIGHT DEADLY SINS IN MY BLADES--
I BANISH YOU, DEMON!

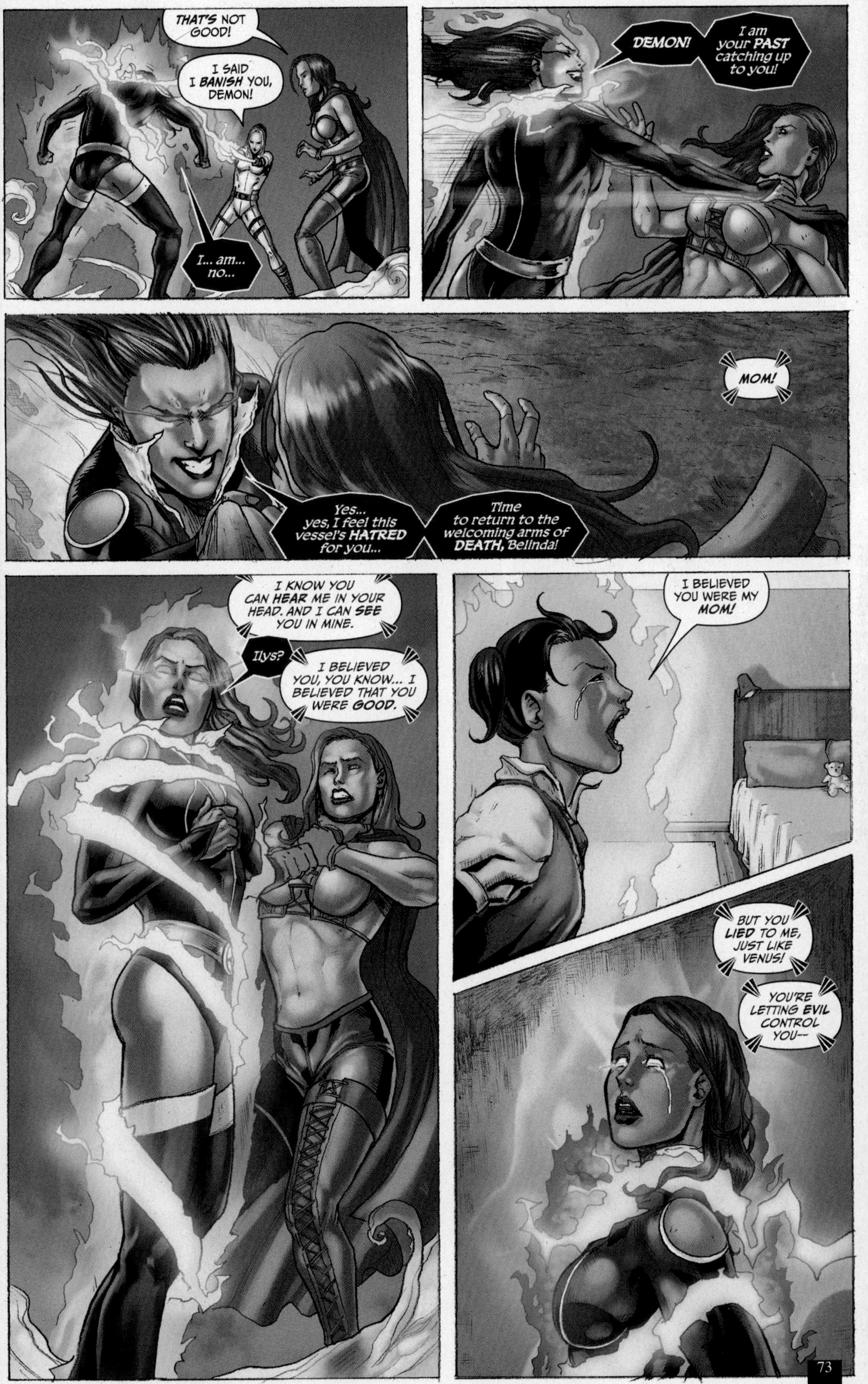
THAT'S NOT GOOD!
I SAID I BANISH YOU, DEMON!
I... am... no...
DEMON!
I am your PAST catching up to you!
MOM!
Yes... yes, I feel this vessel's HATRED for you...
Time to return to the welcoming arms of DEATH, Belinda!
I KNOW YOU CAN HEAR ME IN YOUR HEAD. AND I CAN SEE YOU IN MINE.
Ilys?
I BELIEVED YOU, YOU KNOW... I BELIEVED THAT YOU WERE GOOD.
I BELIEVED YOU WERE MY MOM!
BUT YOU LIED TO ME, JUST LIKE VENUS!
YOU'RE LETTING EVIL CONTROL YOU--

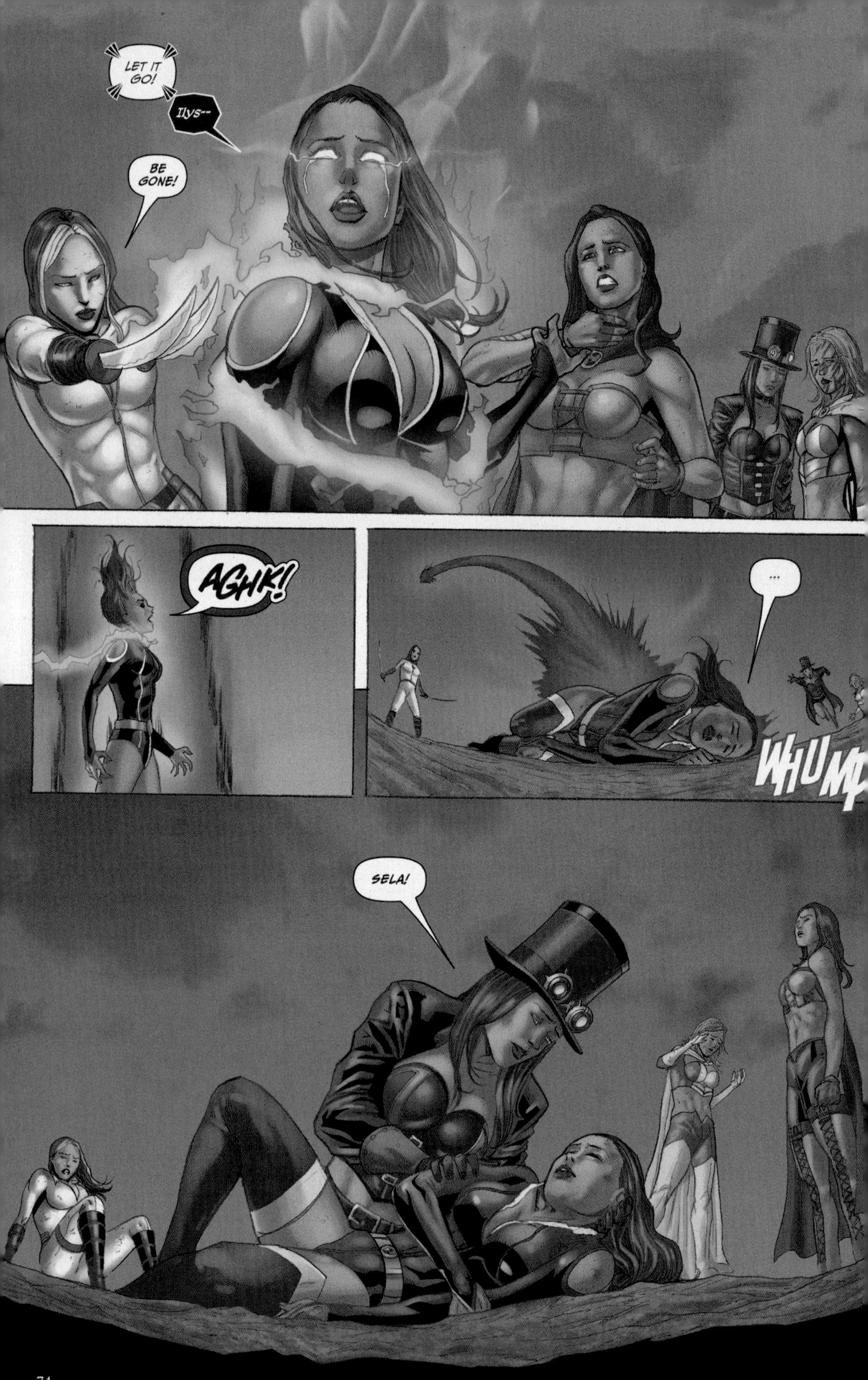
LET IT GO!
Ilys--
BE GONE!
AGHK!
...
WHUM
SELA!

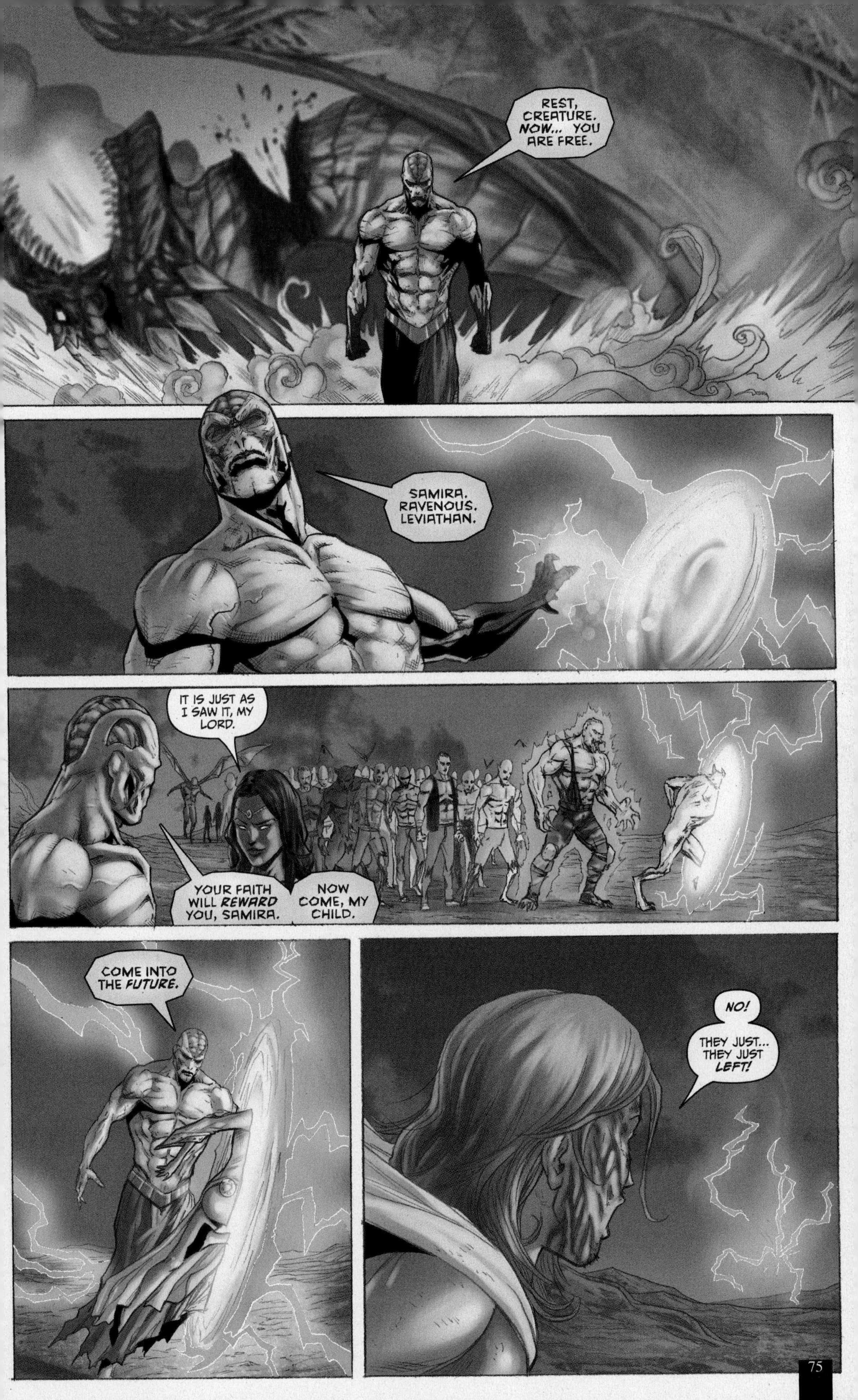

REST, CREATURE. NOW... YOU ARE FREE.
SAMIRA. RAVENOUS. LEVIATHAN.
IT IS JUST AS I SAW IT, MY LORD.
YOUR FAITH WILL REWARD YOU, SAMIRA.
NOW COME, MY CHILD.
COME INTO THE FUTURE.
NO!
THEY JUST... THEY JUST LEFT!

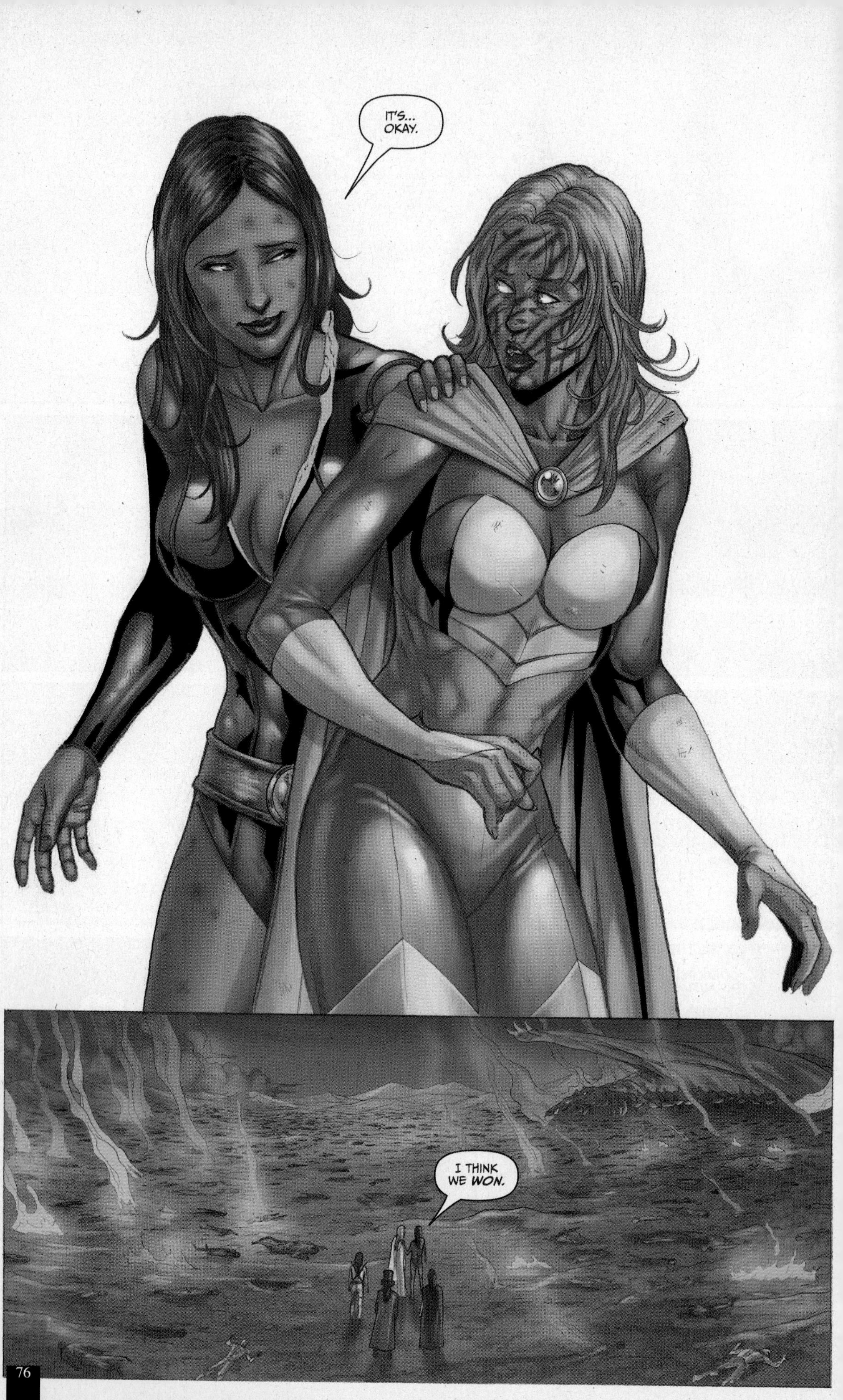
IT'S... OKAY.
I THINK WE WON.

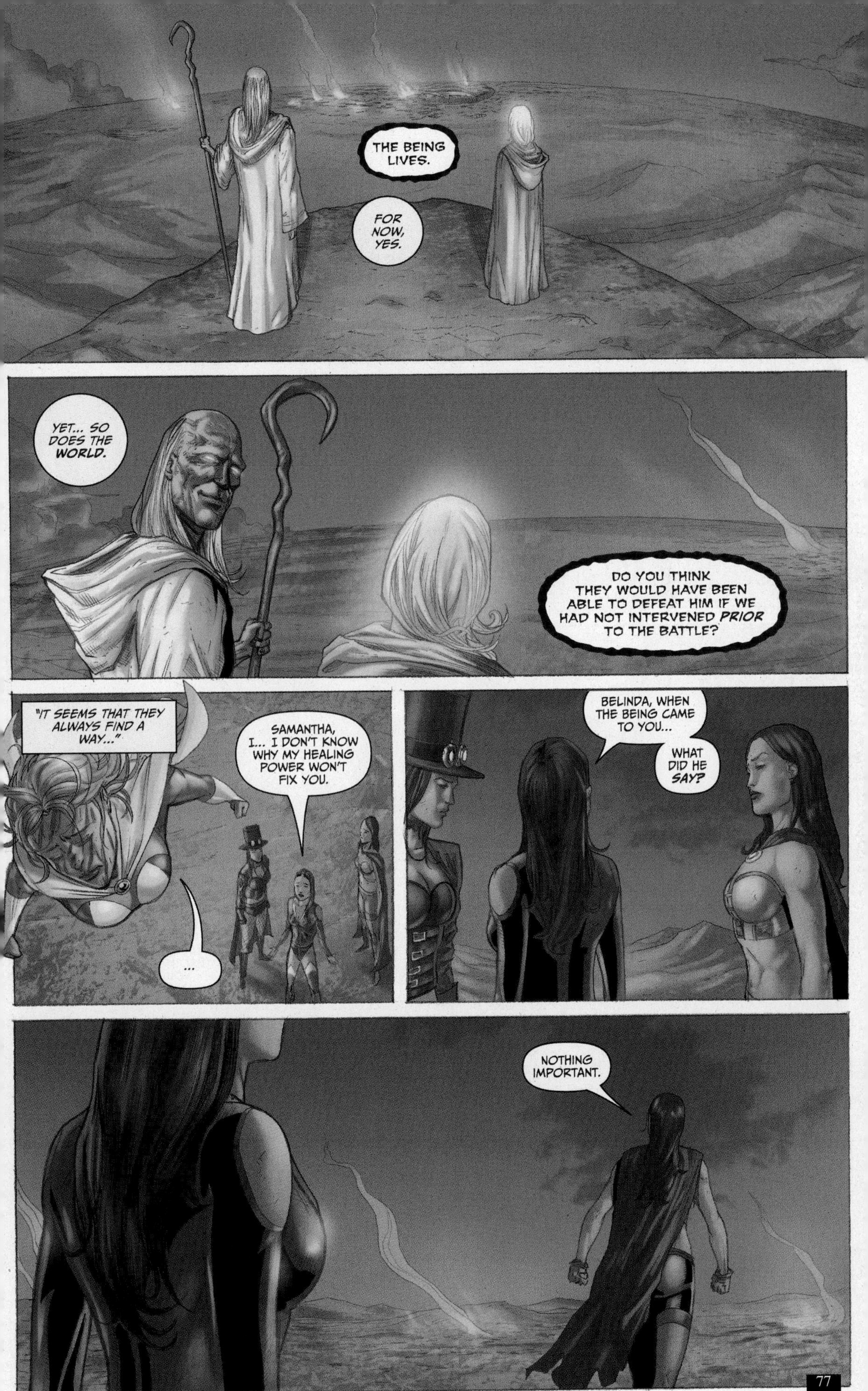
THE BEING LIVES.
FOR NOW, YES.
YET... SO DOES THE WORLD.
DO YOU THINK THEY WOULD HAVE BEEN ABLE TO DEFEAT HIM IF WE HAD NOT INTERVENED PRIOR TO THE BATTLE?
"IT SEEMS THAT THEY ALWAYS FIND A WAY..."
SAMANTHA, I... I DON'T KNOW WHY MY HEALING POWER WON'T FIX YOU.
...
BELINDA, WHEN THE BEING CAME TO YOU...
WHAT DID HE SAY?
NOTHING IMPORTANT.

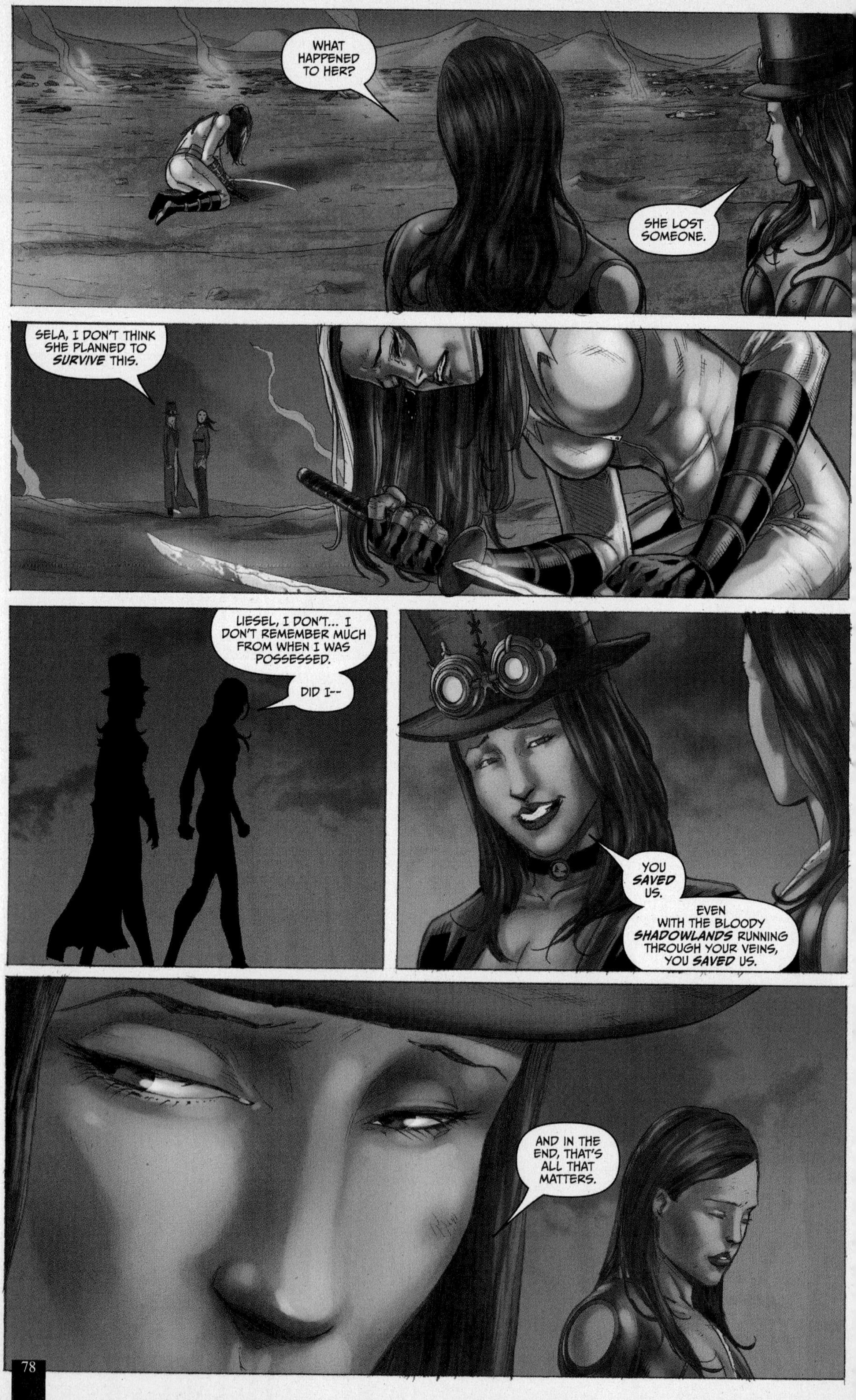
WHAT HAPPENED TO HER?
SHE LOST SOMEONE.
SELA, I DON'T THINK SHE PLANNED TO SURVIVE THIS.
LIESEL, I DON'T... I DON'T REMEMBER MUCH FROM WHEN I WAS POSSESSED.
DID I--
YOU SAVED US.
EVEN WITH THE BLOODY SHADOWLANDS RUNNING THROUGH YOUR VEINS, YOU SAVED US.
AND IN THE END, THAT'S ALL THAT MATTERS.

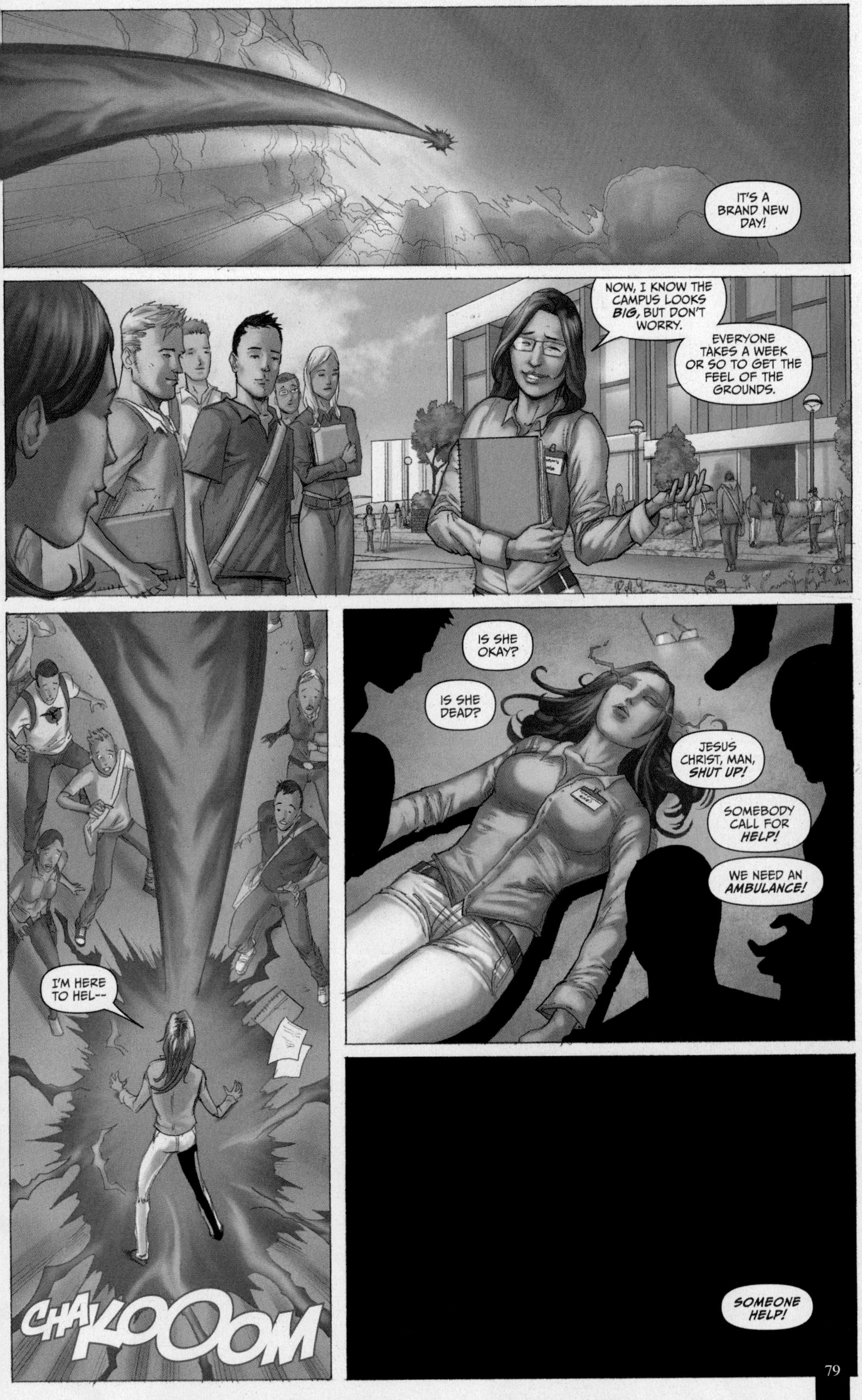
IT'S A BRAND NEW DAY!
NOW, I KNOW THE CAMPUS LOOKS BIG, BUT DON'T WORRY.
EVERYONE TAKES A WEEK OR SO TO GET THE FEEL OF THE GROUNDS.
I'M HERE TO HEL--
CHAKOOOOM
IS SHE OKAY?
IS SHE DEAD?
JESUS CHRIST, MAN, SHUT UP!
SOMEBODY CALL FOR HELP!
WE NEED AN AMBULANCE!
SOMEONE HELP!

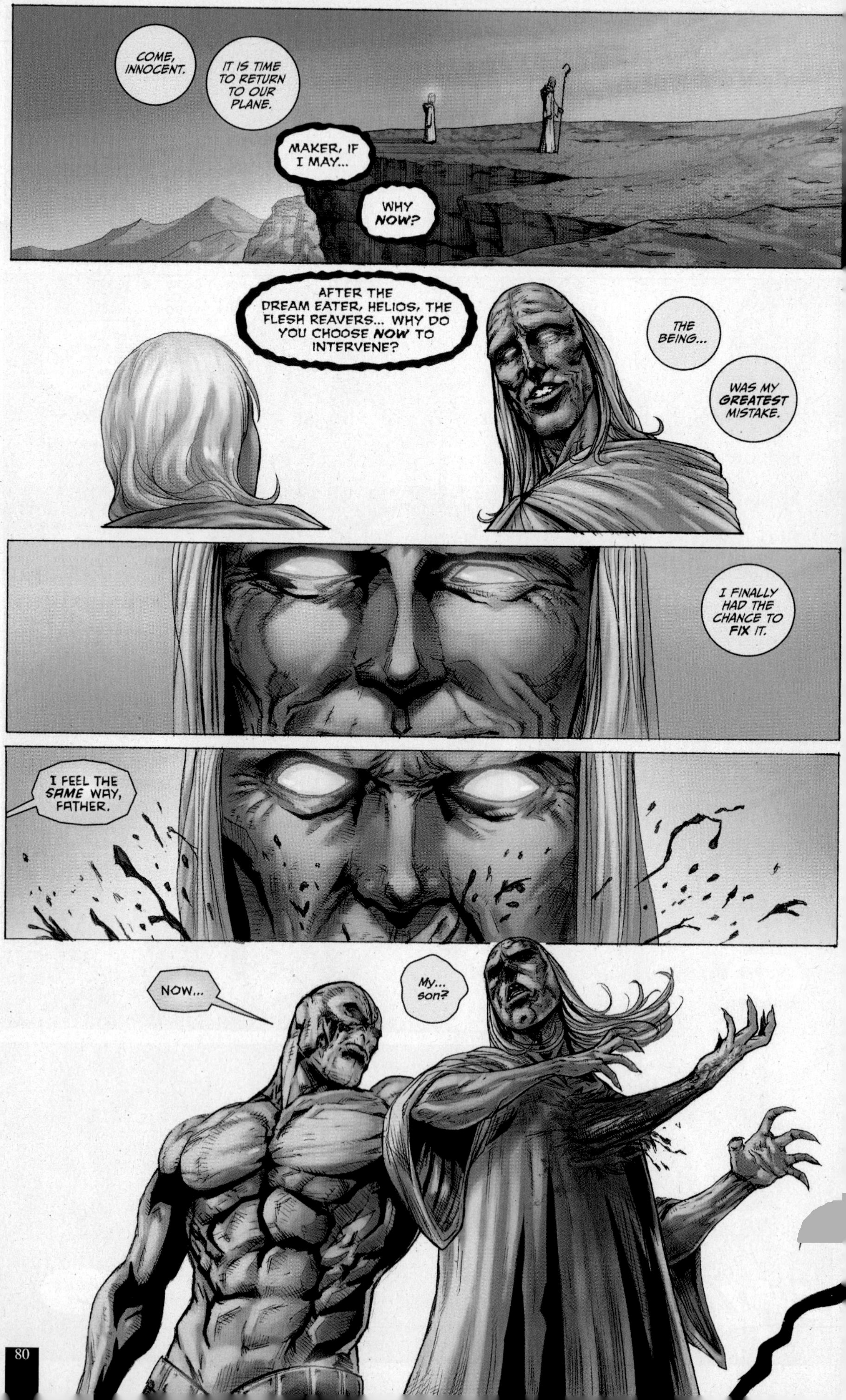
COME, INNOCENT.
IT IS TIME TO RETURN TO OUR PLANE.
MAKER, IF I MAY...
WHY NOW?
AFTER THE DREAM EATER, HELIOS, THE FLESH REAVERS... WHY DO YOU CHOOSE NOW TO INTERVENE?
THE BEING...
WAS MY GREATEST MISTAKE.
I FINALLY HAD THE CHANCE TO FIX IT.
I FEEL THE SAME WAY, FATHER.
NOW...
My... son?

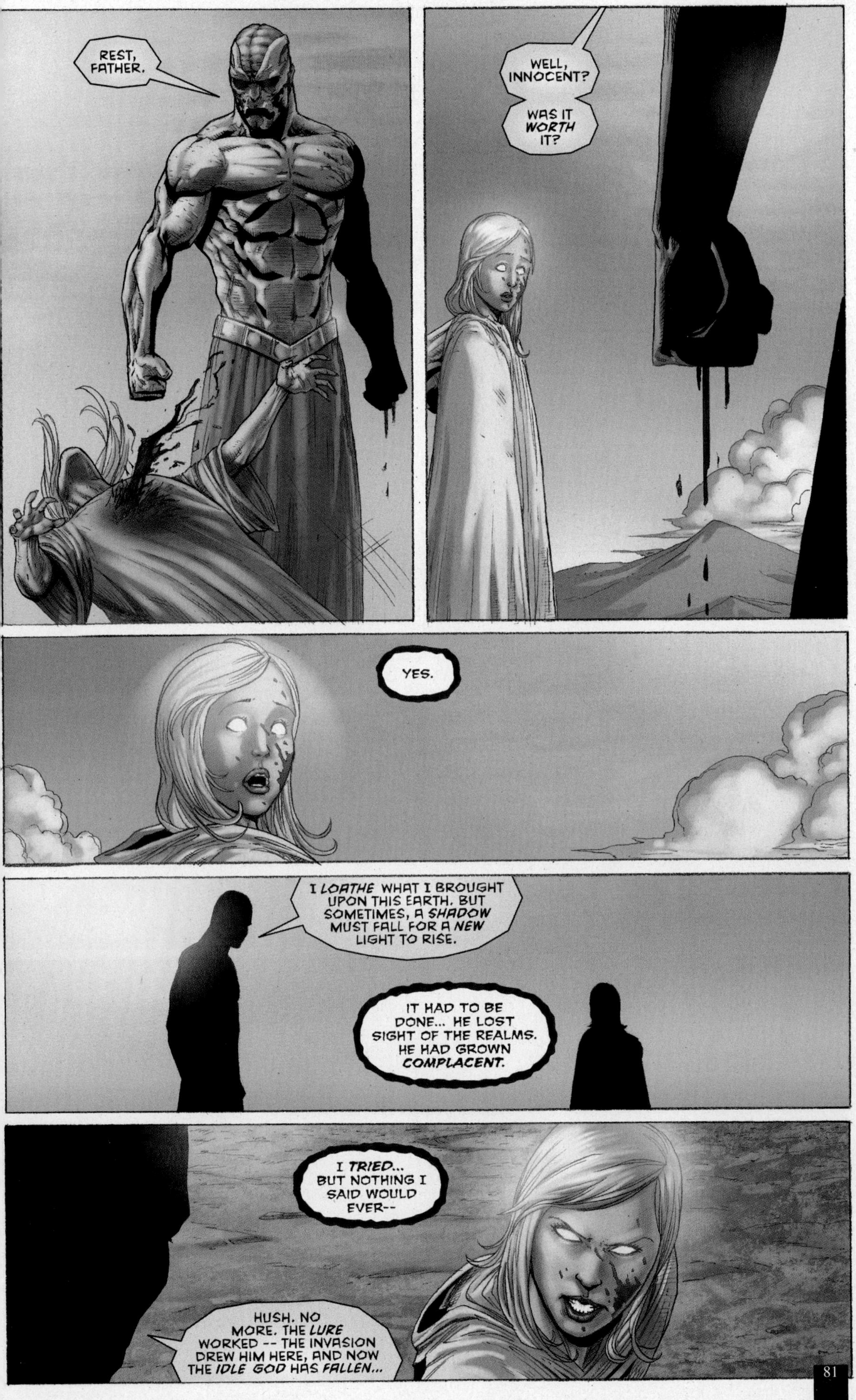
REST, FATHER.
WELL, INNOCENT?
WAS IT WORTH IT?
YES.
I LOATHE WHAT I BROUGHT UPON THIS EARTH. BUT SOMETIMES, A SHADOW MUST FALL FOR A NEW LIGHT TO RISE.
IT HAD TO BE DONE... HE LOST SIGHT OF THE REALMS. HE HAD GROWN COMPLACENT.
I TRIED... BUT NOTHING I SAID WOULD EVER--
HUSH. NO MORE. THE LURE WORKED -- THE INVASION DREW HIM HERE, AND NOW THE IDLE GOD HAS FALLEN...

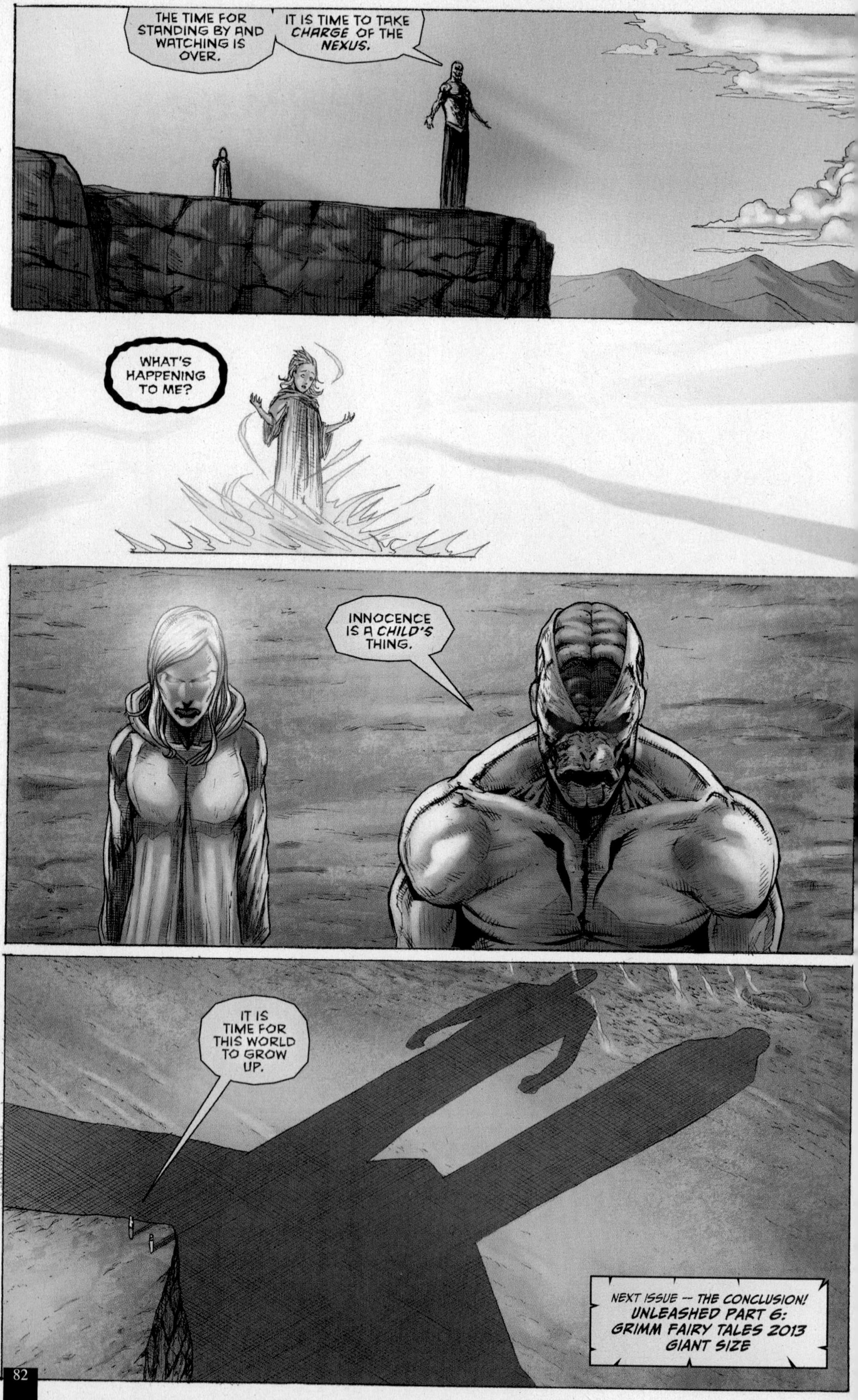
THE TIME FOR STANDING BY AND WATCHING IS OVER.
IT IS TIME TO TAKE CHARGE OF THE NEXUS.
WHAT'S HAPPENING TO ME?
INNOCENCE IS A CHILD'S THING.
IT IS TIME FOR THIS WORLD TO GROW UP.
NEXT ISSUE -- THE CONCLUSION!
UNLEASHED PART 6: GRIMM FAIRY TALES 2013 GIANT SIZE

Grimm Fairy Tales
UNLEASHED

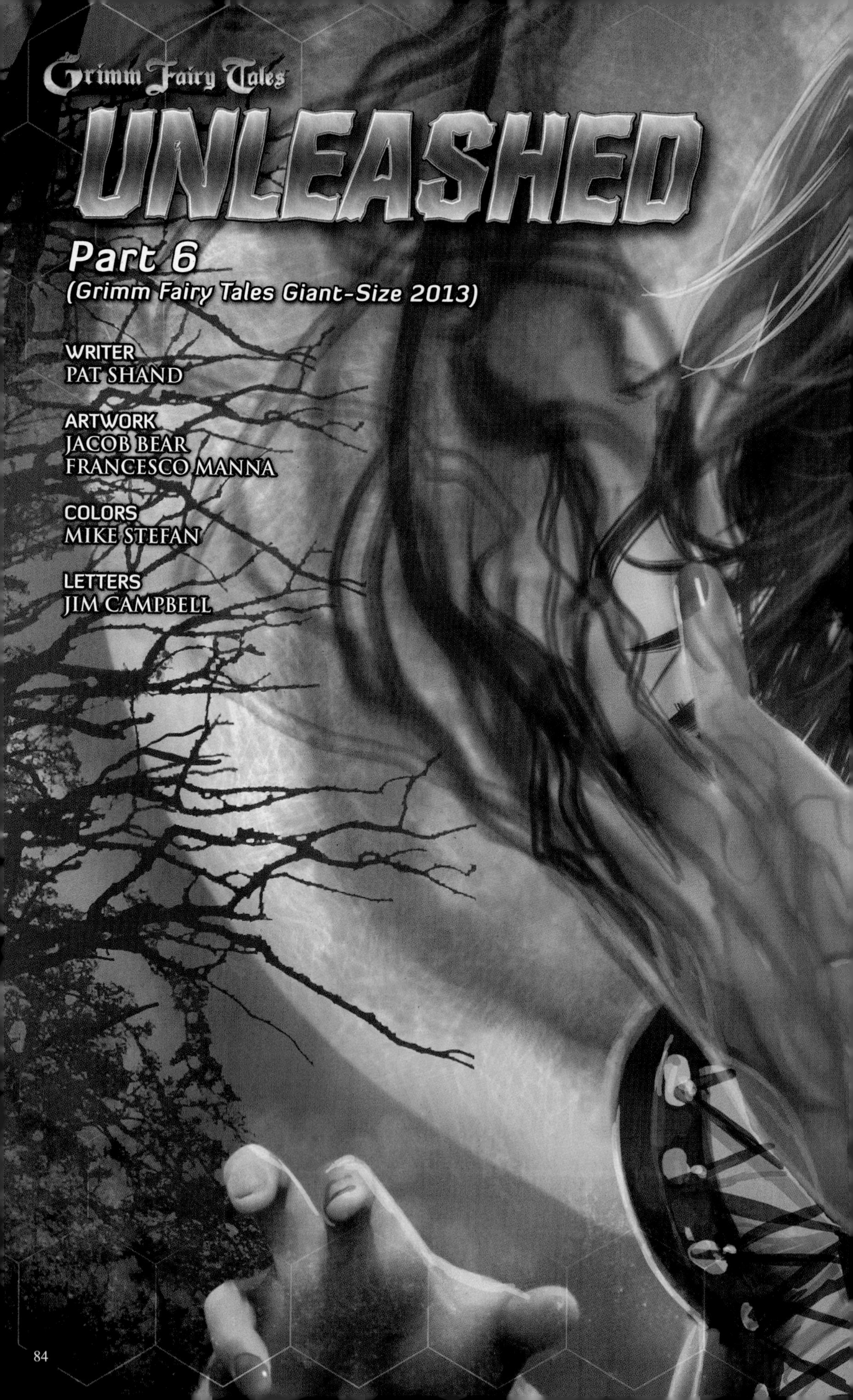
Grimm Fairy Tales
UNLEASHED
Part 6
(Grimm Fairy Tales Giant-Size 2013)
WRITER
PAT SHAND
ARTWORK
JACOB BEAR
FRANCESCO MANNA
COLORS
MIKE STEFAN
LETTERS
JIM CAMPBELL

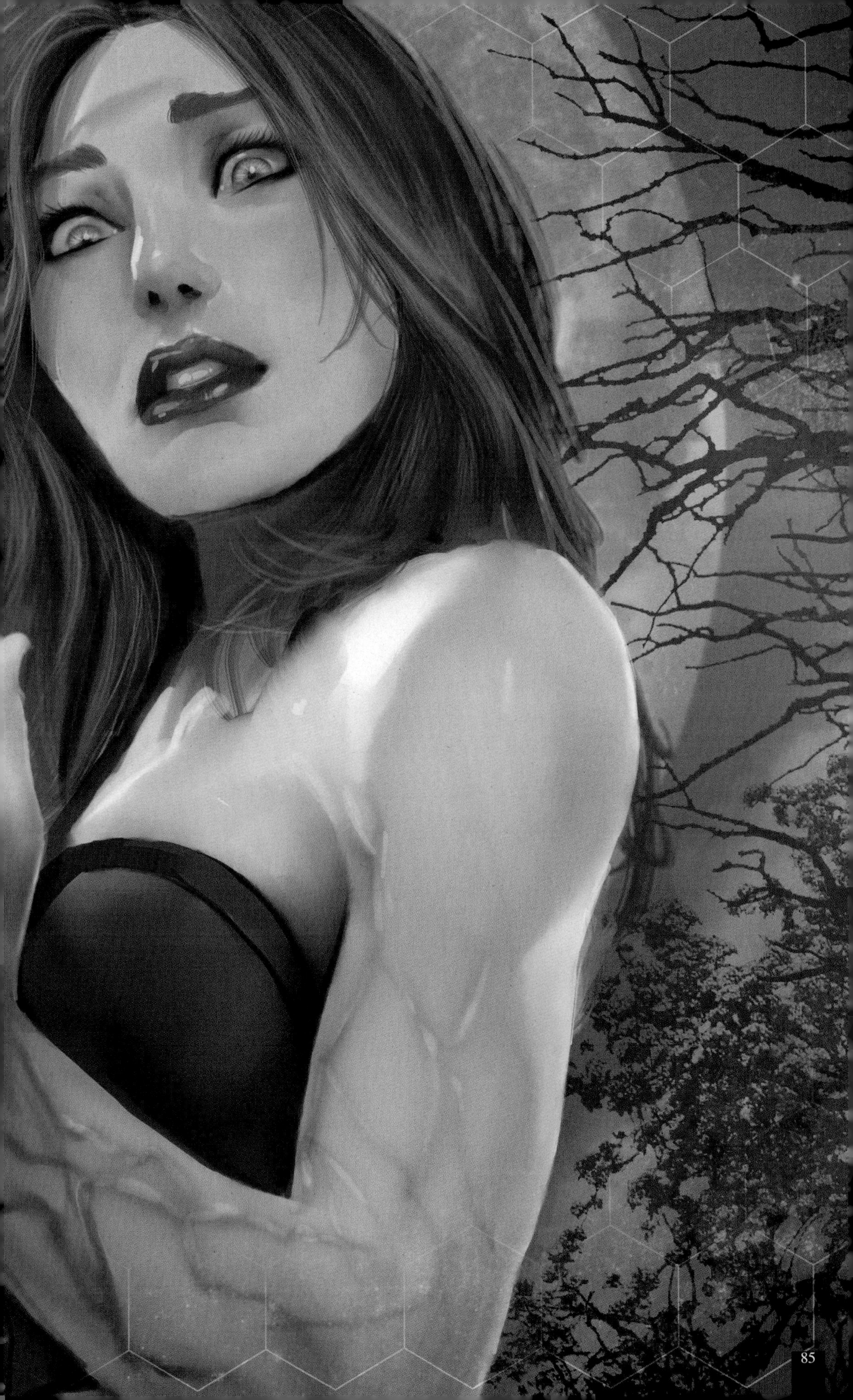

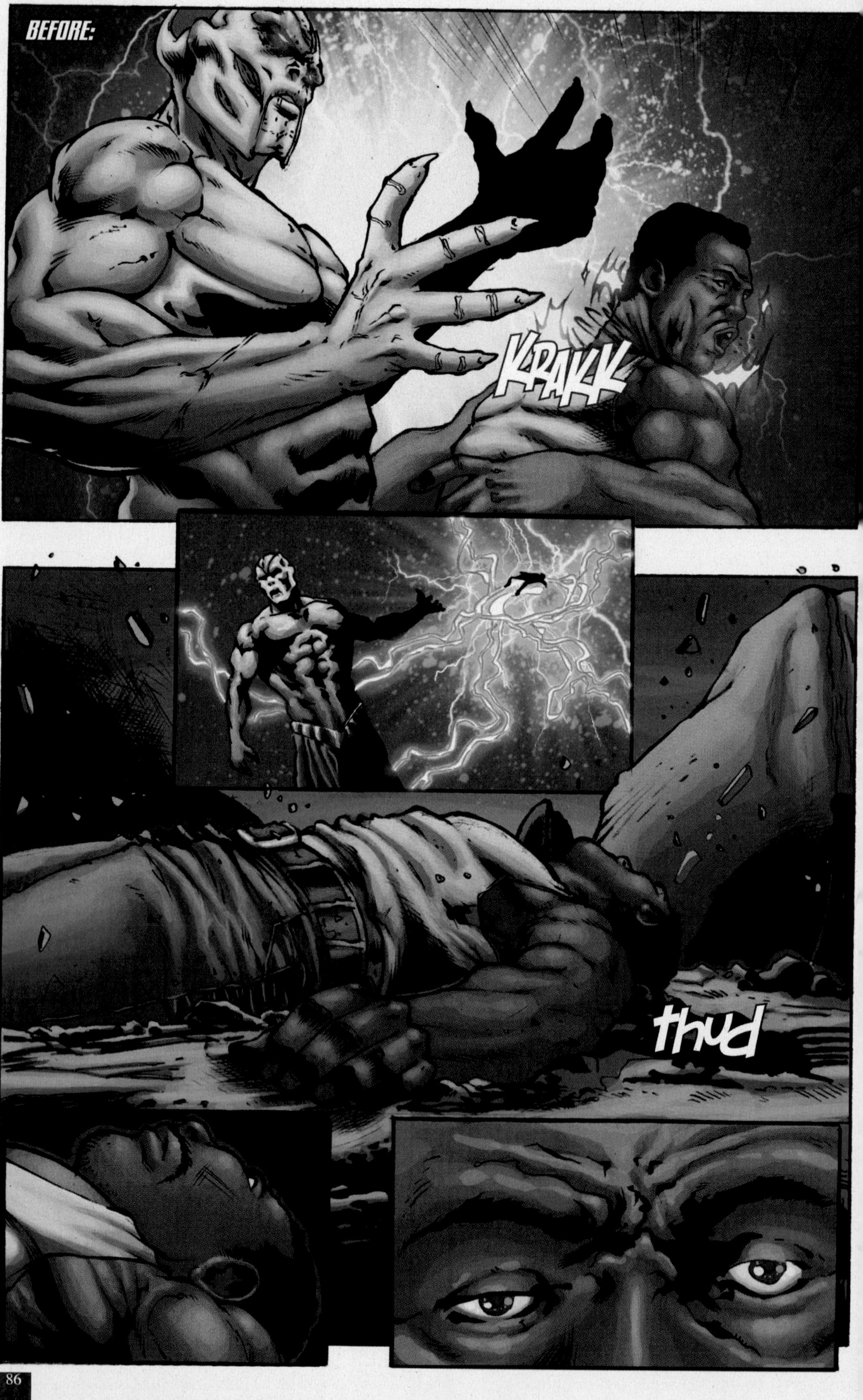
BEFORE:
KRAKK
thud

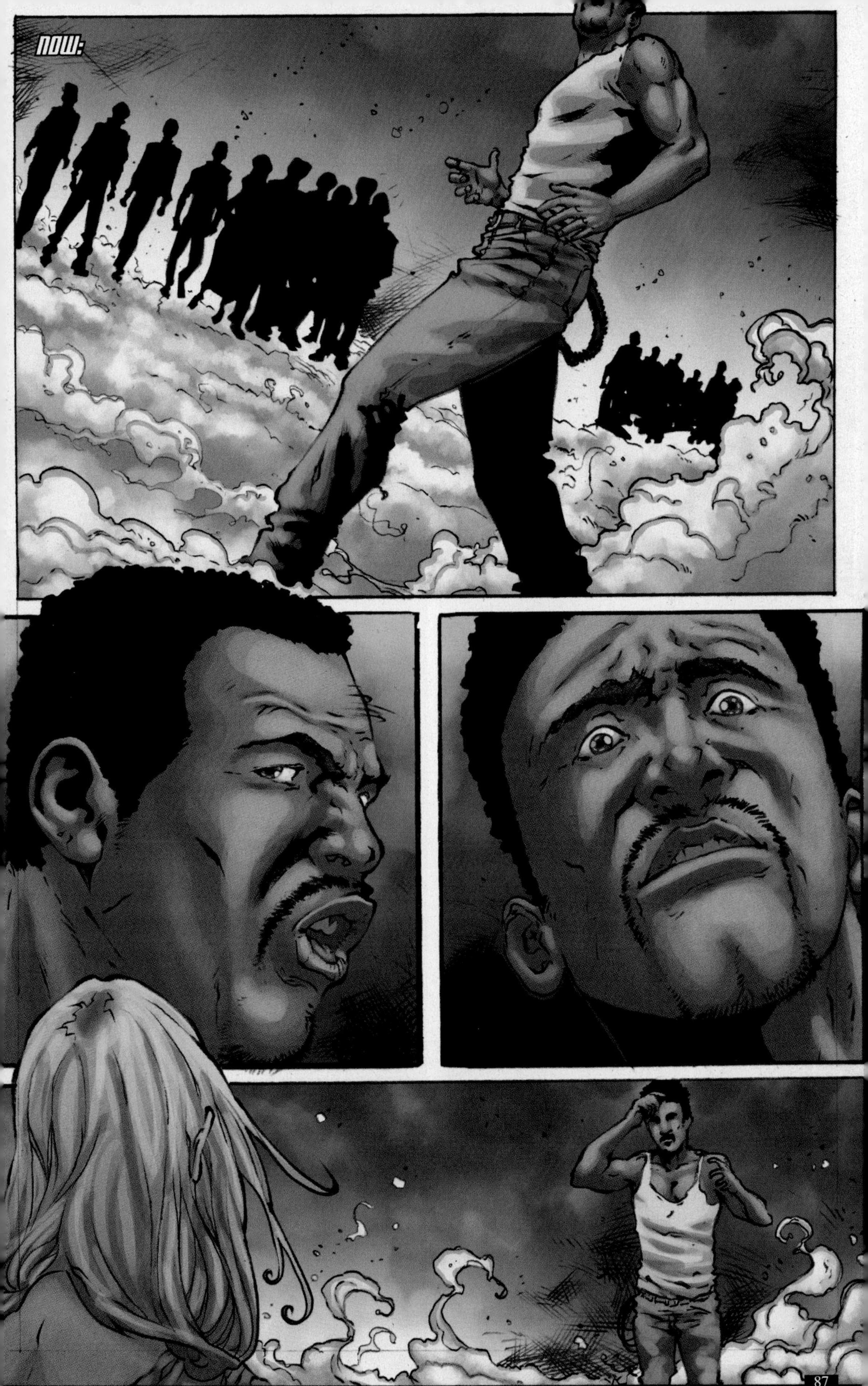
NOW:

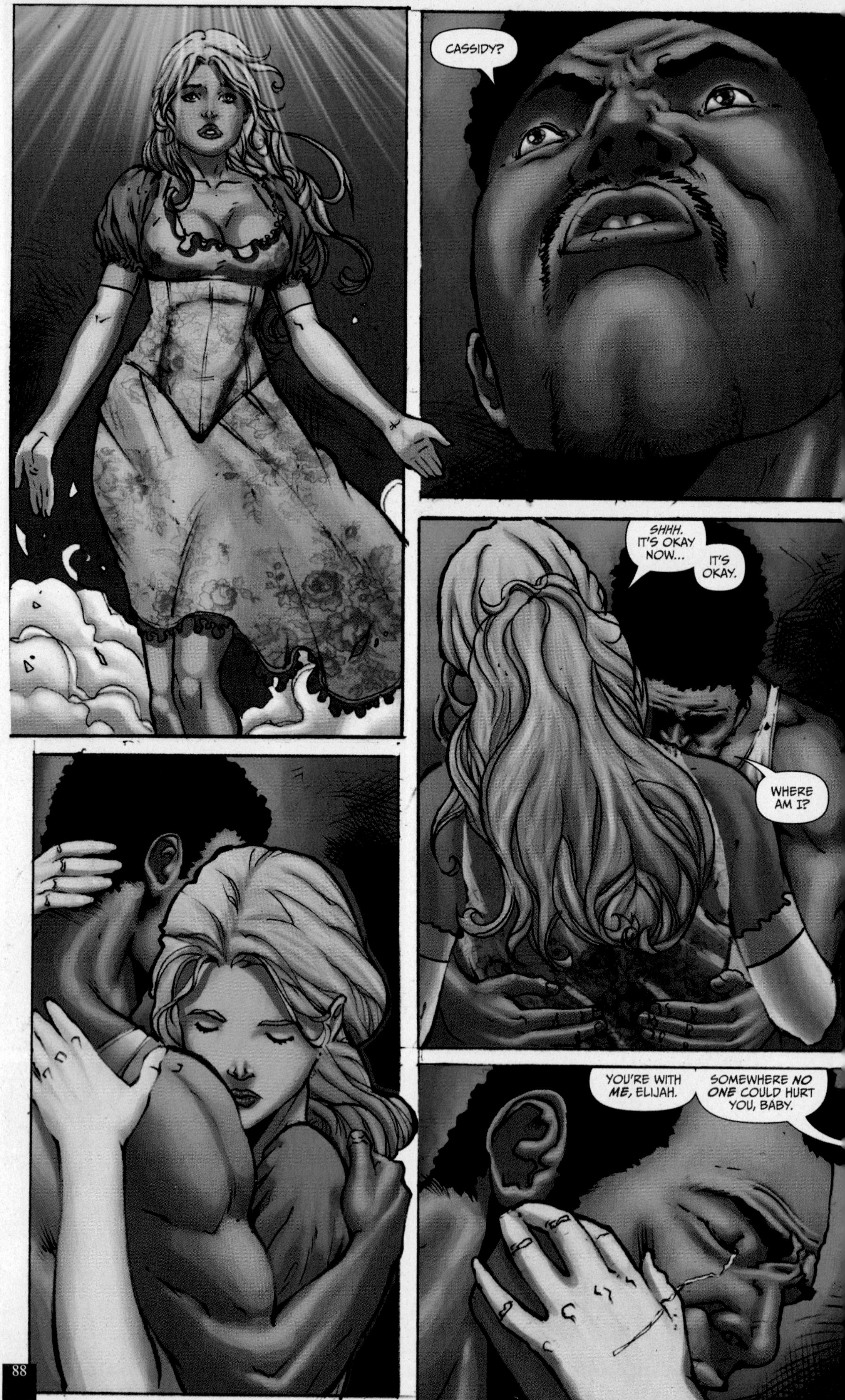
CASSIDY?
SHHH. IT'S OKAY NOW...
IT'S OKAY.
WHERE AM I?
YOU'RE WITH ME, ELIJAH.
SOMEWHERE NO ONE COULD HURT YOU, BABY.

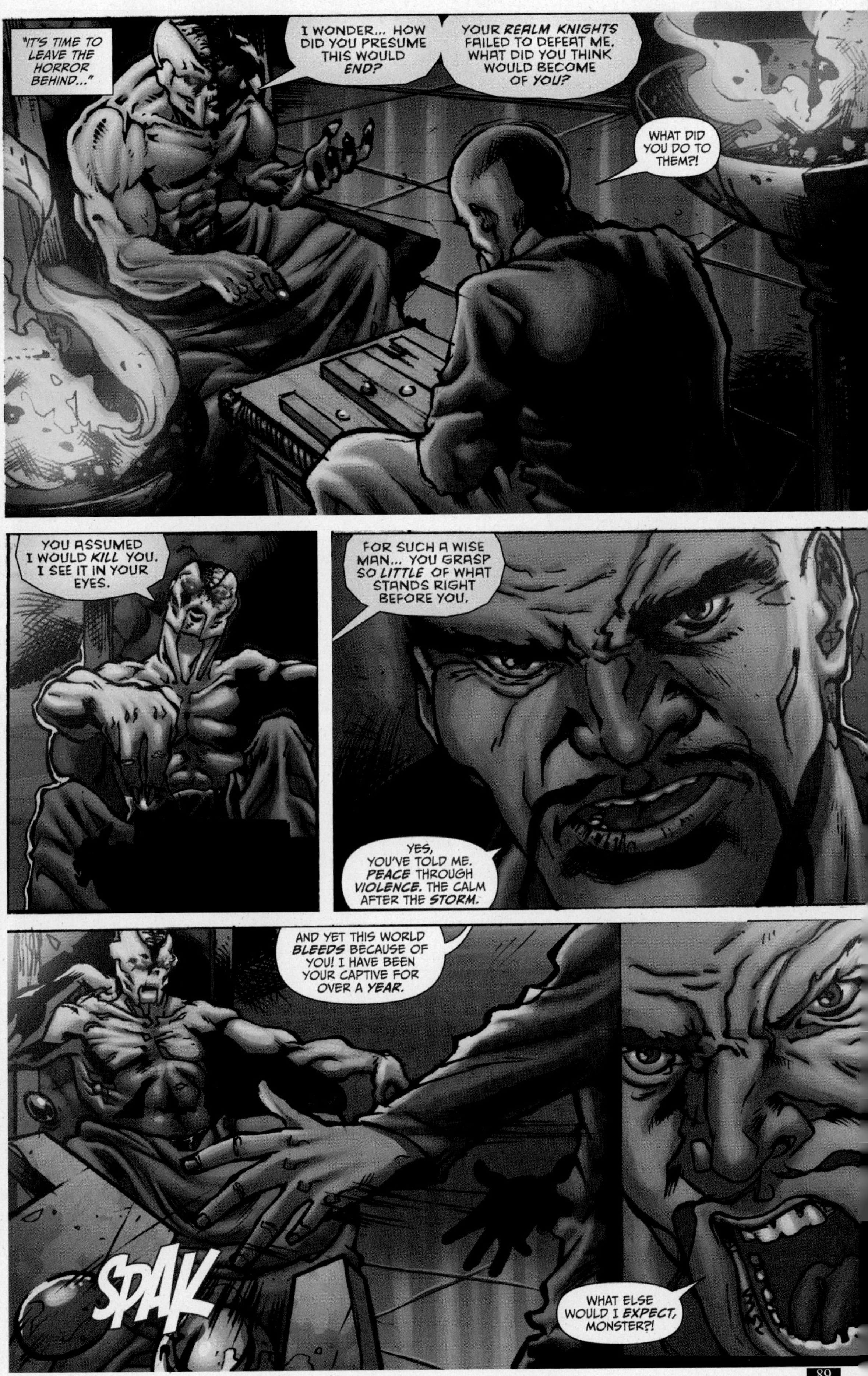
"IT'S TIME TO LEAVE THE HORROR BEHIND..."
I WONDER... HOW DID YOU PRESUME THIS WOULD *END*?
YOUR *REALM KNIGHTS* FAILED TO DEFEAT ME. WHAT DID YOU THINK WOULD BECOME OF *YOU*?
WHAT DID YOU DO TO THEM?!
YOU ASSUMED I WOULD *KILL* YOU. I SEE IT IN YOUR EYES.
FOR SUCH A WISE MAN... YOU GRASP SO *LITTLE* OF WHAT STANDS RIGHT BEFORE YOU.
YES, YOU'VE TOLD ME. *PEACE* THROUGH *VIOLENCE*. THE CALM AFTER THE *STORM*.
AND YET THIS WORLD *BLEEDS* BECAUSE OF YOU! I HAVE BEEN YOUR CAPTIVE FOR OVER A *YEAR*.
SPAK
WHAT ELSE WOULD I *EXPECT*, MONSTER?!

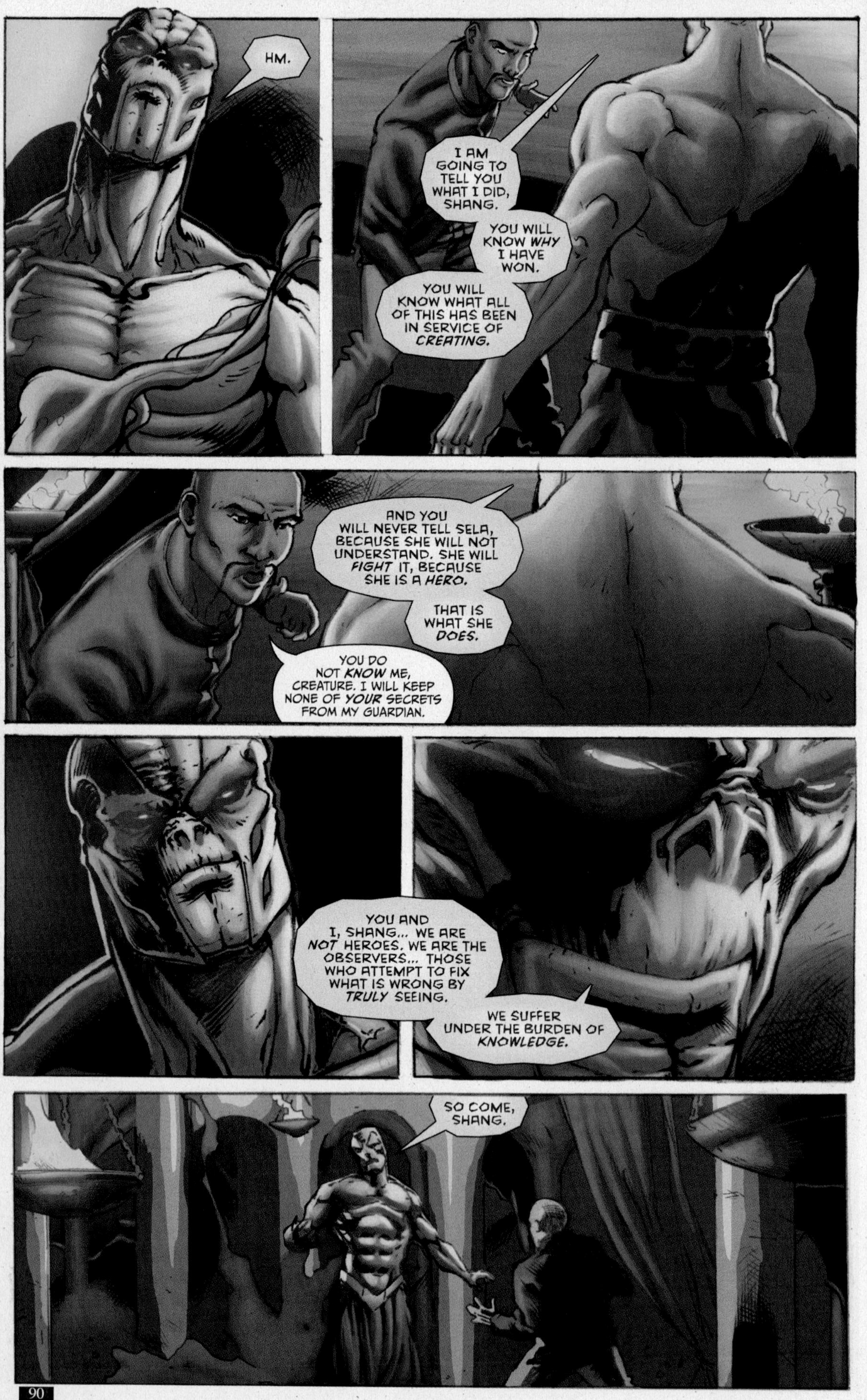
HM.
I AM GOING TO TELL YOU WHAT I DID, SHANG.
YOU WILL KNOW WHY I HAVE WON.
YOU WILL KNOW WHAT ALL OF THIS HAS BEEN IN SERVICE OF CREATING.
AND YOU WILL NEVER TELL SELA, BECAUSE SHE WILL NOT UNDERSTAND. SHE WILL FIGHT IT, BECAUSE SHE IS A HERO.
THAT IS WHAT SHE DOES.
YOU DO NOT KNOW ME, CREATURE. I WILL KEEP NONE OF YOUR SECRETS FROM MY GUARDIAN.
YOU AND I, SHANG... WE ARE NOT HEROES. WE ARE THE OBSERVERS... THOSE WHO ATTEMPT TO FIX WHAT IS WRONG BY TRULY SEEING.
WE SUFFER UNDER THE BURDEN OF KNOWLEDGE.
SO COME, SHANG.

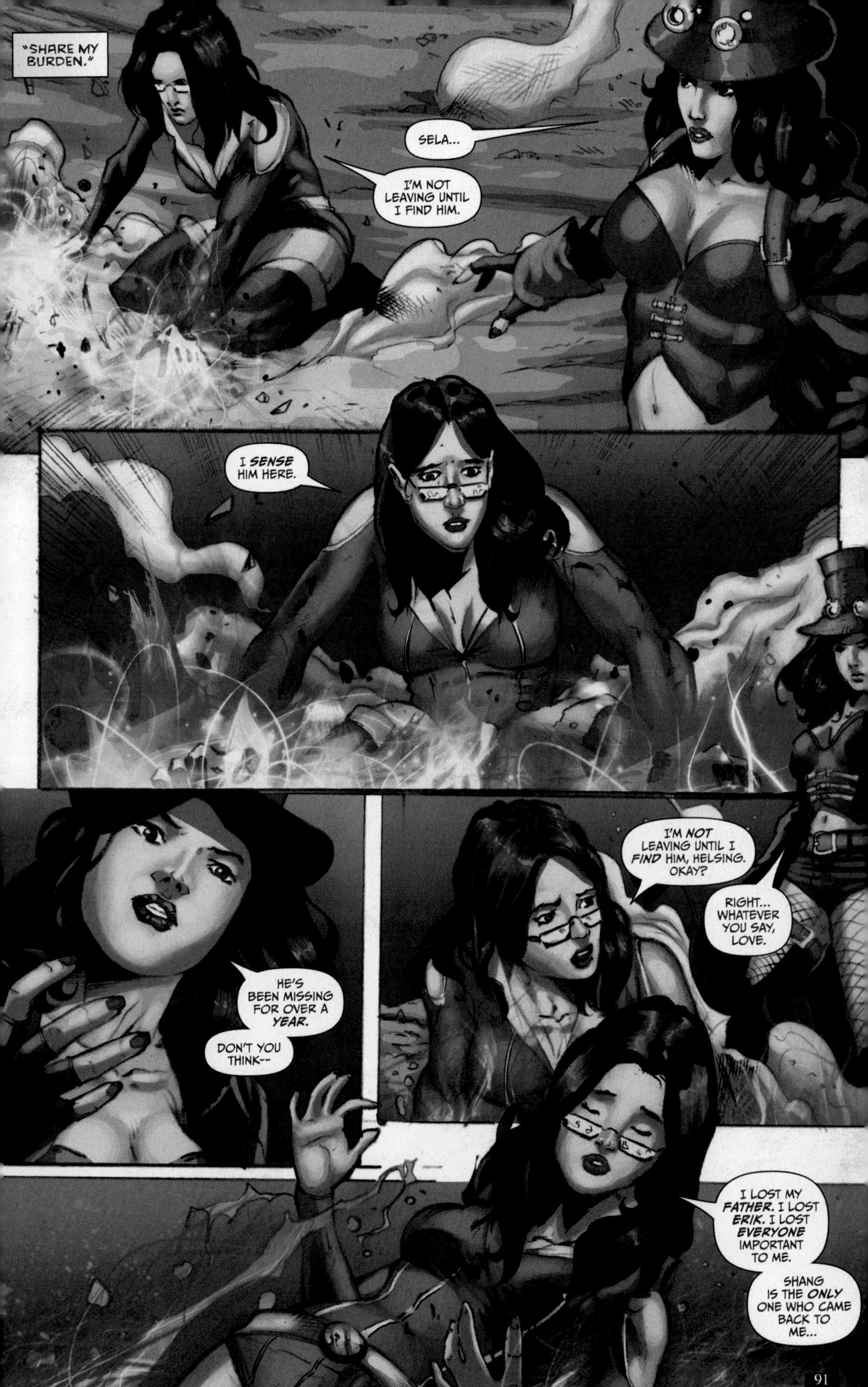
"SHARE MY BURDEN."
SELA...
I'M NOT LEAVING UNTIL I FIND HIM.
I SENSE HIM HERE.
HE'S BEEN MISSING FOR OVER A YEAR.
DON'T YOU THINK--
I'M NOT LEAVING UNTIL I FIND HIM, HELSING. OKAY?
RIGHT... WHATEVER YOU SAY, LOVE.
I LOST MY FATHER. I LOST ERIK. I LOST EVERYONE IMPORTANT TO ME.
SHANG IS THE ONLY ONE WHO CAME BACK TO ME...

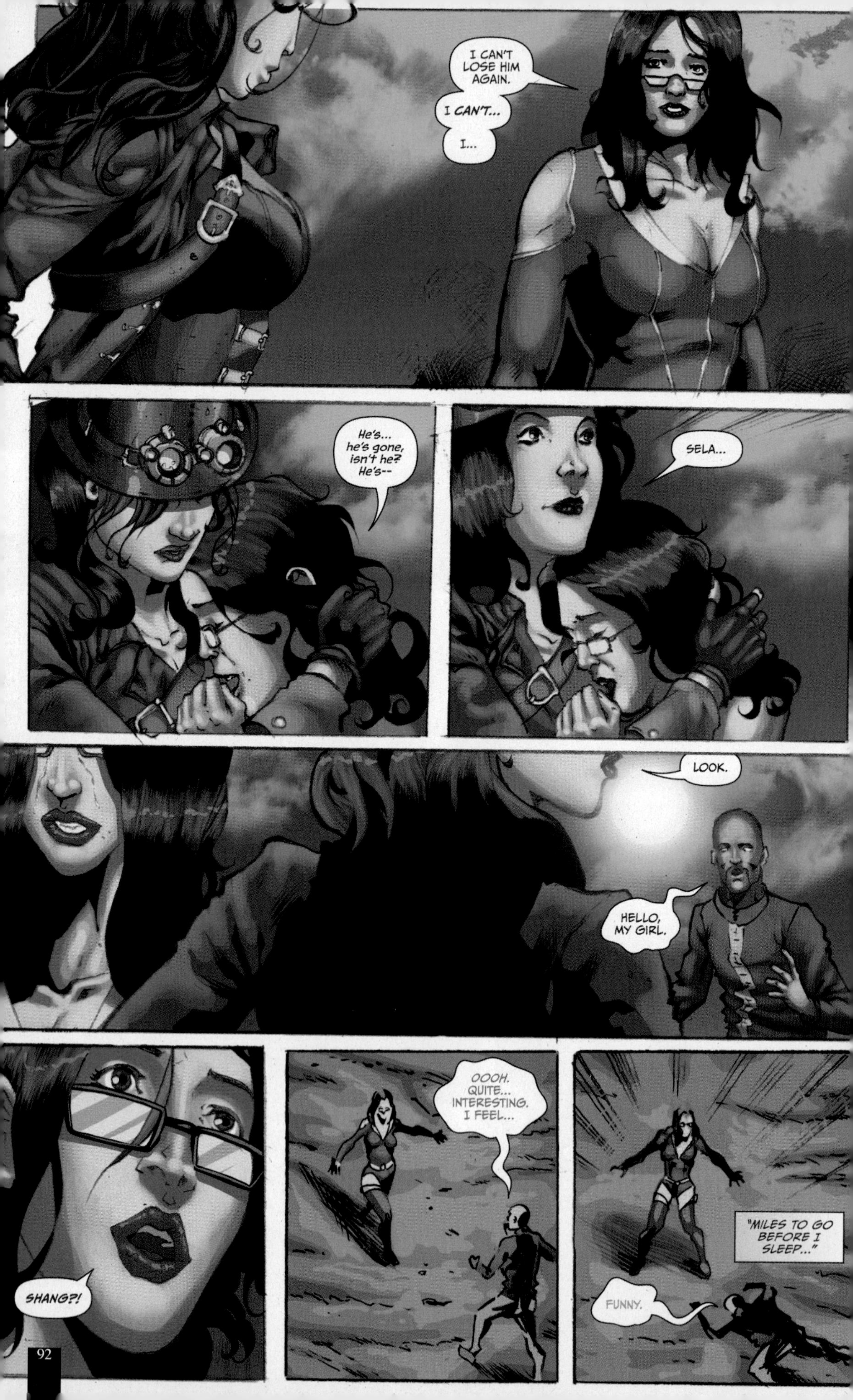
I CAN'T LOSE HIM AGAIN.
I CAN'T...
I...
He's... he's gone, isn't he? He's--
SELA...
LOOK.
HELLO, MY GIRL.
SHANG?!
OOOH. QUITE... INTERESTING. I FEEL...
"MILES TO GO BEFORE I SLEEP..."
FUNNY.

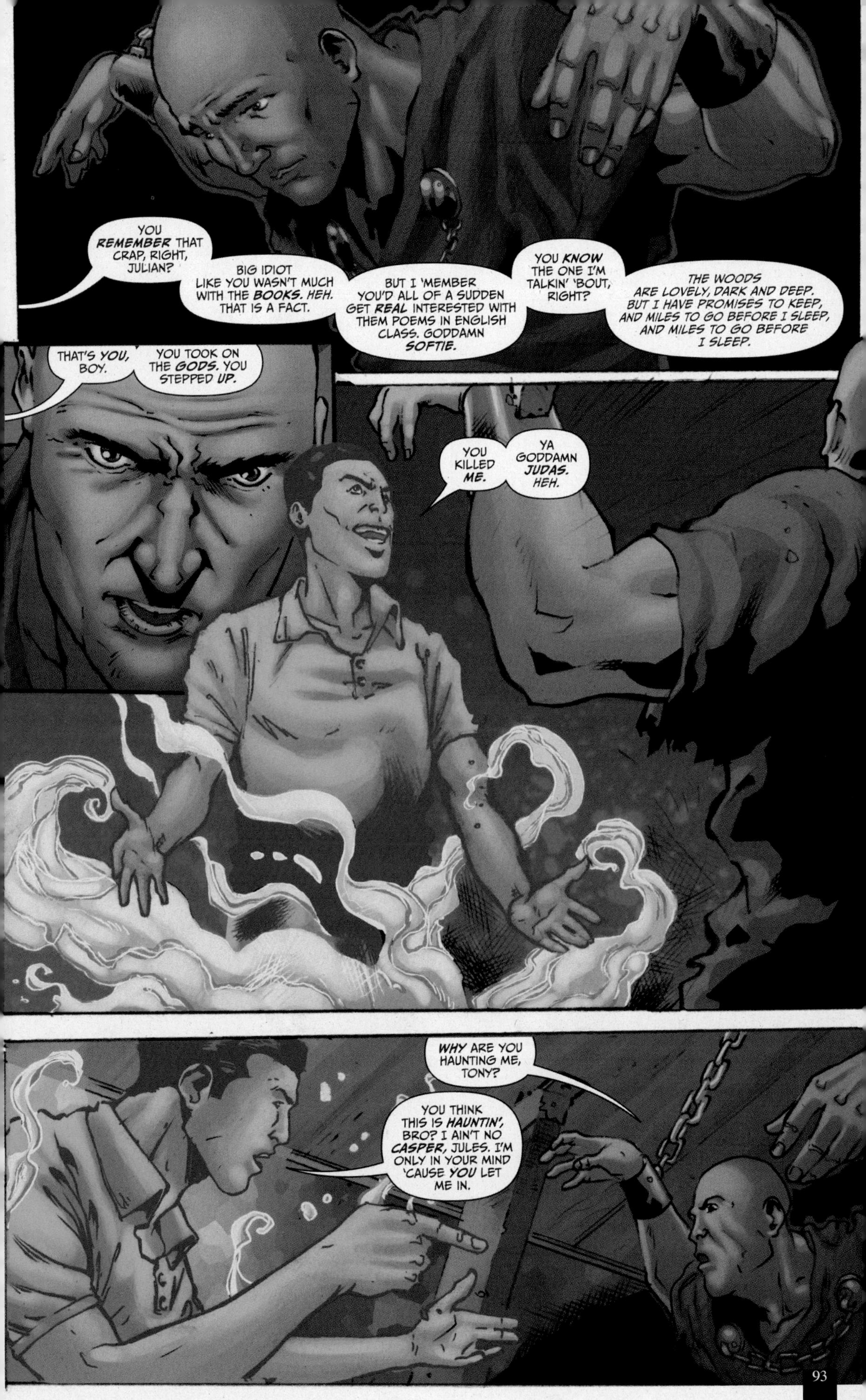
YOU REMEMBER THAT CRAP, RIGHT, JULIAN?
BIG IDIOT LIKE YOU WASN'T MUCH WITH THE BOOKS. HEH. THAT IS A FACT.
BUT I 'MEMBER YOU'D ALL OF A SUDDEN GET REAL INTERESTED WITH THEM POEMS IN ENGLISH CLASS. GODDAMN SOFTIE.
YOU KNOW THE ONE I'M TALKIN' 'BOUT, RIGHT?
THE WOODS ARE LOVELY, DARK AND DEEP. BUT I HAVE PROMISES TO KEEP, AND MILES TO GO BEFORE I SLEEP, AND MILES TO GO BEFORE I SLEEP.
THAT'S YOU, BOY.
YOU TOOK ON THE GODS. YOU STEPPED UP.
YOU KILLED ME.
YA GODDAMN JUDAS. HEH.
WHY ARE YOU HAUNTING ME, TONY?
YOU THINK THIS IS HAUNTIN', BRO? I AIN'T NO CASPER, JULES. I'M ONLY IN YOUR MIND 'CAUSE YOU LET ME IN.

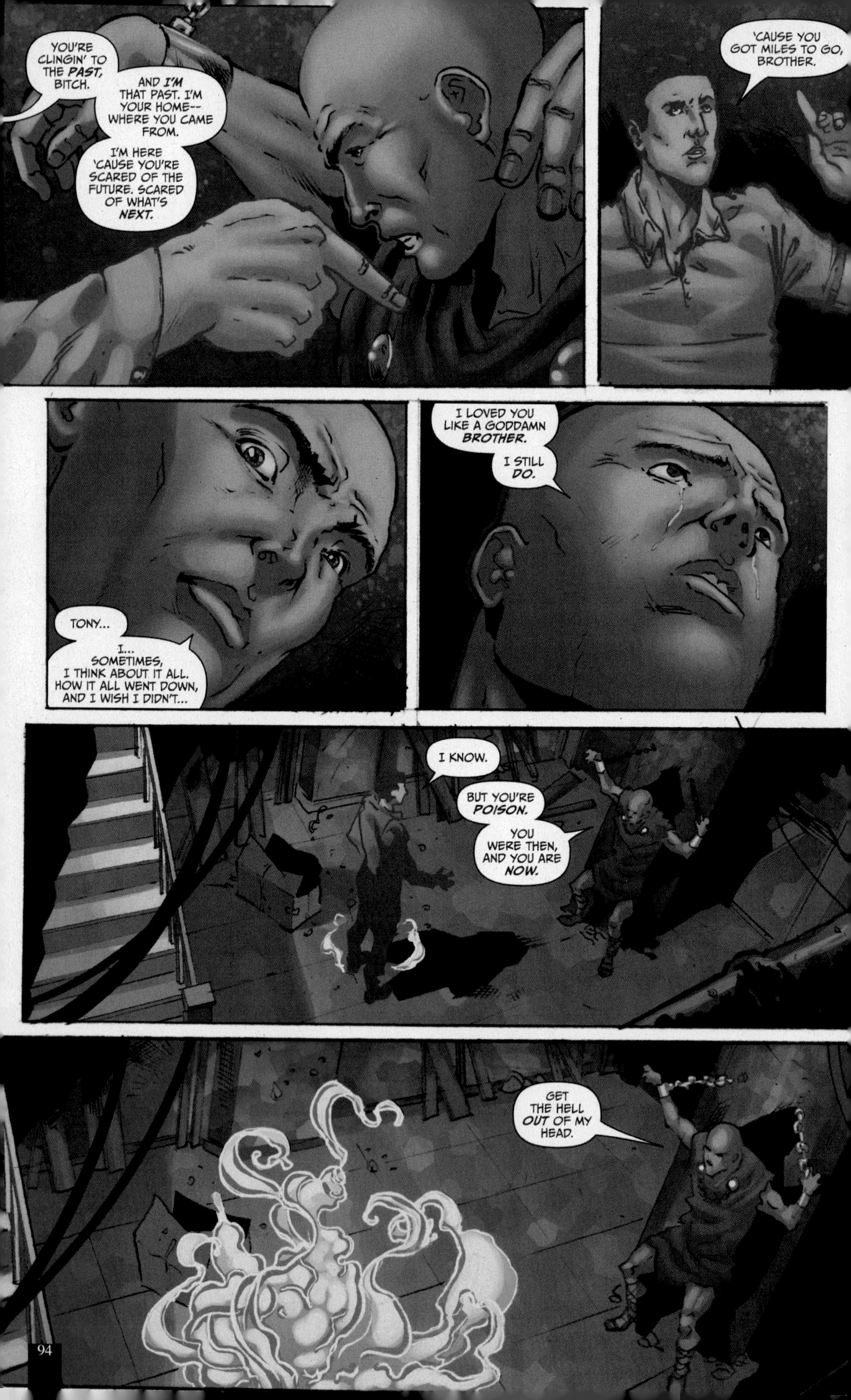
YOU'RE CLINGIN' TO THE PAST, BITCH.
AND I'M THAT PAST. I'M YOUR HOME-- WHERE YOU CAME FROM.
I'M HERE 'CAUSE YOU'RE SCARED OF THE FUTURE. SCARED OF WHAT'S NEXT.
'CAUSE YOU GOT MILES TO GO, BROTHER.
TONY...
I... SOMETIMES, I THINK ABOUT IT ALL. HOW IT ALL WENT DOWN, AND I WISH I DIDN'T...
I LOVED YOU LIKE A GODDAMN BROTHER.
I STILL DO.
I KNOW.
BUT YOU'RE POISON.
YOU WERE THEN, AND YOU ARE NOW.
GET THE HELL OUT OF MY HEAD.

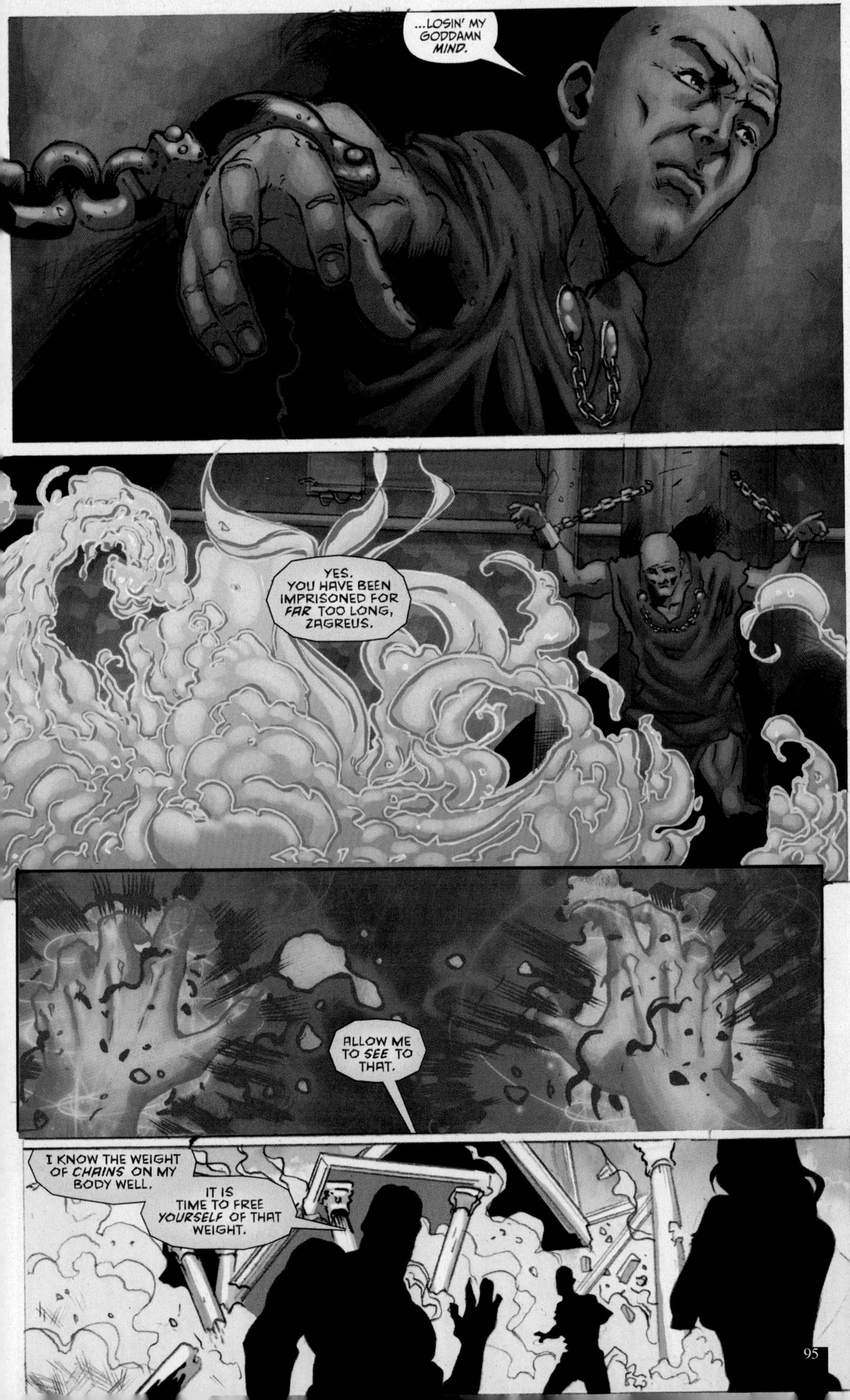
...LOSIN' MY GODDAMN MIND.
YES. YOU HAVE BEEN IMPRISONED FOR FAR TOO LONG, ZAGREUS.
ALLOW ME TO SEE TO THAT.
I KNOW THE WEIGHT OF CHAINS ON MY BODY WELL.
IT IS TIME TO FREE YOURSELF OF THAT WEIGHT.

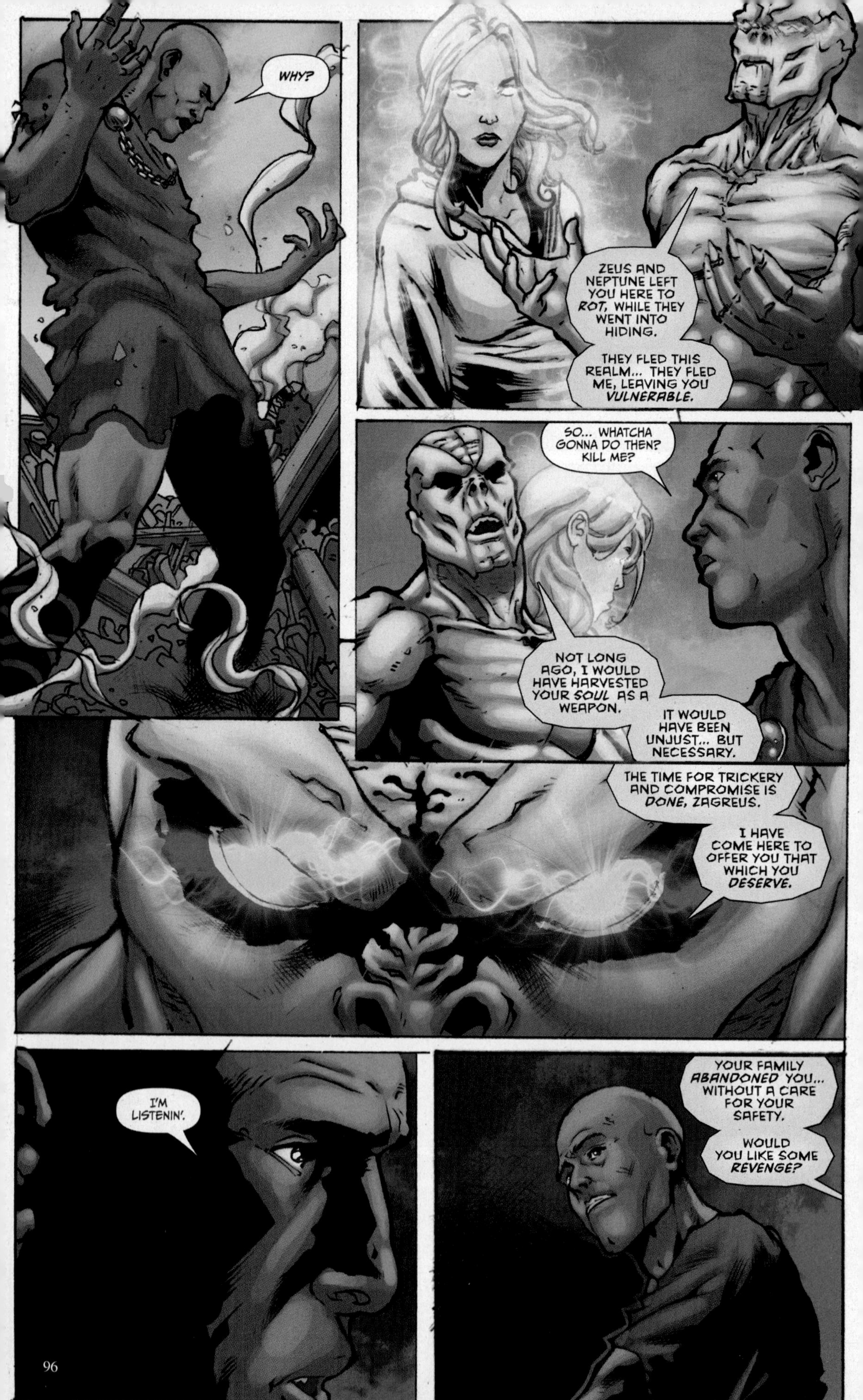

WHY?
ZEUS AND NEPTUNE LEFT YOU HERE TO ROT, WHILE THEY WENT INTO HIDING.
THEY FLED THIS REALM... THEY FLED ME, LEAVING YOU VULNERABLE.
SO... WHATCHA GONNA DO THEN? KILL ME?
NOT LONG AGO, I WOULD HAVE HARVESTED YOUR SOUL AS A WEAPON.
IT WOULD HAVE BEEN UNJUST... BUT NECESSARY.
THE TIME FOR TRICKERY AND COMPROMISE IS DONE, ZAGREUS.
I HAVE COME HERE TO OFFER YOU THAT WHICH YOU DESERVE.
I'M LISTENIN'.
YOUR FAMILY ABANDONED YOU... WITHOUT A CARE FOR YOUR SAFETY.
WOULD YOU LIKE SOME REVENGE?

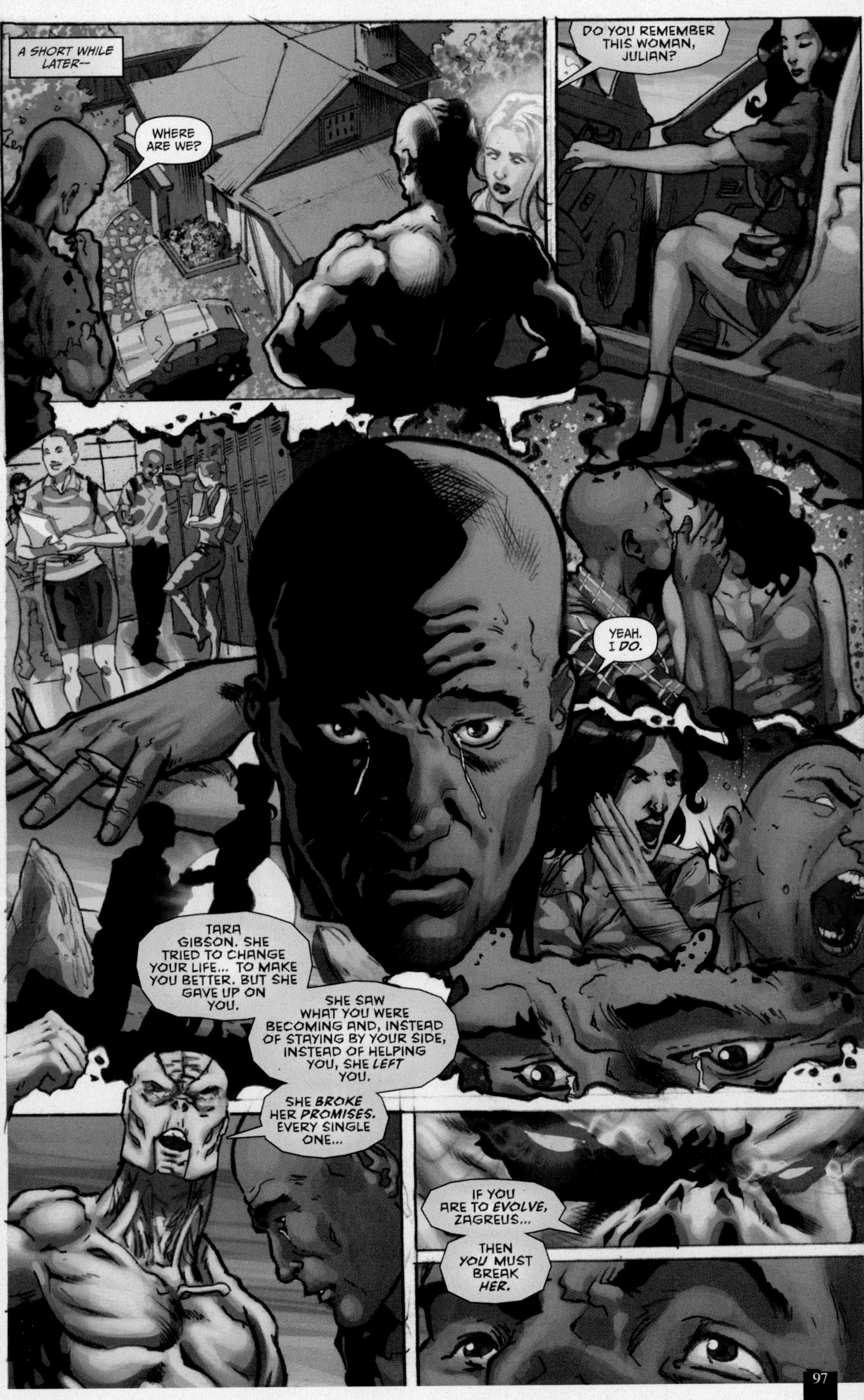
A SHORT WHILE LATER--
WHERE ARE WE?
DO YOU REMEMBER THIS WOMAN, JULIAN?
YEAH. I DO.
TARA GIBSON. SHE TRIED TO CHANGE YOUR LIFE... TO MAKE YOU BETTER. BUT SHE GAVE UP ON YOU.
SHE SAW WHAT YOU WERE BECOMING AND, INSTEAD OF STAYING BY YOUR SIDE, INSTEAD OF HELPING YOU, SHE LEFT YOU.
SHE BROKE HER PROMISES. EVERY SINGLE ONE...
IF YOU ARE TO EVOLVE, ZAGREUS...
THEN YOU MUST BREAK HER.

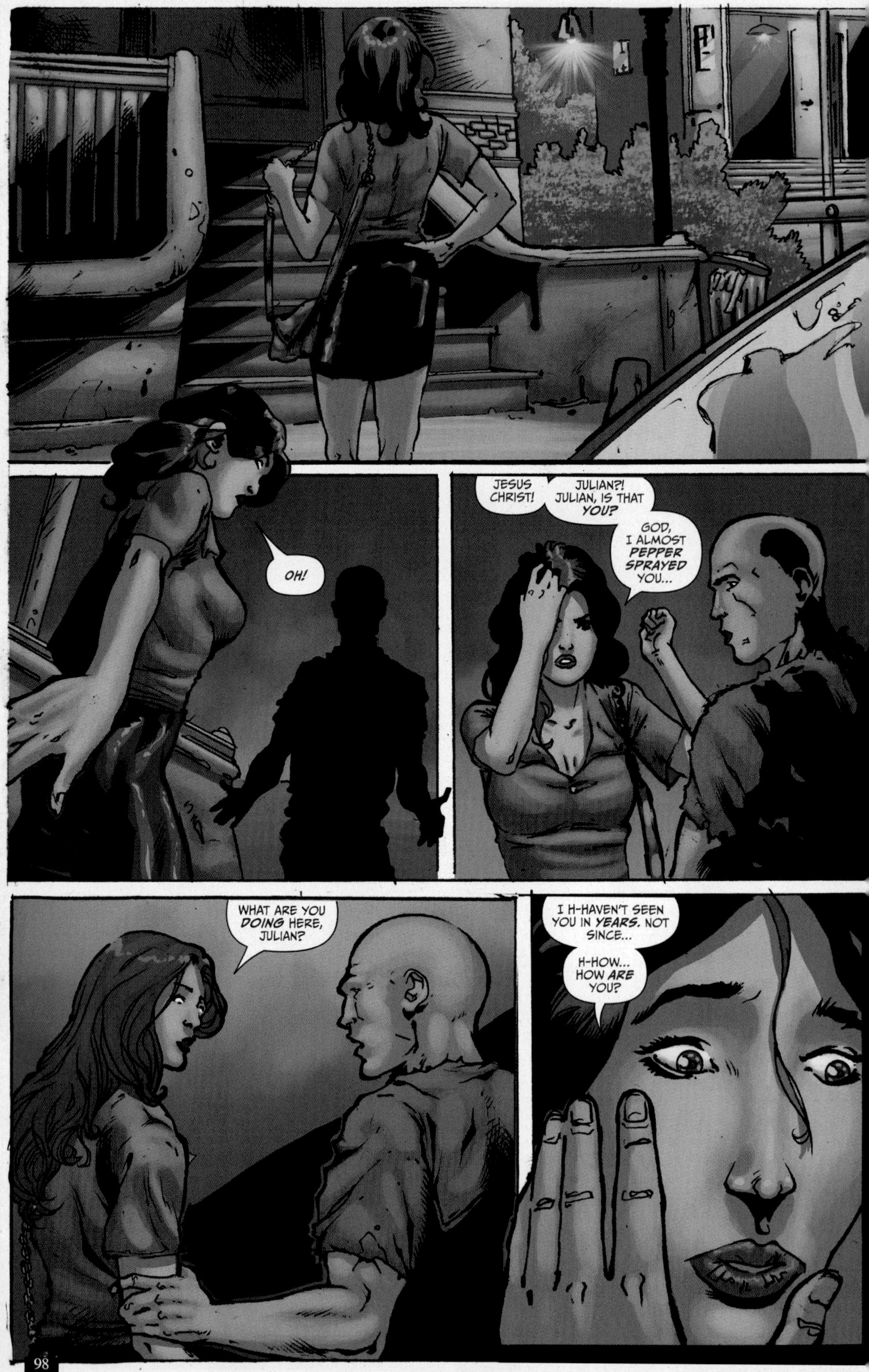
OH!
JESUS CHRIST!
JULIAN?! JULIAN, IS THAT YOU?
GOD, I ALMOST PEPPER SPRAYED YOU...
WHAT ARE YOU DOING HERE, JULIAN?
I H-HAVEN'T SEEN YOU IN YEARS. NOT SINCE...
H-HOW... HOW ARE YOU?

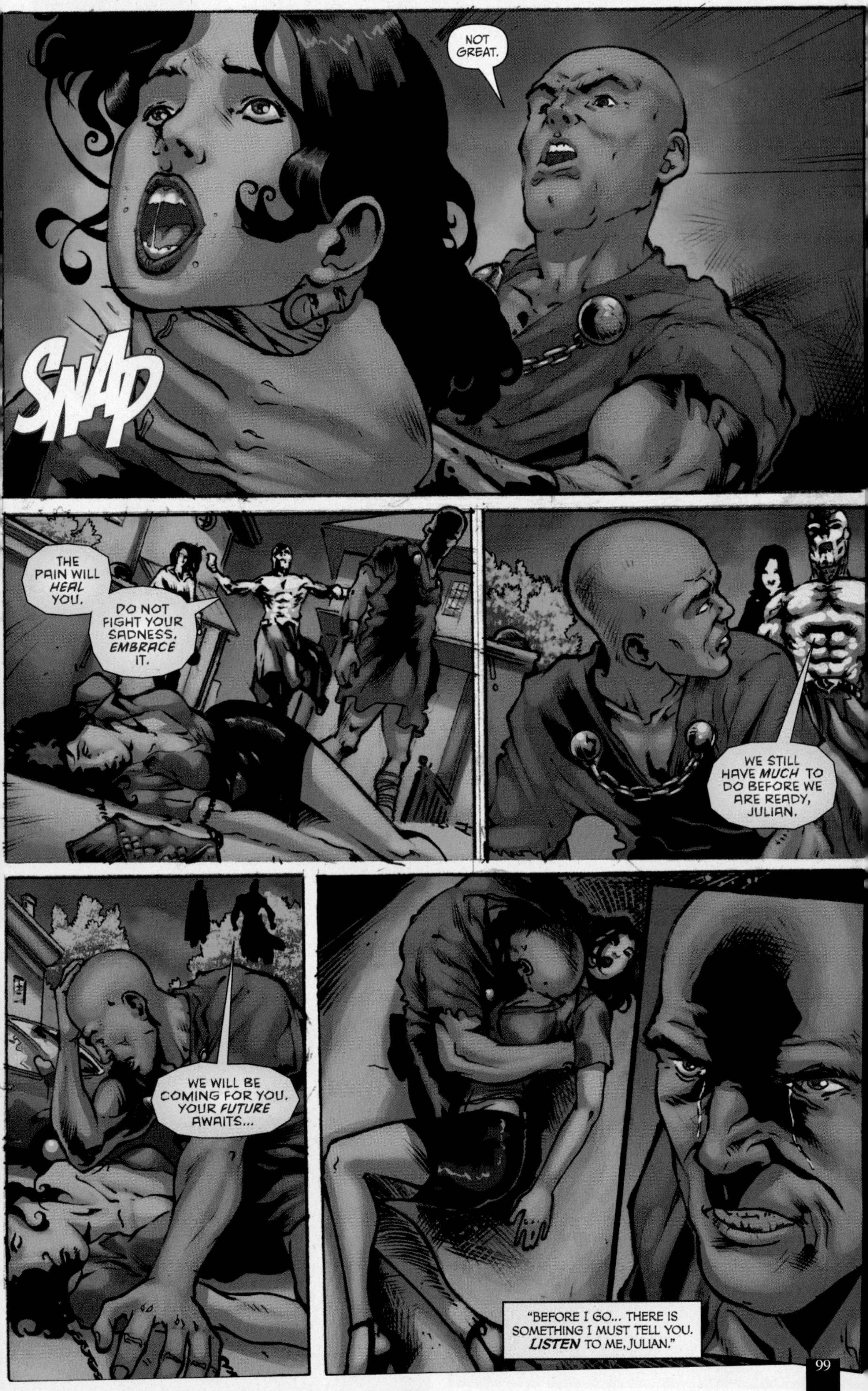
NOT GREAT.
SNAP
THE PAIN WILL HEAL YOU.
DO NOT FIGHT YOUR SADNESS. EMBRACE IT.
WE STILL HAVE MUCH TO DO BEFORE WE ARE READY, JULIAN.
WE WILL BE COMING FOR YOU. YOUR FUTURE AWAITS...
"BEFORE I GO... THERE IS SOMETHING I MUST TELL YOU. LISTEN TO ME, JULIAN."

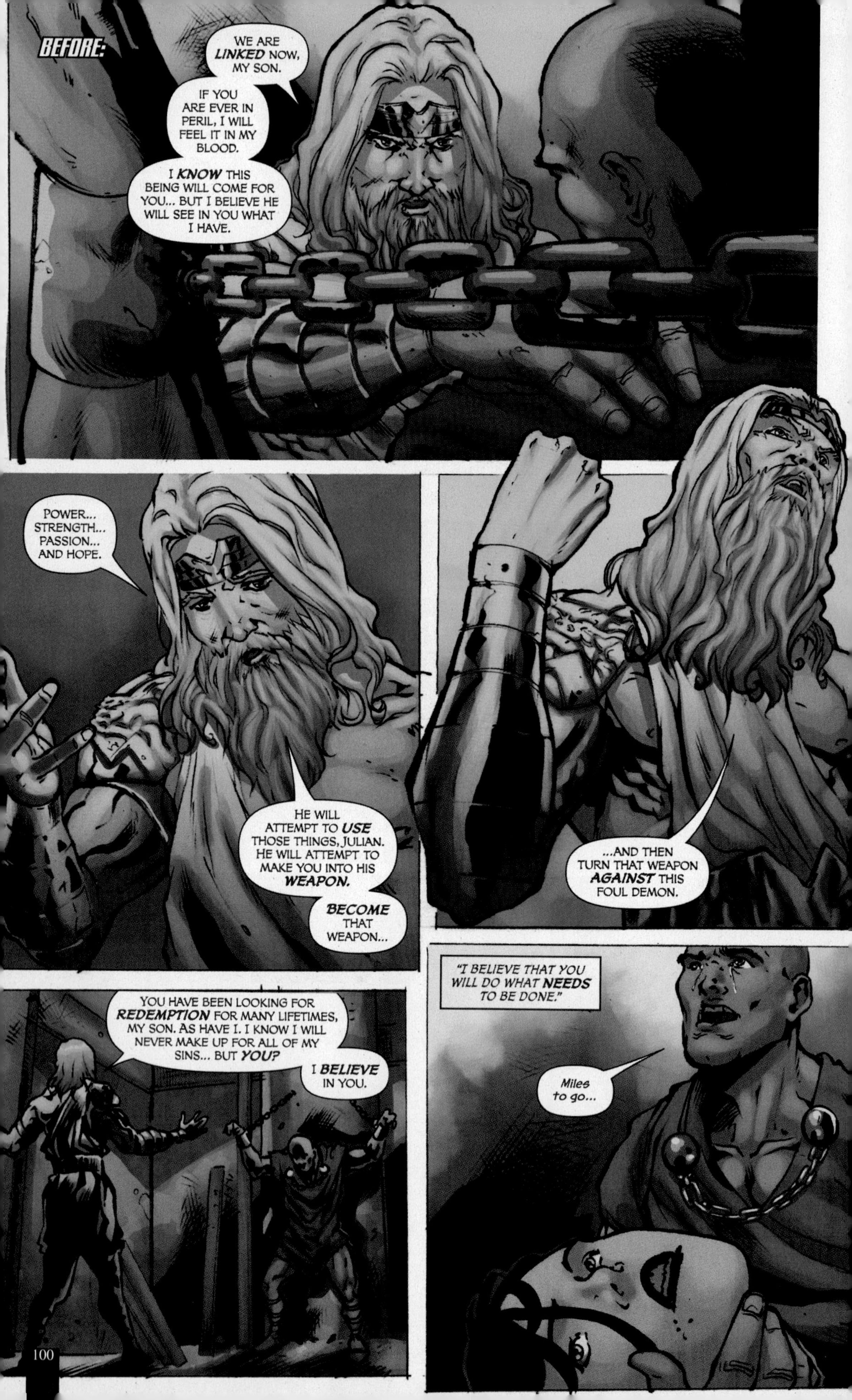
BEFORE:
WE ARE LINKED NOW, MY SON.
IF YOU ARE EVER IN PERIL, I WILL FEEL IT IN MY BLOOD.
I KNOW THIS BEING WILL COME FOR YOU... BUT I BELIEVE HE WILL SEE IN YOU WHAT I HAVE.
POWER... STRENGTH... PASSION... AND HOPE.
HE WILL ATTEMPT TO USE THOSE THINGS, JULIAN. HE WILL ATTEMPT TO MAKE YOU INTO HIS WEAPON.
BECOME THAT WEAPON...
...AND THEN TURN THAT WEAPON AGAINST THIS FOUL DEMON.
YOU HAVE BEEN LOOKING FOR REDEMPTION FOR MANY LIFETIMES, MY SON. AS HAVE I. I KNOW I WILL NEVER MAKE UP FOR ALL OF MY SINS... BUT YOU?
I BELIEVE IN YOU.
"I BELIEVE THAT YOU WILL DO WHAT NEEDS TO BE DONE."
Miles to go...

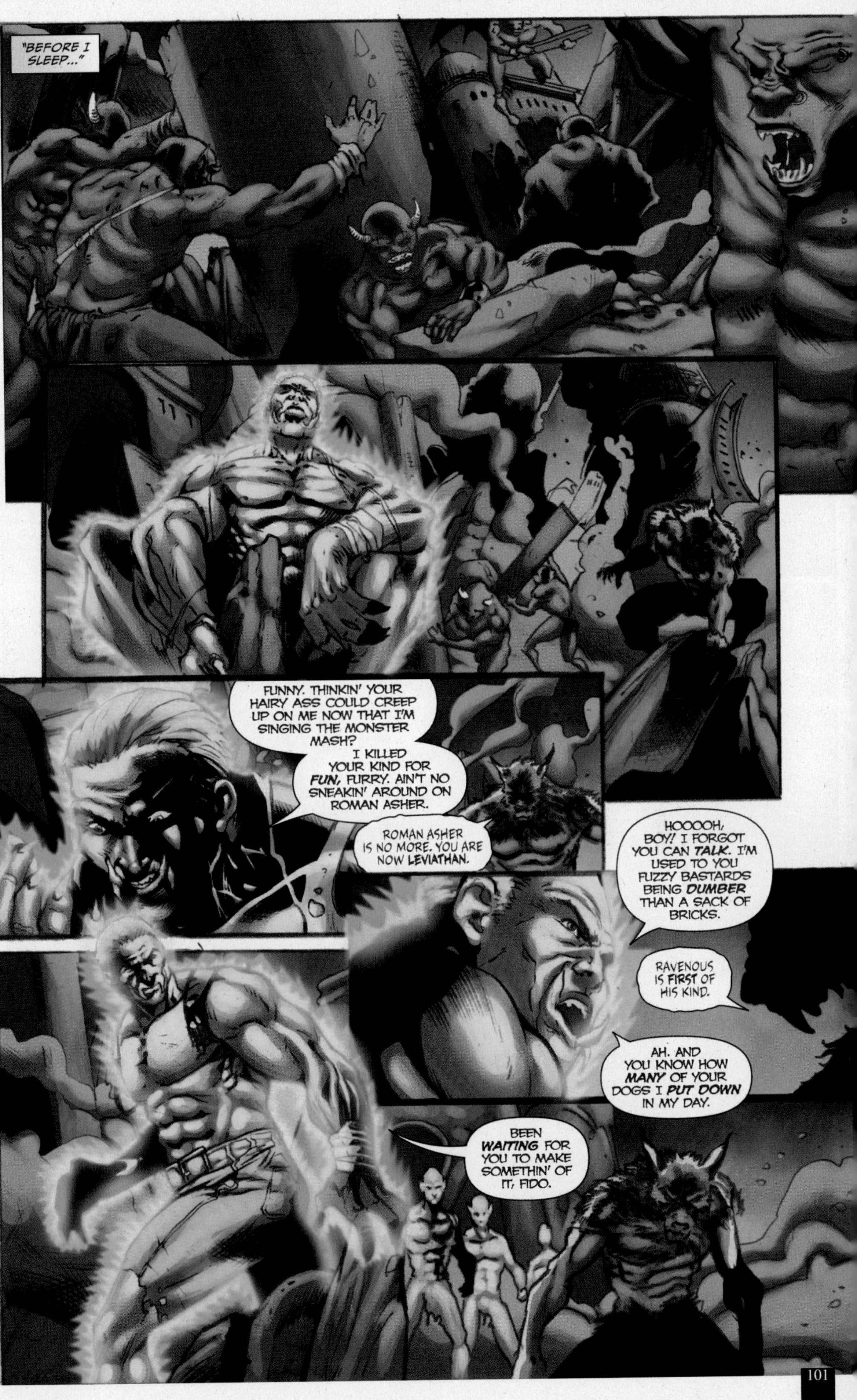
"BEFORE I SLEEP..."
FUNNY. THINKIN' YOUR HAIRY ASS COULD CREEP UP ON ME NOW THAT I'M SINGING THE MONSTER MASH?
I KILLED YOUR KIND FOR FUN, FURRY. AIN'T NO SNEAKIN' AROUND ON ROMAN ASHER.
ROMAN ASHER IS NO MORE. YOU ARE NOW LEVIATHAN.
HOOOOOH, BOY!! I FORGOT YOU CAN TALK. I'M USED TO YOU FUZZY BASTARDS BEING DUMBER THAN A SACK OF BRICKS.
RAVENOUS IS FIRST OF HIS KIND.
AH. AND YOU KNOW HOW MANY OF YOUR DOGS I PUT DOWN IN MY DAY.
BEEN WAITING FOR YOU TO MAKE SOMETHIN' OF IT, FIDO.

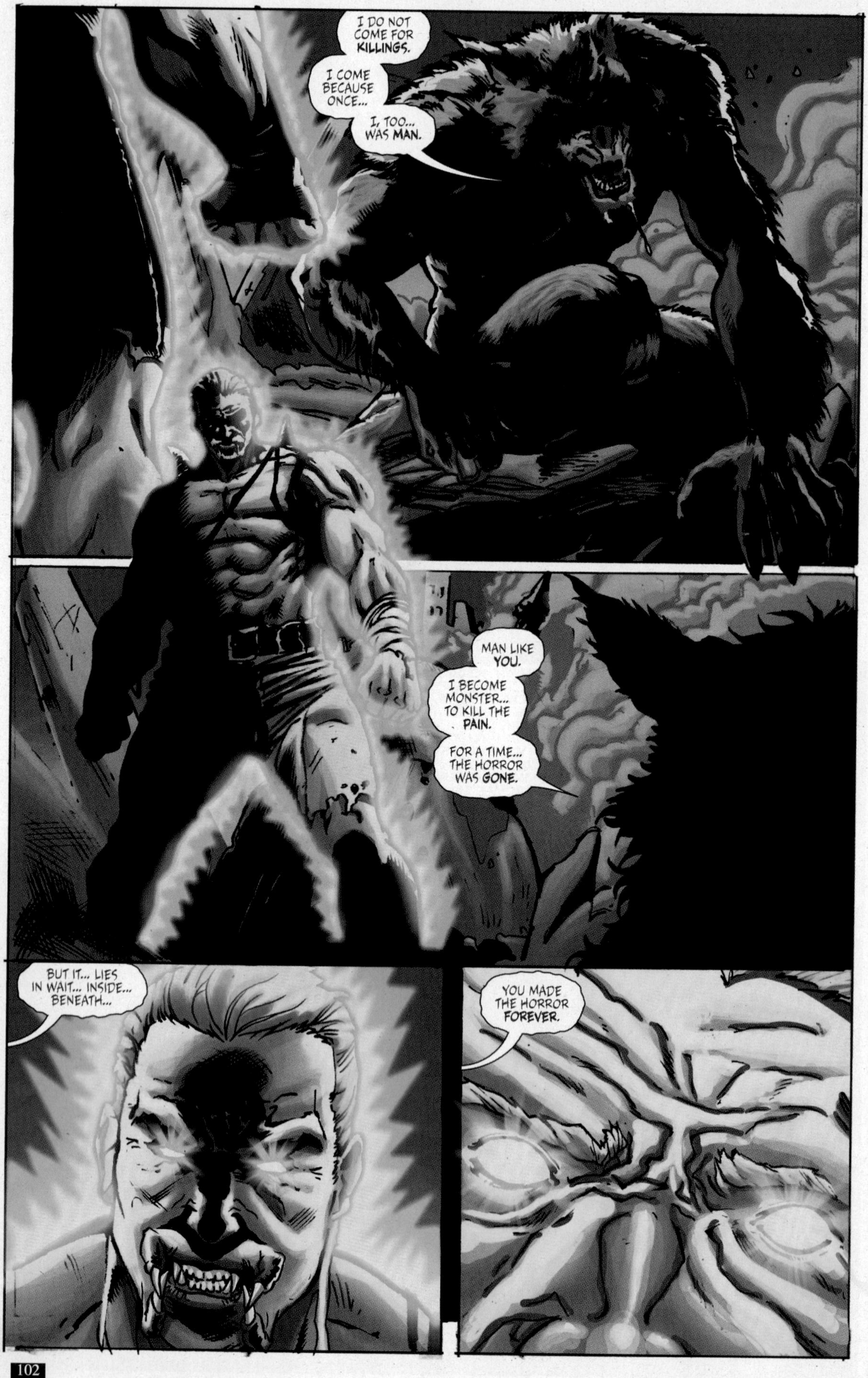
I DO NOT COME FOR KILLINGS.
I COME BECAUSE ONCE...
I, TOO... WAS MAN.
MAN LIKE YOU.
I BECOME MONSTER... TO KILL THE PAIN.
FOR A TIME... THE HORROR WAS GONE.
BUT IT... LIES IN WAIT... INSIDE... BENEATH...
YOU MADE THE HORROR FOREVER.

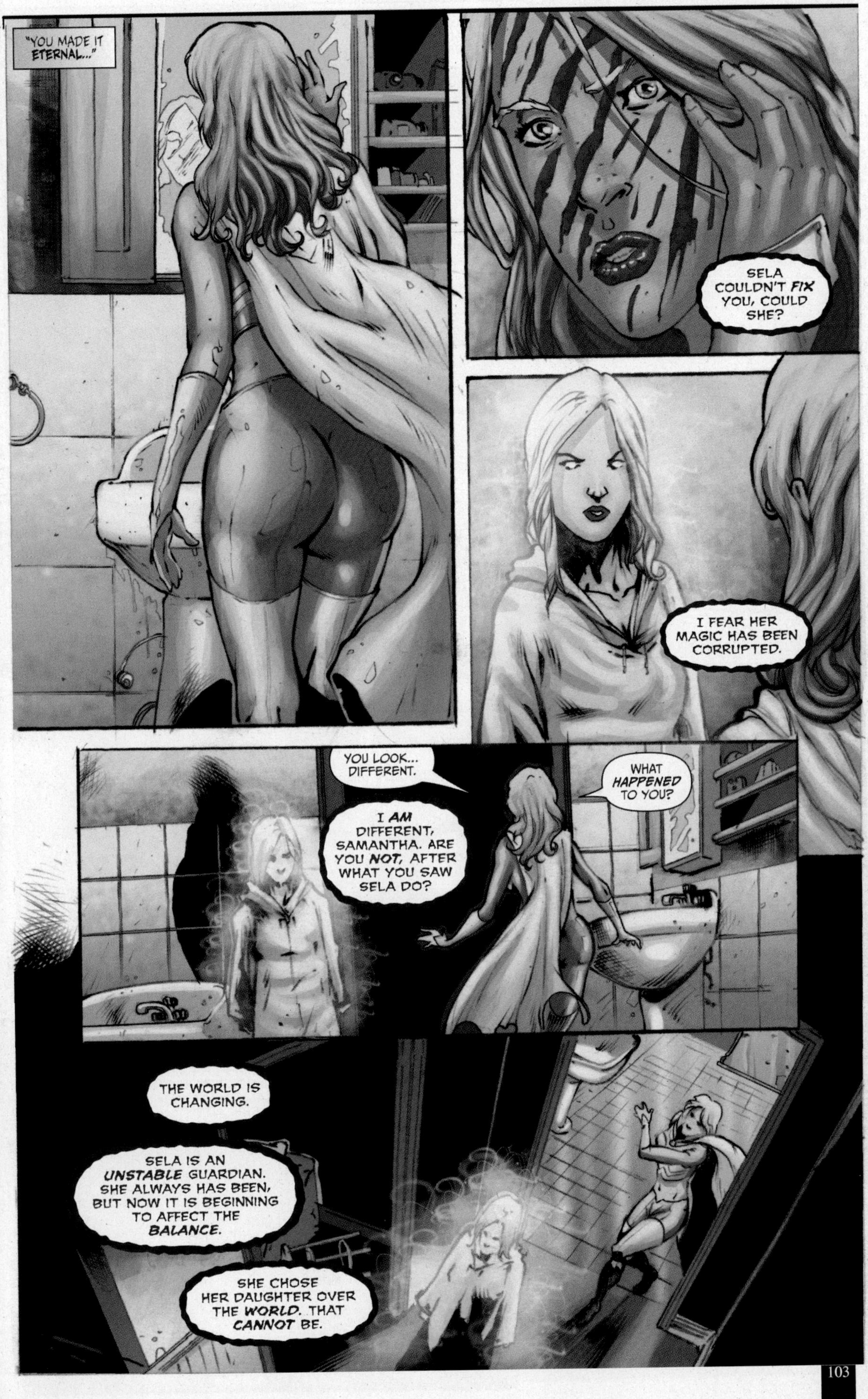
"YOU MADE IT ETERNAL..."
SELA COULDN'T FIX YOU, COULD SHE?
I FEAR HER MAGIC HAS BEEN CORRUPTED.
YOU LOOK... DIFFERENT.
I AM DIFFERENT, SAMANTHA. ARE YOU NOT, AFTER WHAT YOU SAW SELA DO?
WHAT HAPPENED TO YOU?
THE WORLD IS CHANGING.
SELA IS AN UNSTABLE GUARDIAN. SHE ALWAYS HAS BEEN, BUT NOW IT IS BEGINNING TO AFFECT THE BALANCE.
SHE CHOSE HER DAUGHTER OVER THE WORLD. THAT CANNOT BE.

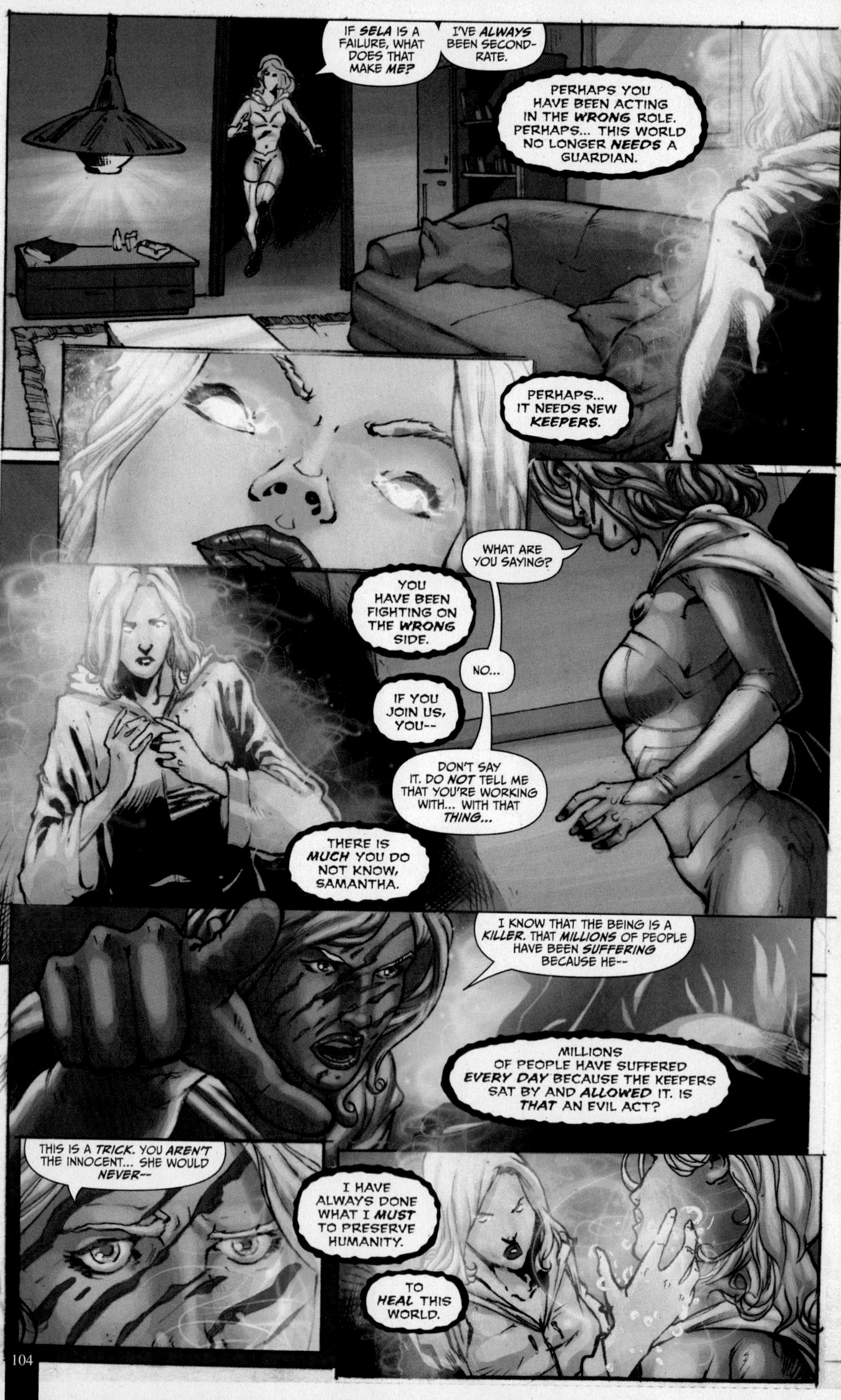

IF SELA IS A FAILURE, WHAT DOES THAT MAKE ME?
I'VE ALWAYS BEEN SECOND-RATE.
PERHAPS YOU HAVE BEEN ACTING IN THE WRONG ROLE. PERHAPS... THIS WORLD NO LONGER NEEDS A GUARDIAN.
PERHAPS... IT NEEDS NEW KEEPERS.
WHAT ARE YOU SAYING?
YOU HAVE BEEN FIGHTING ON THE WRONG SIDE.
NO...
IF YOU JOIN US, YOU--
DON'T SAY IT. DO NOT TELL ME THAT YOU'RE WORKING WITH... WITH THAT THING...
THERE IS MUCH YOU DO NOT KNOW, SAMANTHA.
I KNOW THAT THE BEING IS A KILLER. THAT MILLIONS OF PEOPLE HAVE BEEN SUFFERING BECAUSE HE--
MILLIONS OF PEOPLE HAVE SUFFERED EVERY DAY BECAUSE THE KEEPERS SAT BY AND ALLOWED IT. IS THAT AN EVIL ACT?
THIS IS A TRICK. YOU AREN'T THE INNOCENT... SHE WOULD NEVER--
I HAVE ALWAYS DONE WHAT I MUST TO PRESERVE HUMANITY.
TO HEAL THIS WORLD.

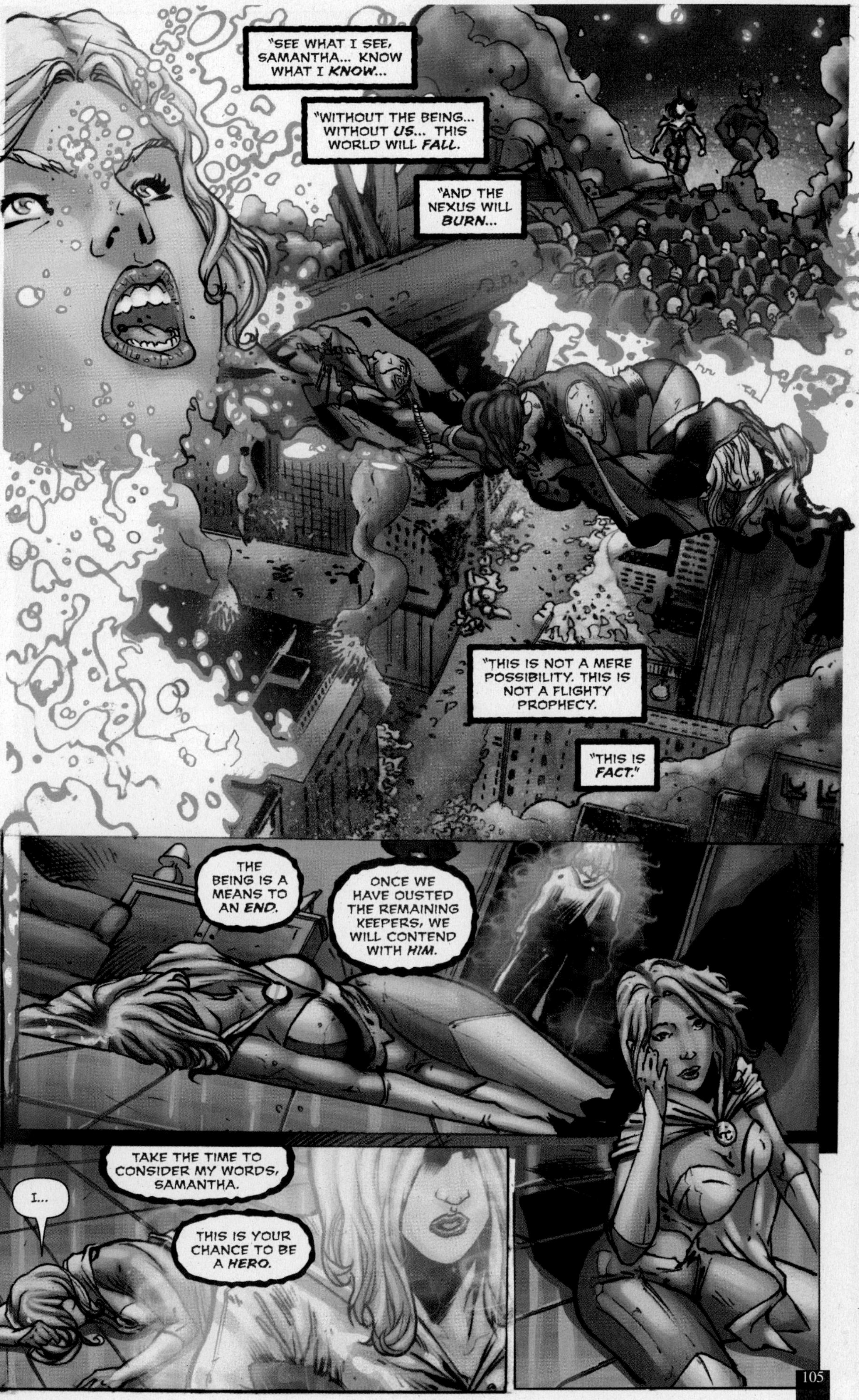
"SEE WHAT I SEE, SAMANTHA... KNOW WHAT I KNOW...
"WITHOUT THE BEING... WITHOUT US... THIS WORLD WILL FALL.
"AND THE NEXUS WILL BURN...
"THIS IS NOT A MERE POSSIBILITY. THIS IS NOT A FLIGHTY PROPHECY.
"THIS IS FACT."
THE BEING IS A MEANS TO AN END.
ONCE WE HAVE OUSTED THE REMAINING KEEPERS, WE WILL CONTEND WITH HIM.
TAKE THE TIME TO CONSIDER MY WORDS, SAMANTHA.
I...
THIS IS YOUR CHANCE TO BE A HERO.

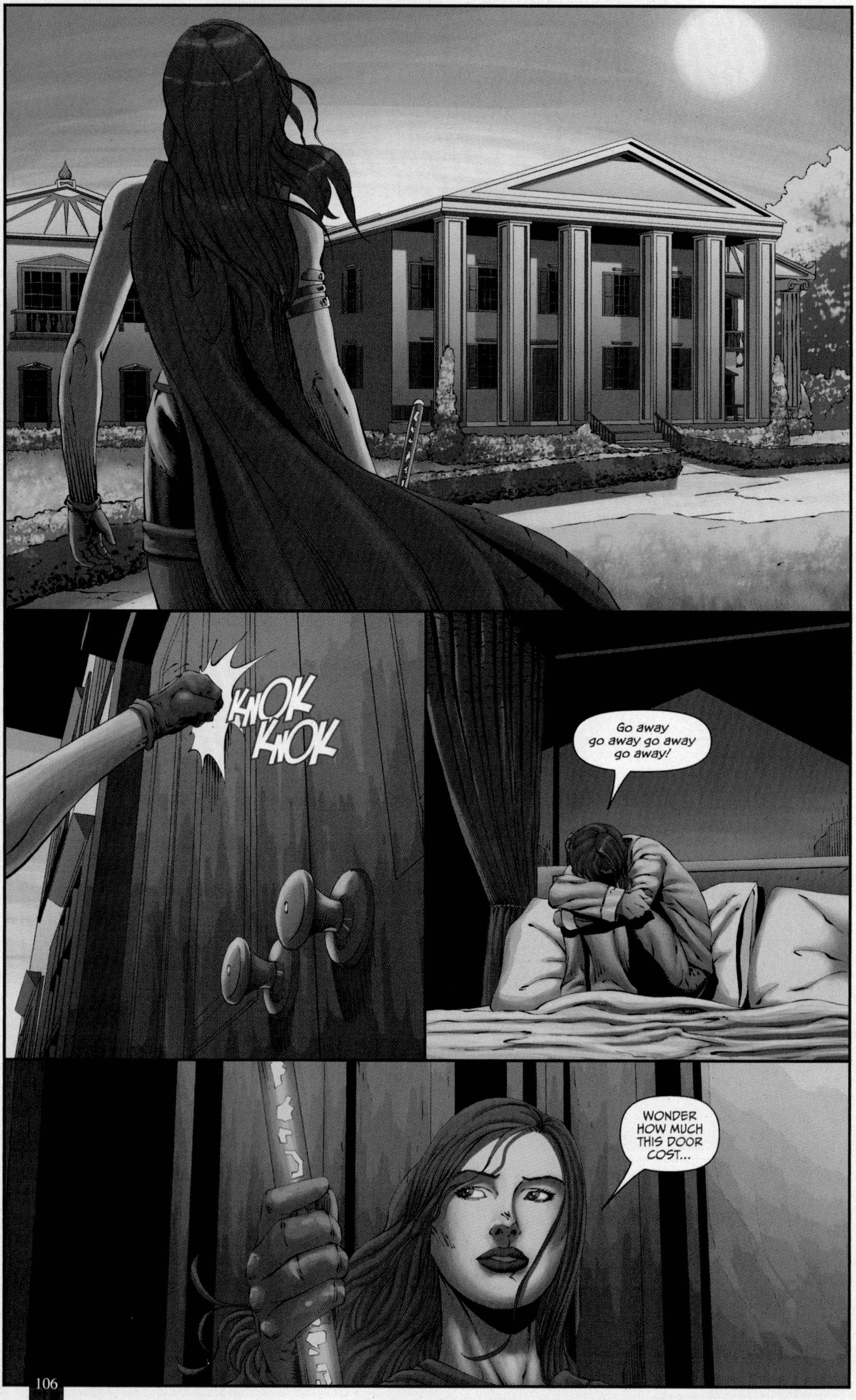
KNOK KNOK
Go away go away go away go away!
WONDER HOW MUCH THIS DOOR COST...

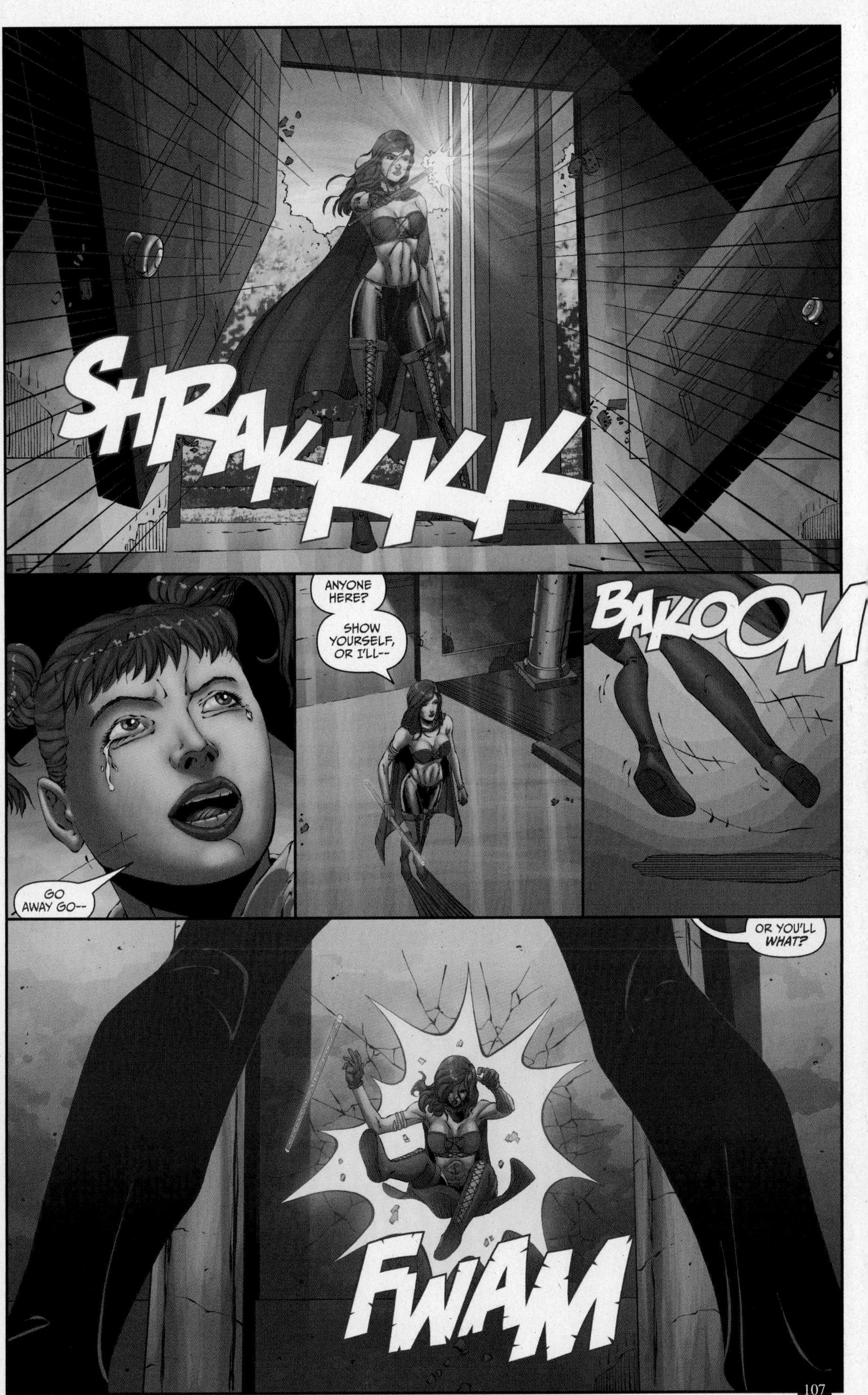
SHRAKKKK
GO AWAY GO--
ANYONE HERE?
SHOW YOURSELF, OR I'LL--
BAKOOM
OR YOU'LL WHAT?
FWAM

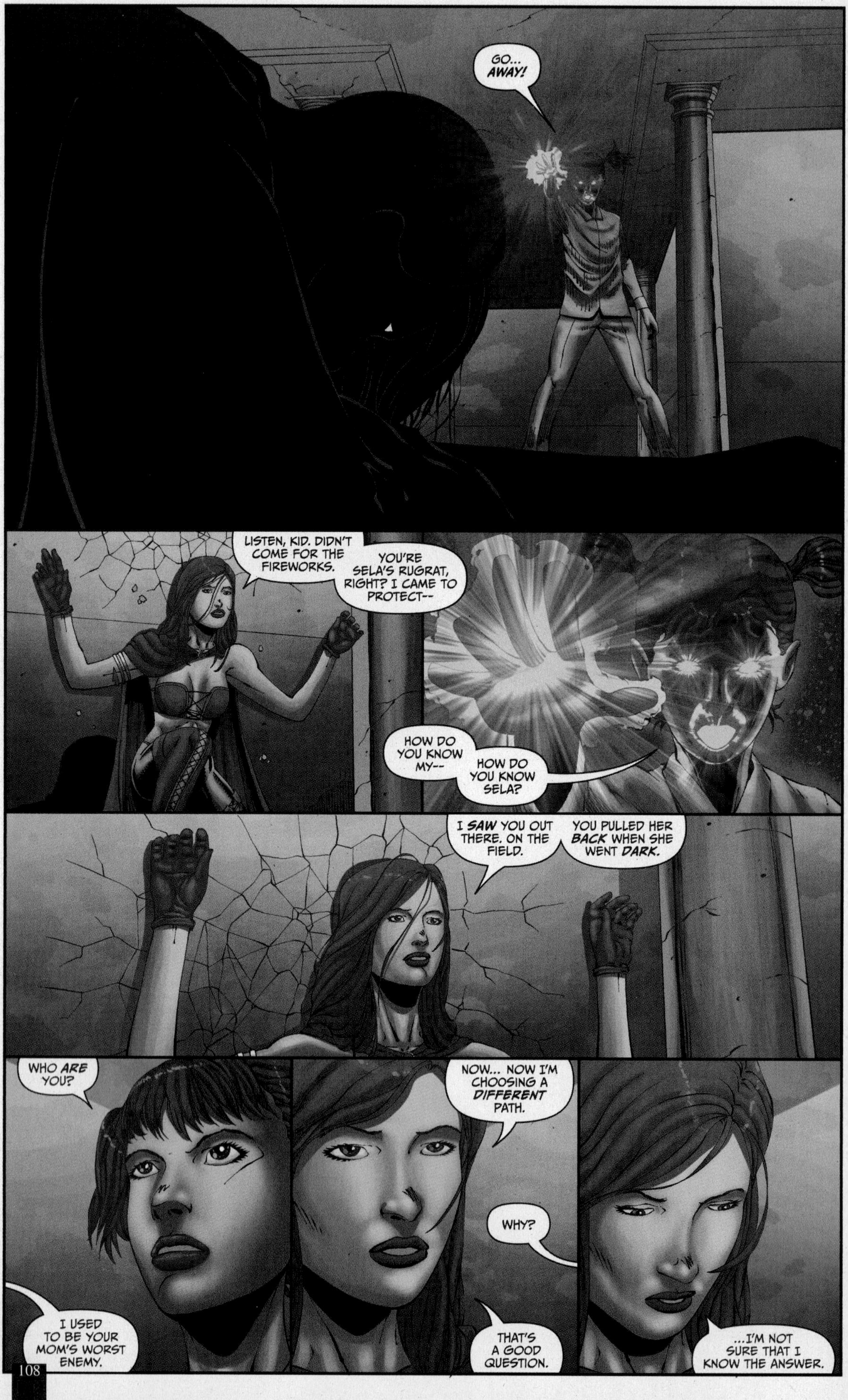
GO... AWAY!
LISTEN, KID. DIDN'T COME FOR THE FIREWORKS.
YOU'RE SELA'S RUGRAT, RIGHT? I CAME TO PROTECT--
HOW DO YOU KNOW MY--
HOW DO YOU KNOW SELA?
I SAW YOU OUT THERE. ON THE FIELD.
YOU PULLED HER BACK WHEN SHE WENT DARK.
WHO ARE YOU?
I USED TO BE YOUR MOM'S WORST ENEMY.
NOW... NOW I'M CHOOSING A DIFFERENT PATH.
WHY?
THAT'S A GOOD QUESTION.
...I'M NOT SURE THAT I KNOW THE ANSWER.

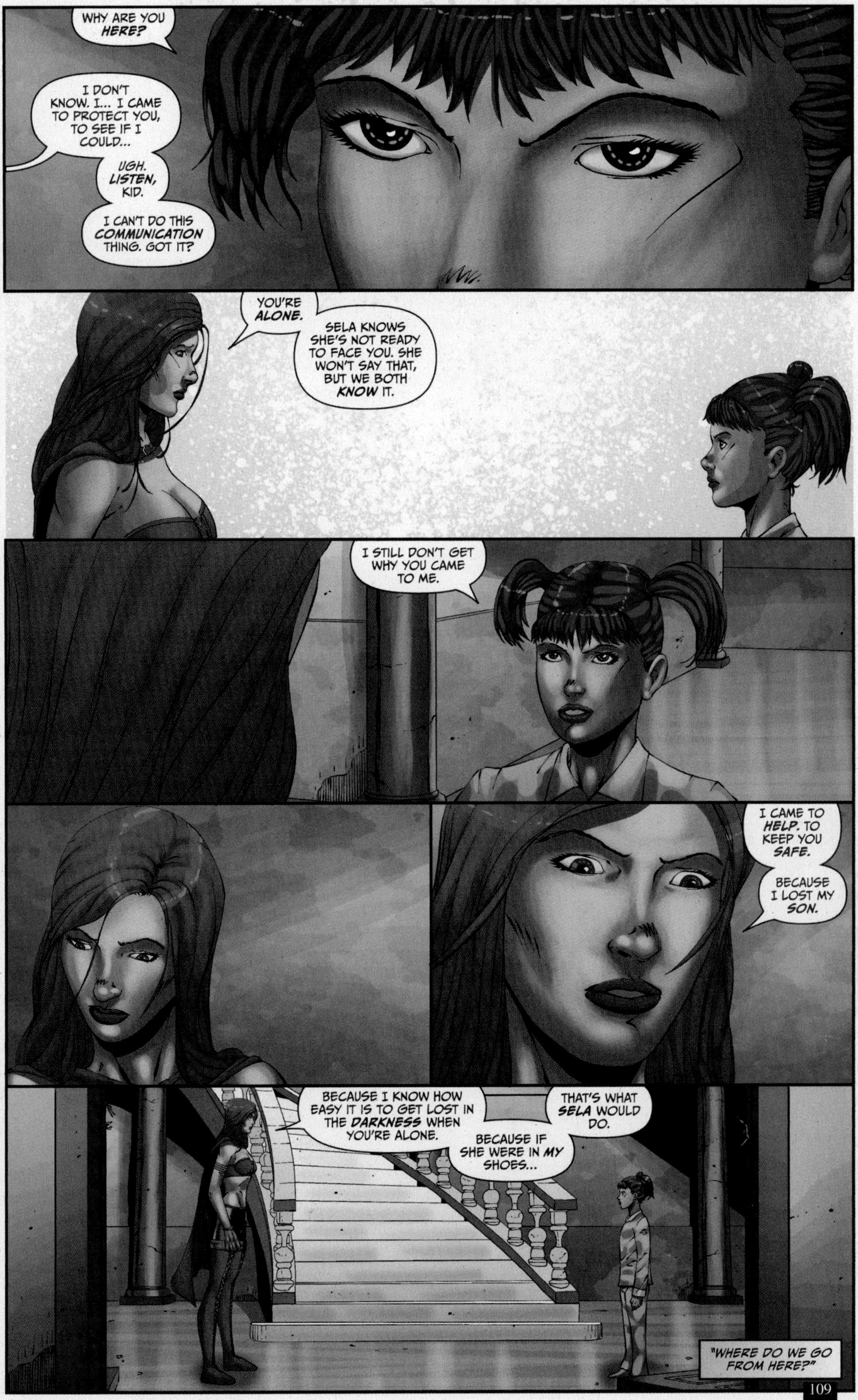
WHY ARE YOU HERE?
I DON'T KNOW. I... I CAME TO PROTECT YOU, TO SEE IF I COULD...
UGH. LISTEN, KID.
I CAN'T DO THIS COMMUNICATION THING. GOT IT?
YOU'RE ALONE.
SELA KNOWS SHE'S NOT READY TO FACE YOU. SHE WON'T SAY THAT, BUT WE BOTH KNOW IT.
I STILL DON'T GET WHY YOU CAME TO ME.
I CAME TO HELP. TO KEEP YOU SAFE.
BECAUSE I LOST MY SON.
BECAUSE I KNOW HOW EASY IT IS TO GET LOST IN THE DARKNESS WHEN YOU'RE ALONE.
BECAUSE IF SHE WERE IN MY SHOES...
THAT'S WHAT SELA WOULD DO.
"WHERE DO WE GO FROM HERE?"

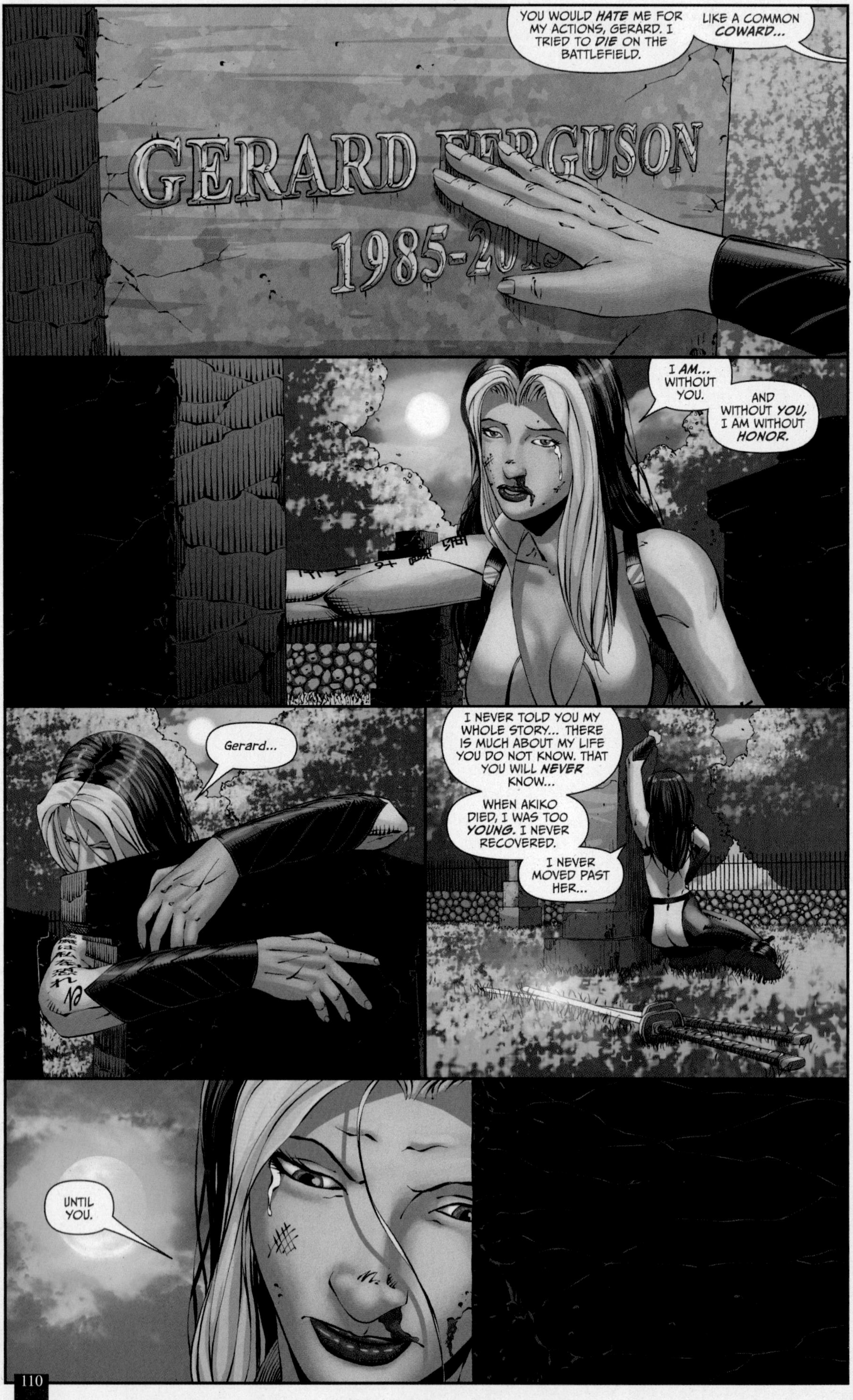
YOU WOULD HATE ME FOR MY ACTIONS, GERARD. I TRIED TO DIE ON THE BATTLEFIELD.
LIKE A COMMON COWARD...
GERARD FERGUSON
1985-201
I AM... WITHOUT YOU.
AND WITHOUT YOU, I AM WITHOUT HONOR.
Gerard...
I NEVER TOLD YOU MY WHOLE STORY... THERE IS MUCH ABOUT MY LIFE YOU DO NOT KNOW. THAT YOU WILL NEVER KNOW...
WHEN AKIKO DIED, I WAS TOO YOUNG. I NEVER RECOVERED.
I NEVER MOVED PAST HER...
UNTIL YOU.

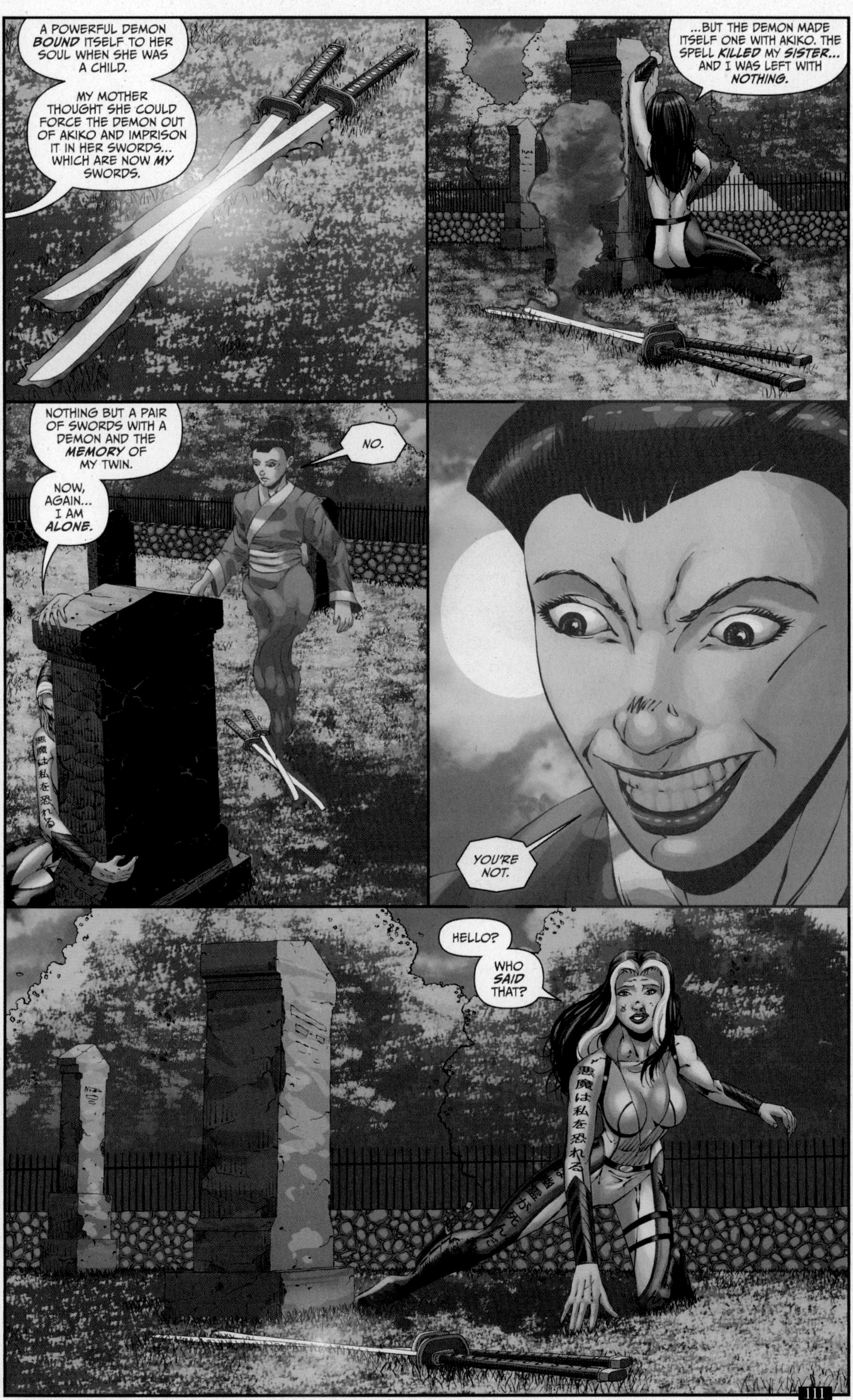
A POWERFUL DEMON *BOUND* ITSELF TO HER SOUL WHEN SHE WAS A CHILD.
MY MOTHER THOUGHT SHE COULD FORCE THE DEMON OUT OF AKIKO AND IMPRISON IT IN HER SWORDS... WHICH ARE NOW *MY* SWORDS.
...BUT THE DEMON MADE ITSELF ONE WITH AKIKO. THE SPELL *KILLED* MY *SISTER...* AND I WAS LEFT WITH *NOTHING.*
NOTHING BUT A PAIR OF SWORDS WITH A DEMON AND THE *MEMORY* OF MY TWIN.
NOW, AGAIN... I AM *ALONE.*
NO.
悪魔は私を恐れる
YOU'RE NOT.
HELLO?
WHO *SAID* THAT?

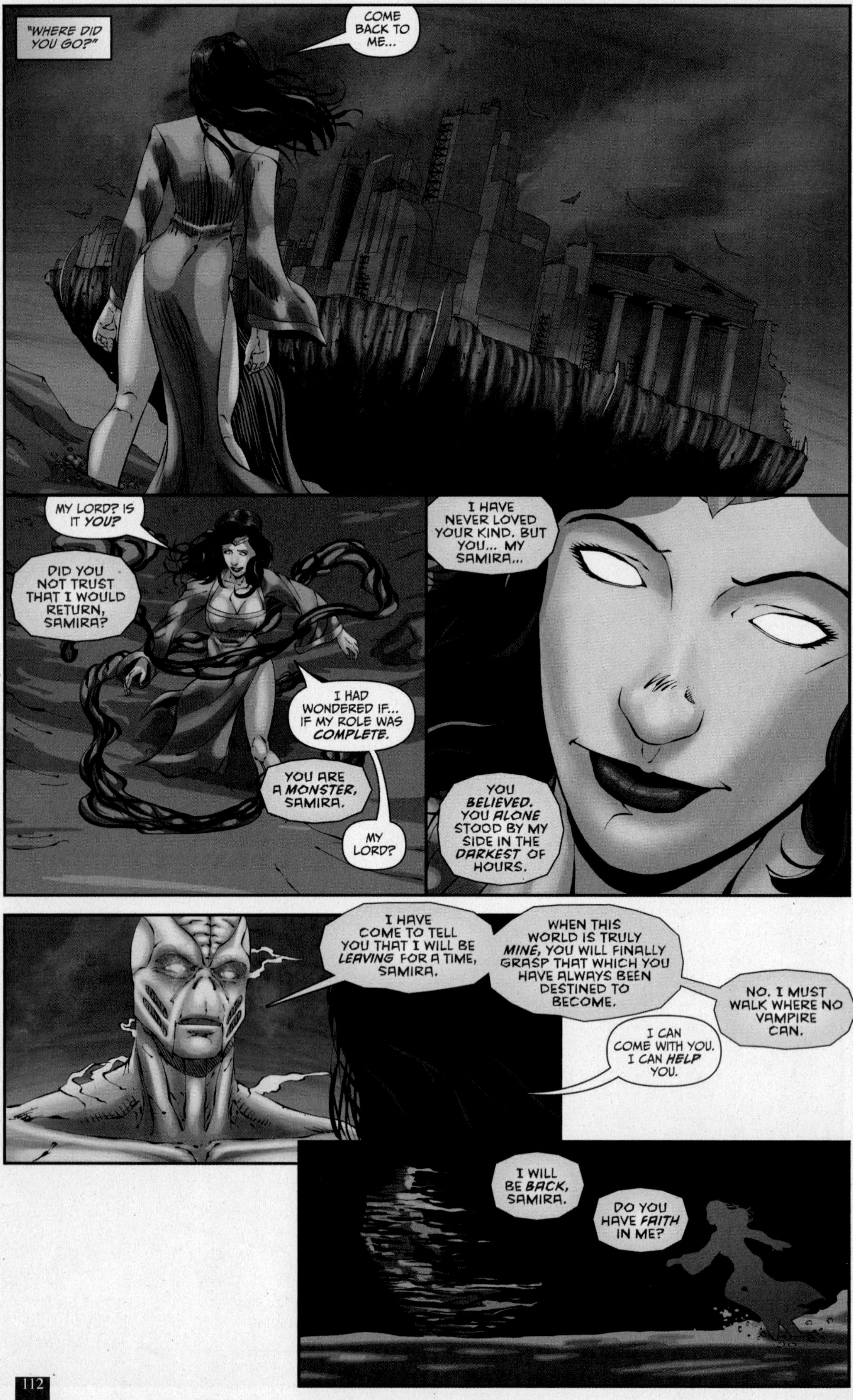
"WHERE DID YOU GO?"
COME BACK TO ME...
MY LORD? IS IT YOU?
DID YOU NOT TRUST THAT I WOULD RETURN, SAMIRA?
I HAD WONDERED IF... IF MY ROLE WAS COMPLETE.
YOU ARE A MONSTER, SAMIRA.
MY LORD?
I HAVE NEVER LOVED YOUR KIND. BUT YOU... MY SAMIRA...
YOU BELIEVED. YOU ALONE STOOD BY MY SIDE IN THE DARKEST OF HOURS.
I HAVE COME TO TELL YOU THAT I WILL BE LEAVING FOR A TIME, SAMIRA.
WHEN THIS WORLD IS TRULY MINE, YOU WILL FINALLY GRASP THAT WHICH YOU HAVE ALWAYS BEEN DESTINED TO BECOME.
I CAN COME WITH YOU. I CAN HELP YOU.
NO. I MUST WALK WHERE NO VAMPIRE CAN.
I WILL BE BACK, SAMIRA.
DO YOU HAVE FAITH IN ME?

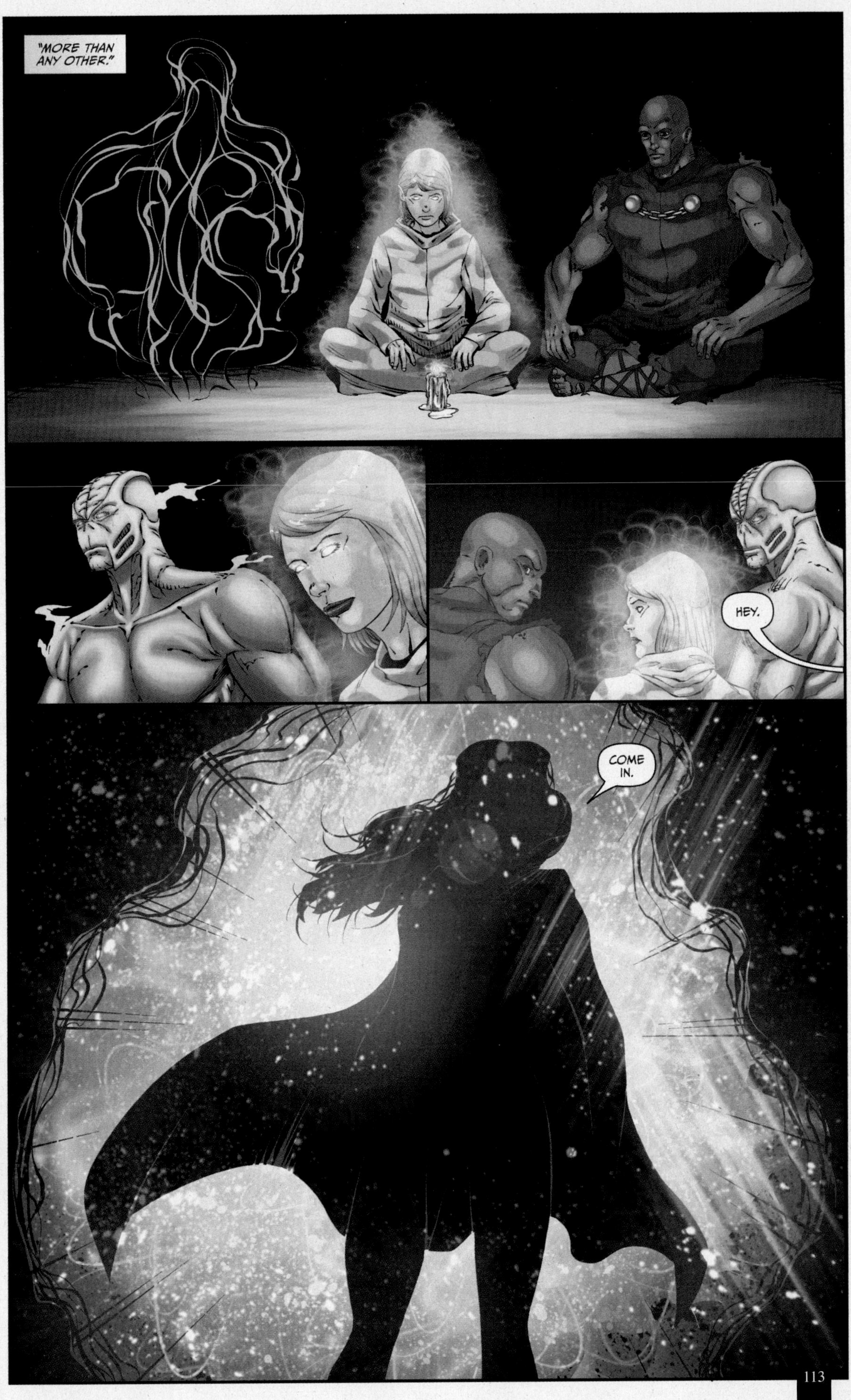
"MORE THAN ANY OTHER."
HEY.
COME IN.

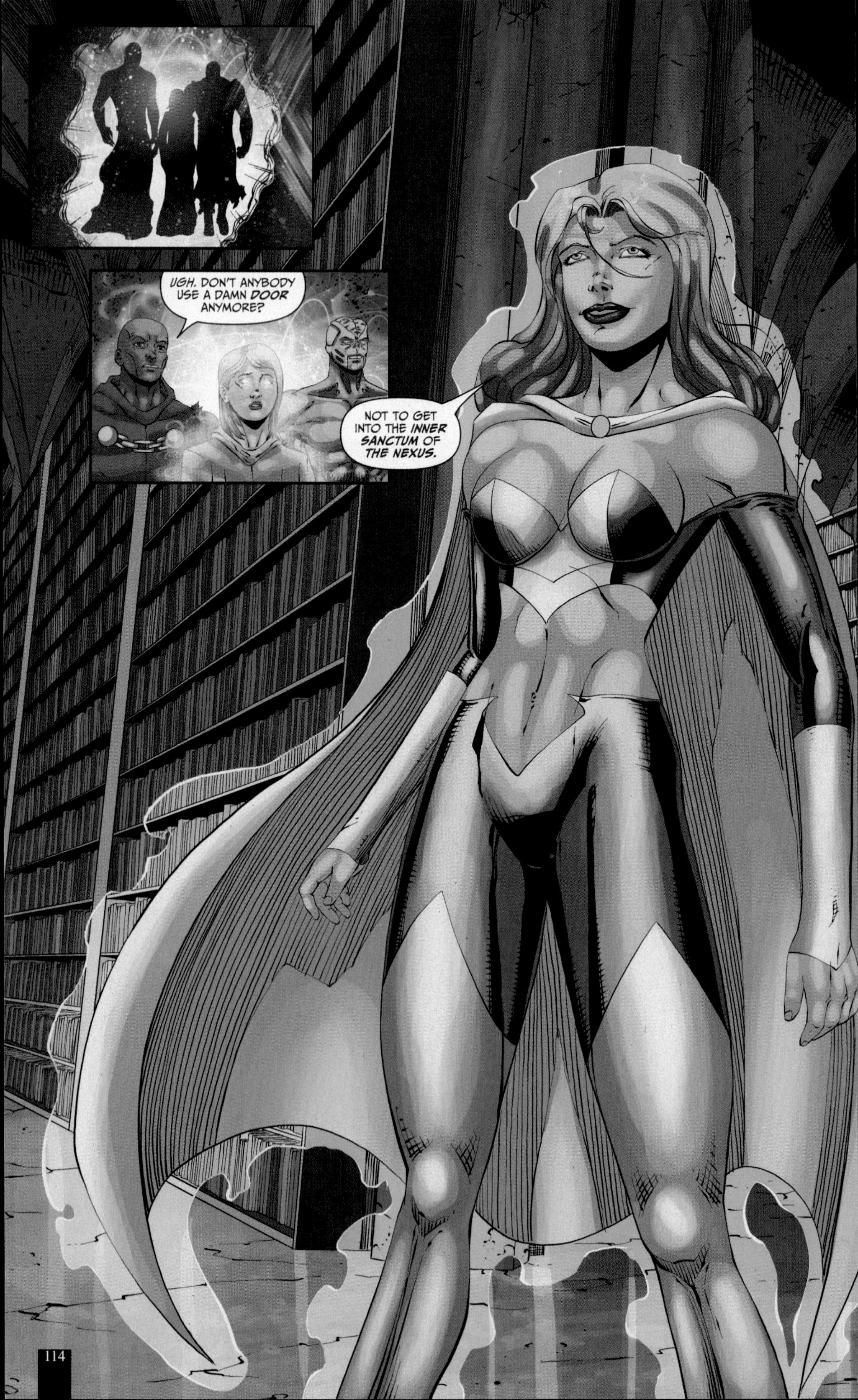
UGH. DON'T ANYBODY USE A DAMN DOOR ANYMORE?
NOT TO GET INTO THE INNER SANCTUM OF THE NEXUS.

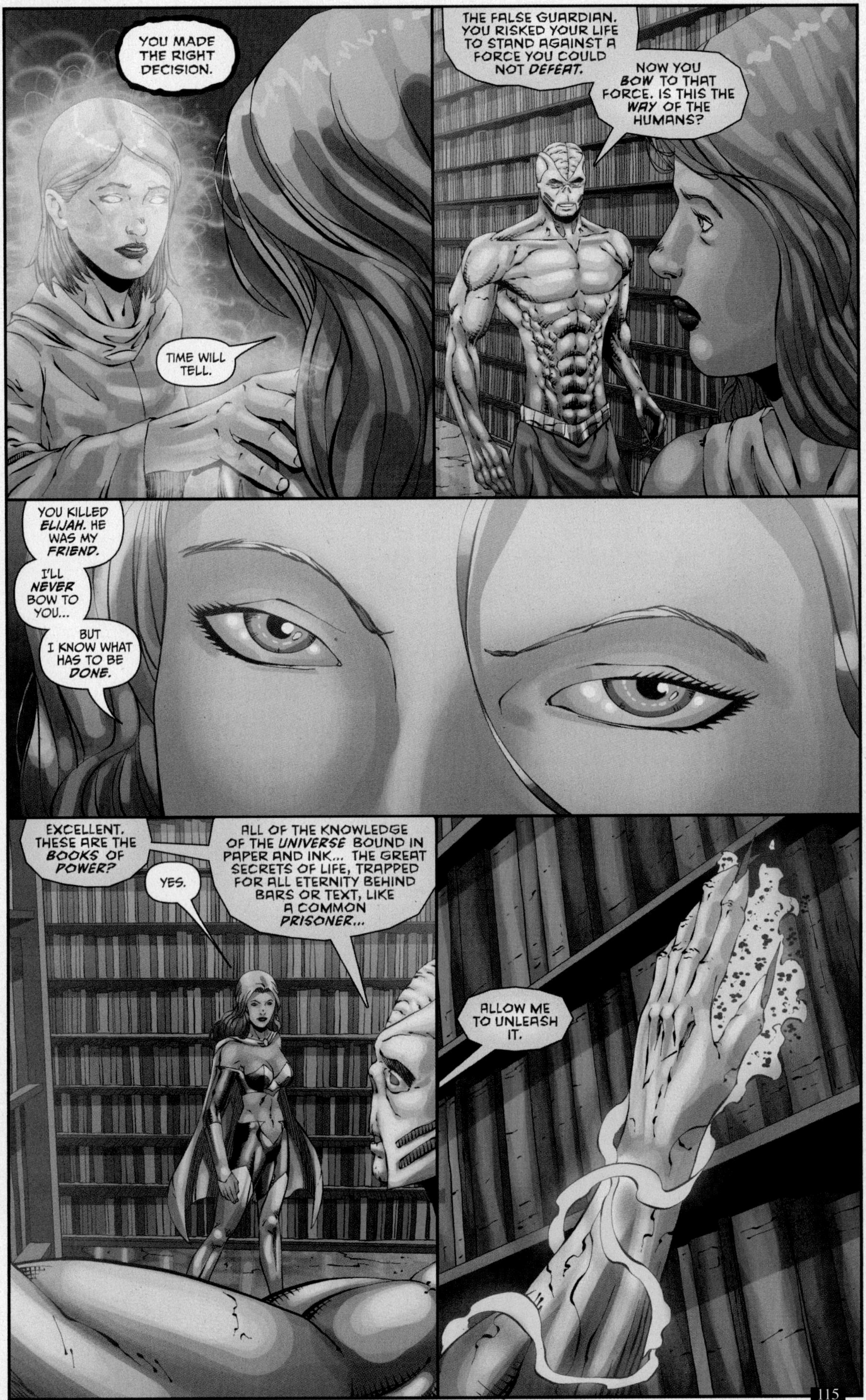
YOU MADE THE RIGHT DECISION.
TIME WILL TELL.
THE FALSE GUARDIAN. YOU RISKED YOUR LIFE TO STAND AGAINST A FORCE YOU COULD NOT DEFEAT.
NOW YOU BOW TO THAT FORCE. IS THIS THE WAY OF THE HUMANS?
YOU KILLED ELIJAH. HE WAS MY FRIEND.
I'LL NEVER BOW TO YOU...
BUT I KNOW WHAT HAS TO BE DONE.
EXCELLENT. THESE ARE THE BOOKS OF POWER?
YES.
ALL OF THE KNOWLEDGE OF THE UNIVERSE BOUND IN PAPER AND INK... THE GREAT SECRETS OF LIFE, TRAPPED FOR ALL ETERNITY BEHIND BARS OR TEXT, LIKE A COMMON PRISONER...
ALLOW ME TO UNLEASH IT.

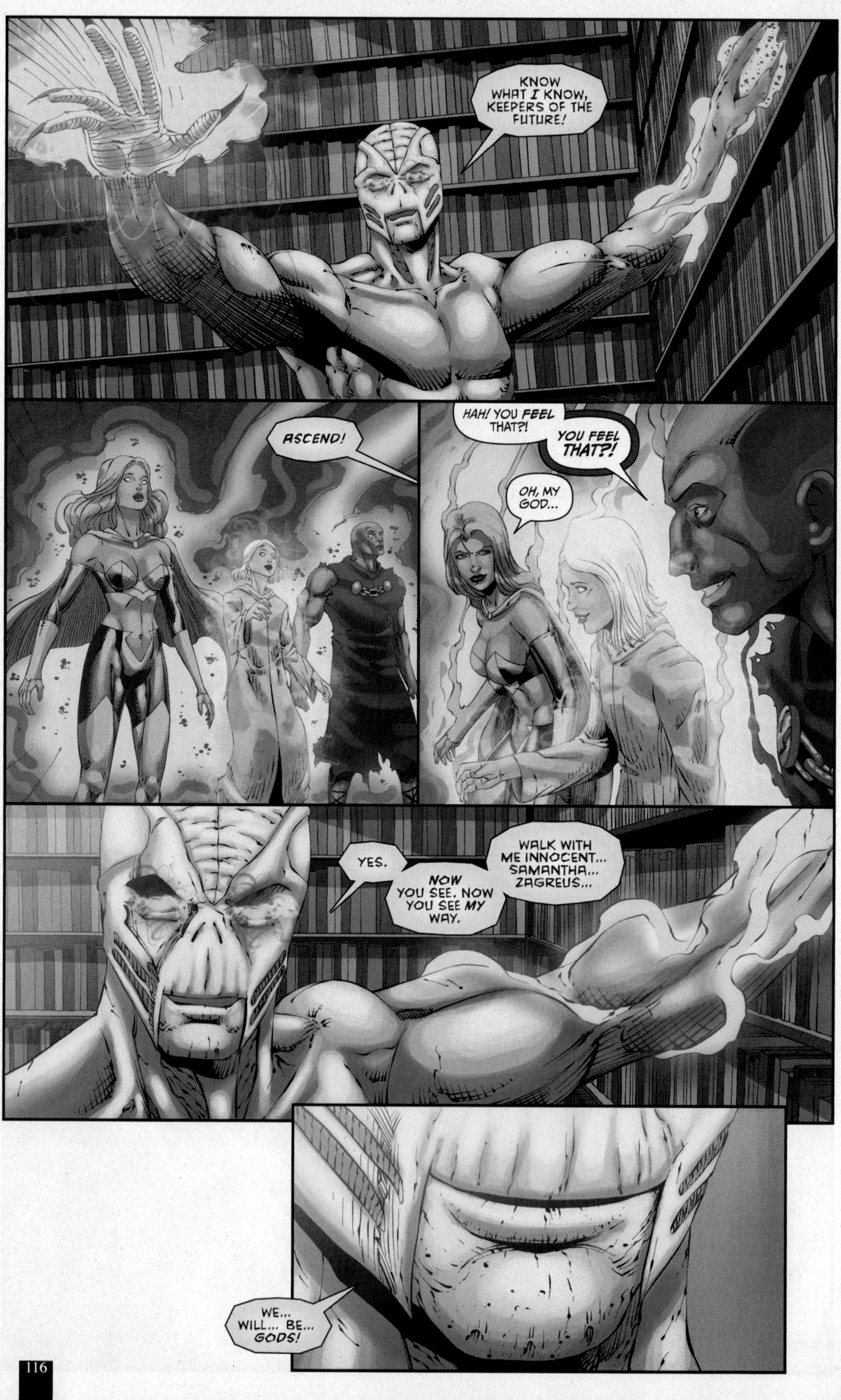
KNOW WHAT I KNOW, KEEPERS OF THE FUTURE!
ASCEND!
HAH! YOU FEEL THAT?!
YOU FEEL THAT?!
OH, MY GOD...
YES.
NOW YOU SEE. NOW YOU SEE MY WAY.
WALK WITH ME INNOCENT... SAMANTHA... ZAGREUS...
WE... WILL... BE... GODS!

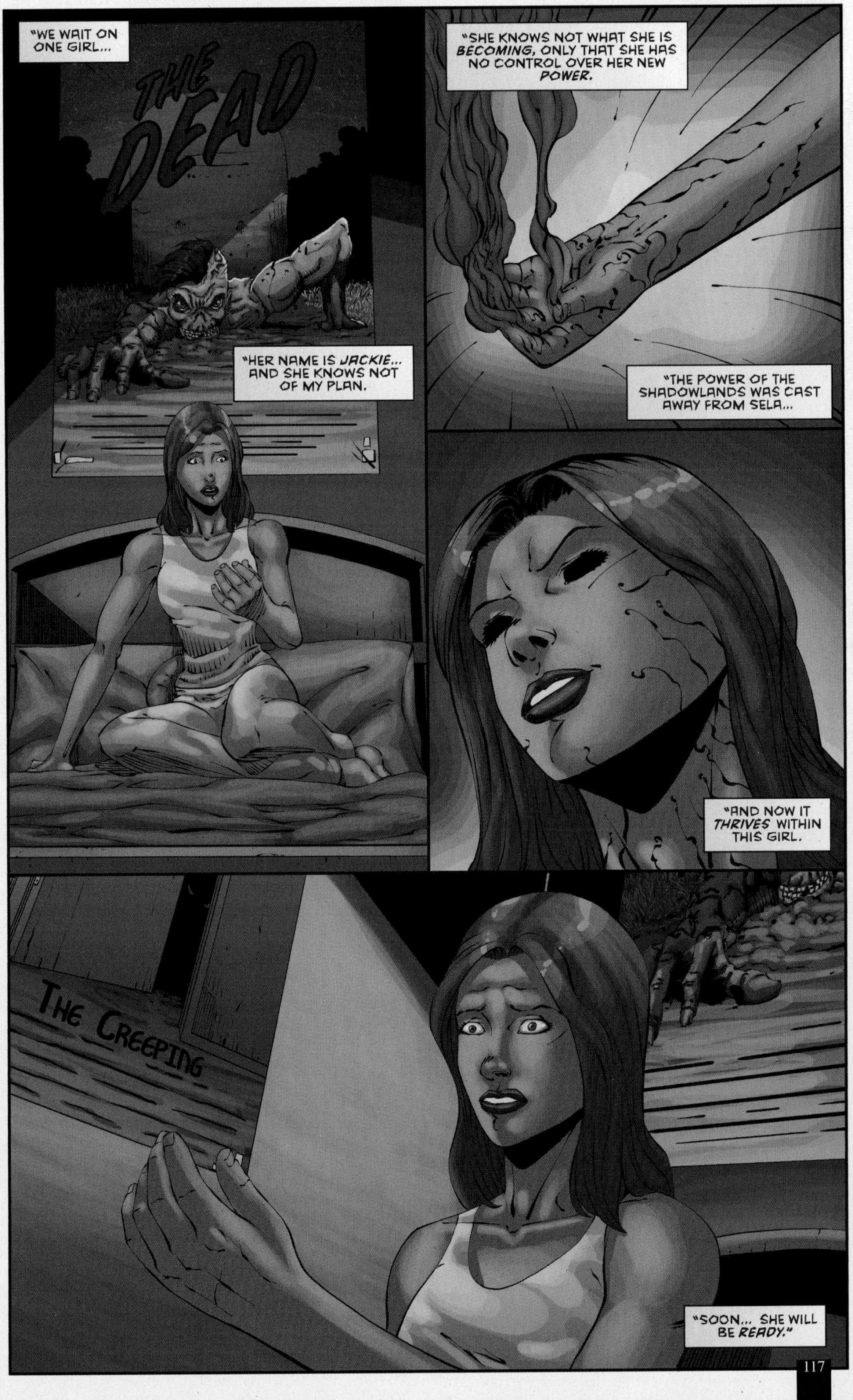
"WE WAIT ON ONE GIRL...
THE DEAD
"HER NAME IS JACKIE... AND SHE KNOWS NOT OF MY PLAN.
"SHE KNOWS NOT WHAT SHE IS BECOMING, ONLY THAT SHE HAS NO CONTROL OVER HER NEW POWER.
"THE POWER OF THE SHADOWLANDS WAS CAST AWAY FROM SELA...
"AND NOW IT THRIVES WITHIN THIS GIRL.
THE CREEPING
"SOON... SHE WILL BE READY."

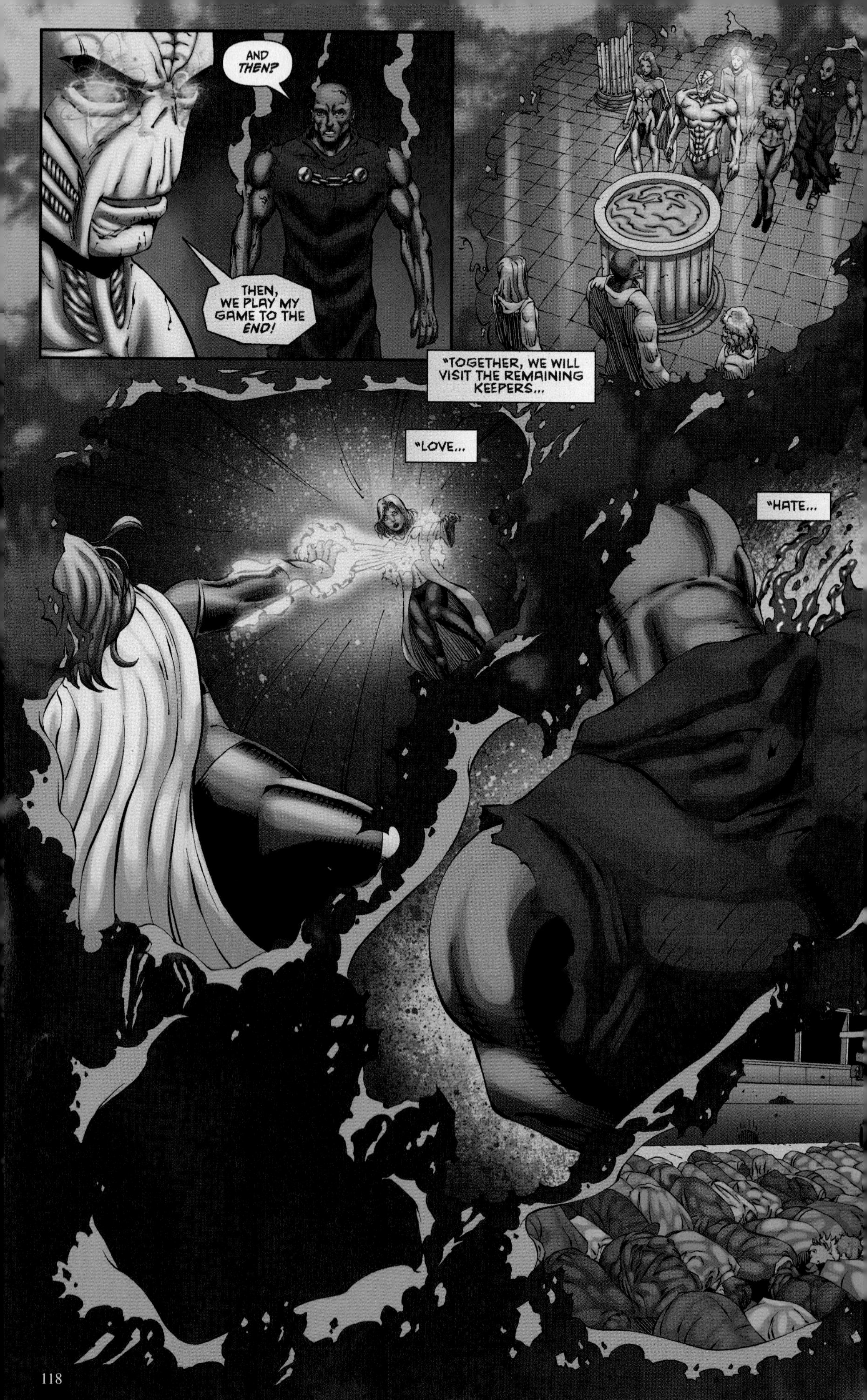
AND THEN?
THEN, WE PLAY MY GAME TO THE END!
"TOGETHER, WE WILL VISIT THE REMAINING KEEPERS...
"LOVE...
"HATE...

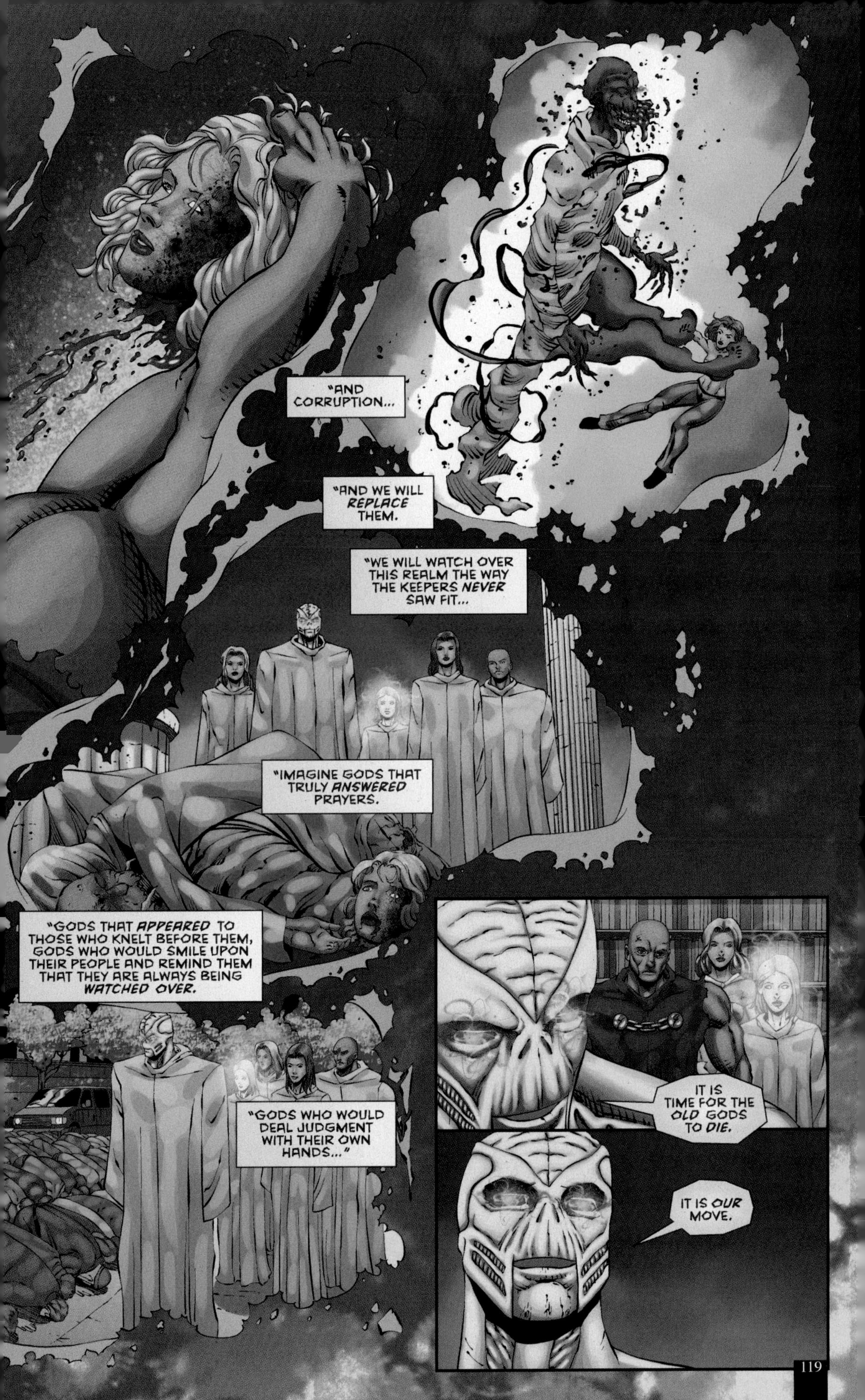

"AND CORRUPTION...
"AND WE WILL REPLACE THEM.
"WE WILL WATCH OVER THIS REALM THE WAY THE KEEPERS NEVER SAW FIT...
"IMAGINE GODS THAT TRULY ANSWERED PRAYERS.
"GODS THAT APPEARED TO THOSE WHO KNELT BEFORE THEM, GODS WHO WOULD SMILE UPON THEIR PEOPLE AND REMIND THEM THAT THEY ARE ALWAYS BEING WATCHED OVER.
"GODS WHO WOULD DEAL JUDGMENT WITH THEIR OWN HANDS..."
IT IS TIME FOR THE OLD GODS TO DIE.
IT IS OUR MOVE.

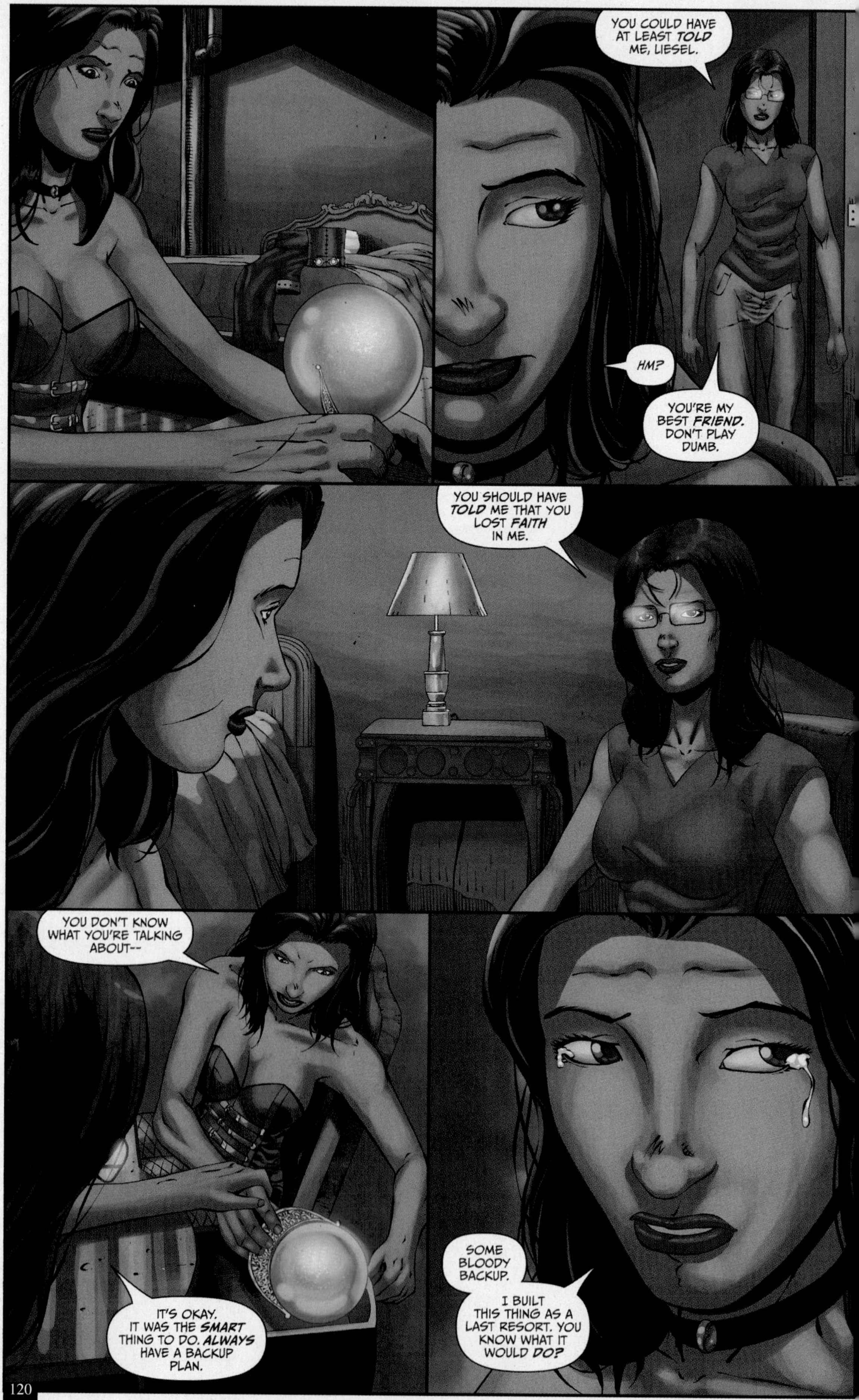
YOU COULD HAVE AT LEAST TOLD ME, LIESEL.
HM?
YOU'RE MY BEST FRIEND. DON'T PLAY DUMB.
YOU SHOULD HAVE TOLD ME THAT YOU LOST FAITH IN ME.
YOU DON'T KNOW WHAT YOU'RE TALKING ABOUT--
IT'S OKAY. IT WAS THE SMART THING TO DO. ALWAYS HAVE A BACKUP PLAN.
SOME BLOODY BACKUP.
I BUILT THIS THING AS A LAST RESORT. YOU KNOW WHAT IT WOULD DO?

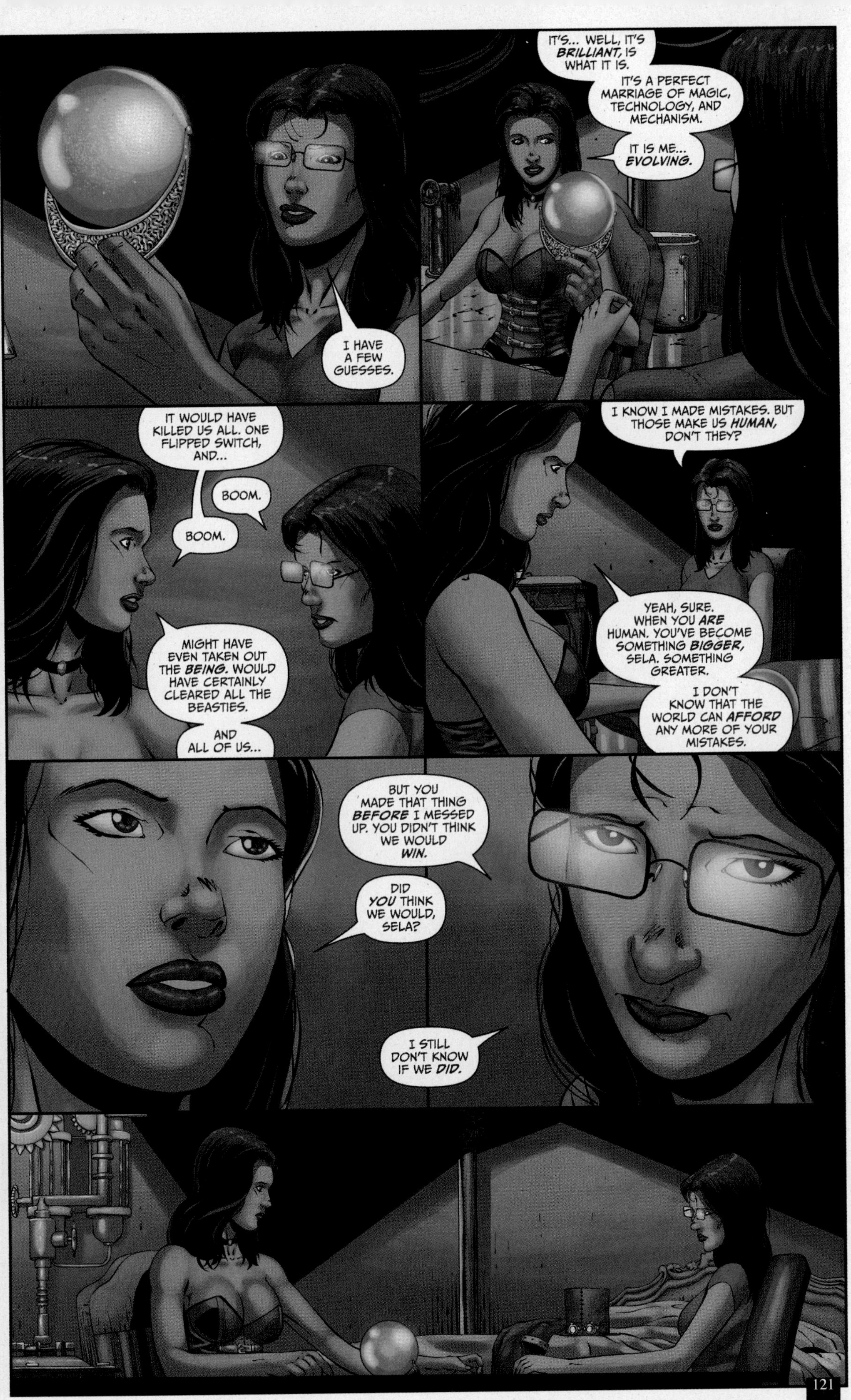
I HAVE A FEW GUESSES.
IT'S... WELL, IT'S BRILLIANT, IS WHAT IT IS.
IT'S A PERFECT MARRIAGE OF MAGIC, TECHNOLOGY, AND MECHANISM.
IT IS ME... EVOLVING.
IT WOULD HAVE KILLED US ALL. ONE FLIPPED SWITCH, AND...
BOOM.
BOOM.
MIGHT HAVE EVEN TAKEN OUT THE BEING. WOULD HAVE CERTAINLY CLEARED ALL THE BEASTIES.
AND ALL OF US...
I KNOW I MADE MISTAKES. BUT THOSE MAKE US HUMAN, DON'T THEY?
YEAH, SURE. WHEN YOU ARE HUMAN. YOU'VE BECOME SOMETHING BIGGER, SELA. SOMETHING GREATER.
I DON'T KNOW THAT THE WORLD CAN AFFORD ANY MORE OF YOUR MISTAKES.
BUT YOU MADE THAT THING BEFORE I MESSED UP. YOU DIDN'T THINK WE WOULD WIN.
DID YOU THINK WE WOULD, SELA?
I STILL DON'T KNOW IF WE DID.

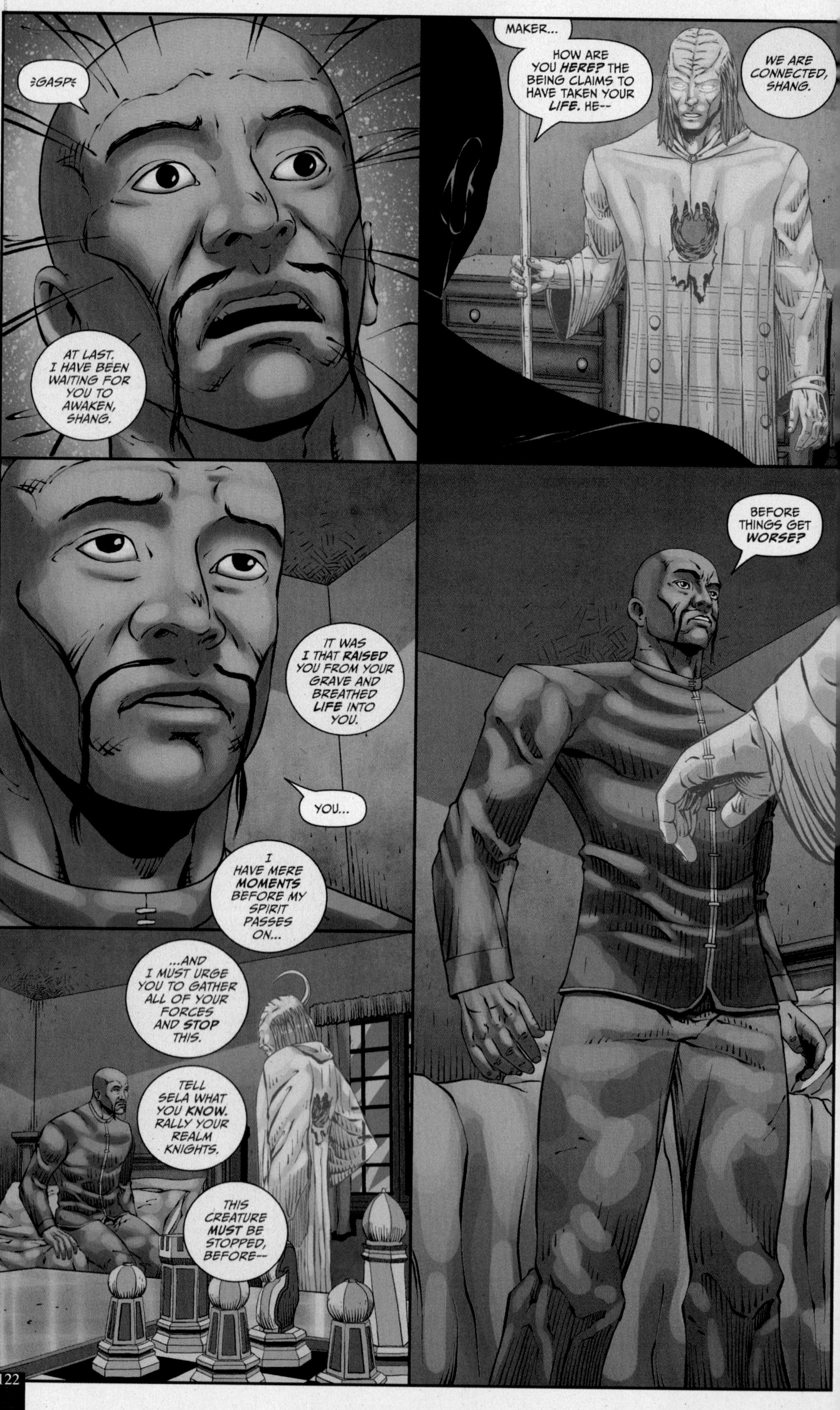

≥GASP≤
AT LAST. I HAVE BEEN WAITING FOR YOU TO AWAKEN, SHANG.
MAKER...
HOW ARE YOU HERE? THE BEING CLAIMS TO HAVE TAKEN YOUR LIFE. HE--
WE ARE CONNECTED, SHANG.
IT WAS I THAT RAISED YOU FROM YOUR GRAVE AND BREATHED LIFE INTO YOU.
YOU...
I HAVE MERE MOMENTS BEFORE MY SPIRIT PASSES ON...
...AND I MUST URGE YOU TO GATHER ALL OF YOUR FORCES AND STOP THIS.
TELL SELA WHAT YOU KNOW. RALLY YOUR REALM KNIGHTS.
THIS CREATURE MUST BE STOPPED, BEFORE--
BEFORE THINGS GET WORSE?

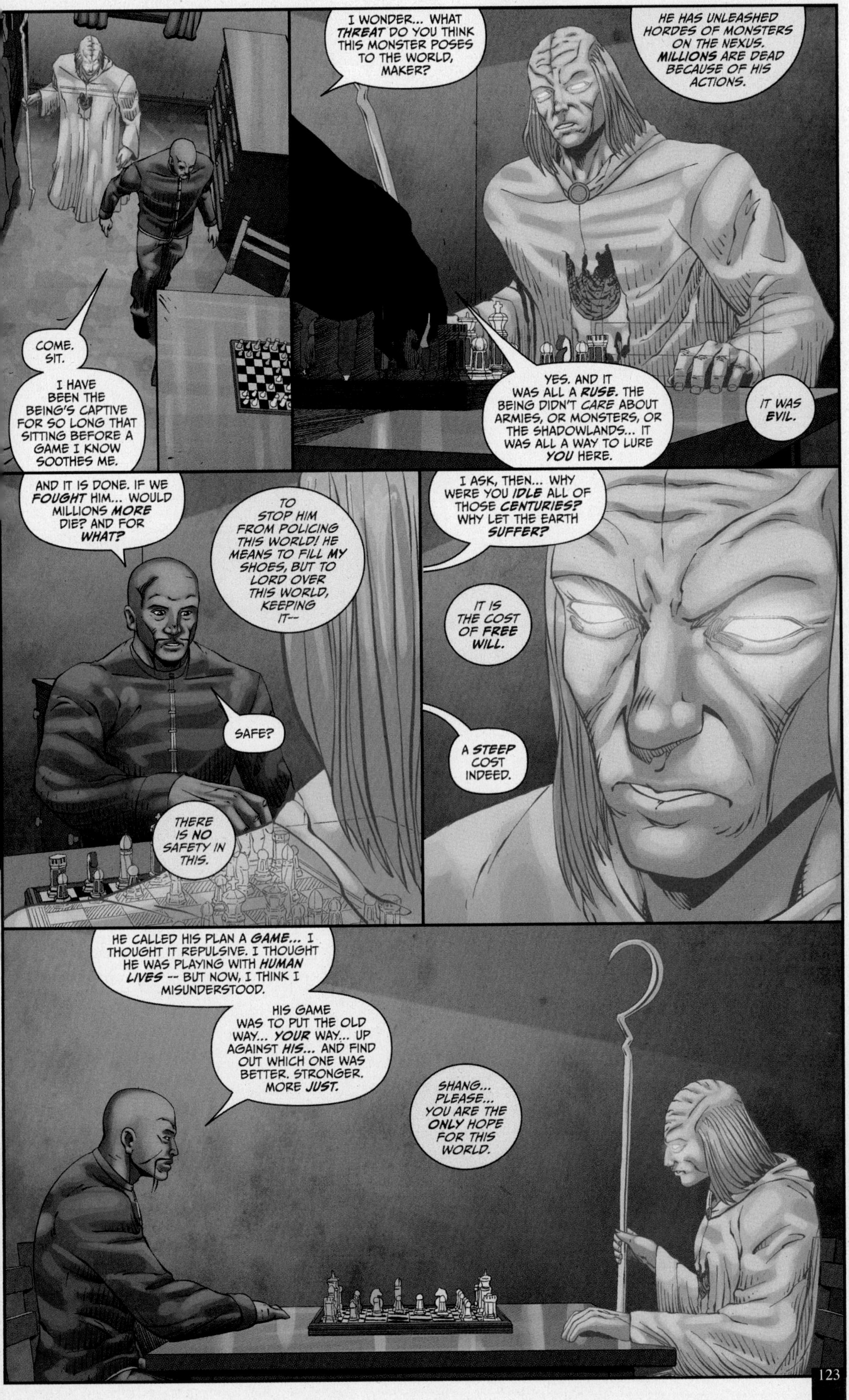
COME. SIT.
I HAVE BEEN THE BEING'S CAPTIVE FOR SO LONG THAT SITTING BEFORE A GAME I KNOW SOOTHES ME.
I WONDER... WHAT THREAT DO YOU THINK THIS MONSTER POSES TO THE WORLD, MAKER?
HE HAS UNLEASHED HORDES OF MONSTERS ON THE NEXUS. MILLIONS ARE DEAD BECAUSE OF HIS ACTIONS.
YES. AND IT WAS ALL A RUSE. THE BEING DIDN'T CARE ABOUT ARMIES, OR MONSTERS, OR THE SHADOWLANDS... IT WAS ALL A WAY TO LURE YOU HERE.
IT WAS EVIL.
AND IT IS DONE. IF WE FOUGHT HIM... WOULD MILLIONS MORE DIE? AND FOR WHAT?
TO STOP HIM FROM POLICING THIS WORLD! HE MEANS TO FILL MY SHOES, BUT TO LORD OVER THIS WORLD, KEEPING IT--
SAFE?
THERE IS NO SAFETY IN THIS.
I ASK, THEN... WHY WERE YOU IDLE ALL OF THOSE CENTURIES? WHY LET THE EARTH SUFFER?
IT IS THE COST OF FREE WILL.
A STEEP COST INDEED.
HE CALLED HIS PLAN A GAME... I THOUGHT IT REPULSIVE. I THOUGHT HE WAS PLAYING WITH HUMAN LIVES -- BUT NOW, I THINK I MISUNDERSTOOD.
HIS GAME WAS TO PUT THE OLD WAY... YOUR WAY... UP AGAINST HIS... AND FIND OUT WHICH ONE WAS BETTER. STRONGER. MORE JUST.
SHANG... PLEASE... YOU ARE THE ONLY HOPE FOR THIS WORLD.

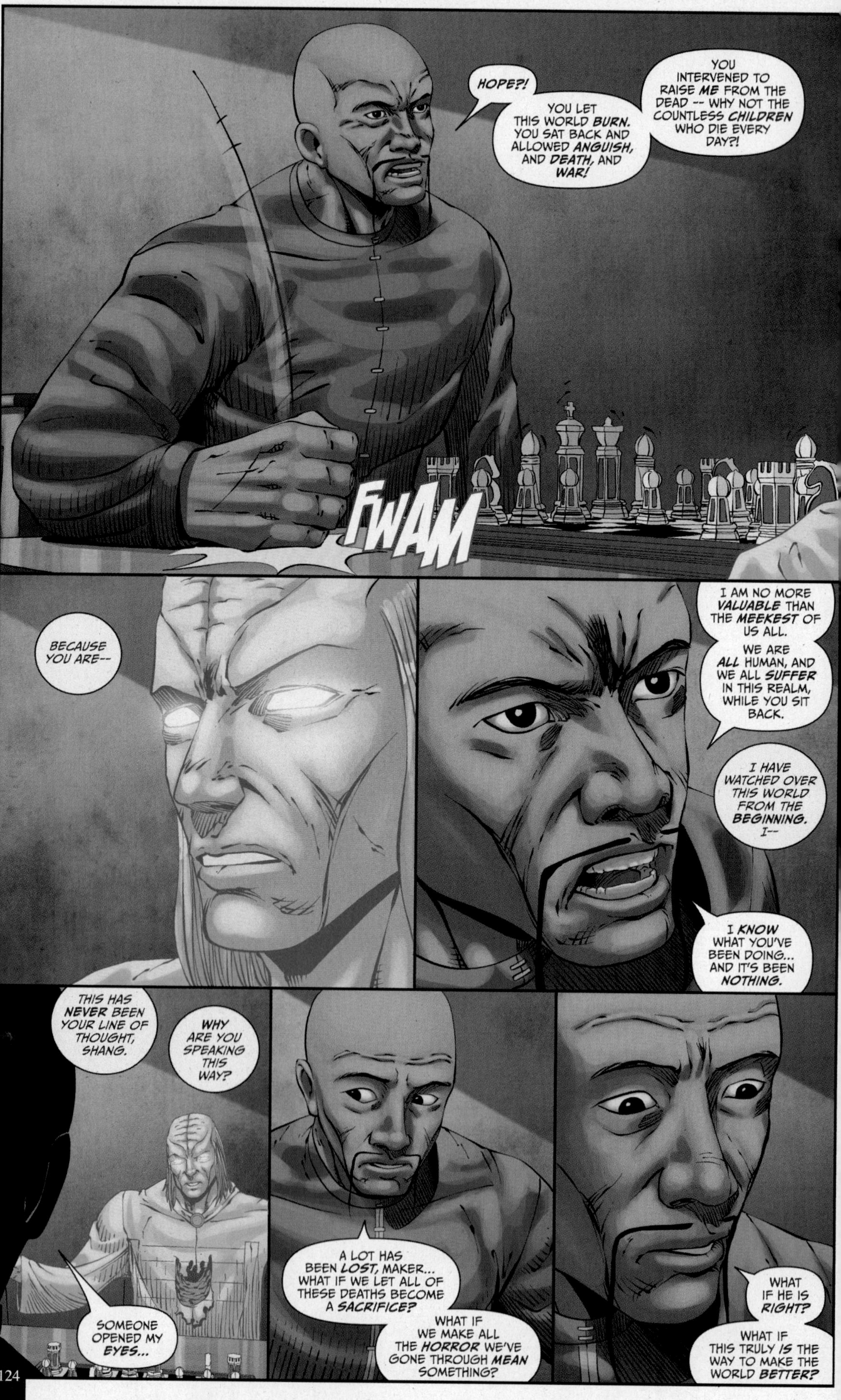
HOPE?!
YOU LET THIS WORLD BURN. YOU SAT BACK AND ALLOWED ANGUISH, AND DEATH, AND WAR!
YOU INTERVENED TO RAISE ME FROM THE DEAD -- WHY NOT THE COUNTLESS CHILDREN WHO DIE EVERY DAY?!
FWAM
BECAUSE YOU ARE--
I AM NO MORE VALUABLE THAN THE MEEKEST OF US ALL.
WE ARE ALL HUMAN, AND WE ALL SUFFER IN THIS REALM, WHILE YOU SIT BACK.
I HAVE WATCHED OVER THIS WORLD FROM THE BEGINNING. I--
I KNOW WHAT YOU'VE BEEN DOING... AND IT'S BEEN NOTHING.
THIS HAS NEVER BEEN YOUR LINE OF THOUGHT, SHANG.
WHY ARE YOU SPEAKING THIS WAY?
SOMEONE OPENED MY EYES...
A LOT HAS BEEN LOST, MAKER... WHAT IF WE LET ALL OF THESE DEATHS BECOME A SACRIFICE?
WHAT IF WE MAKE ALL THE HORROR WE'VE GONE THROUGH MEAN SOMETHING?
WHAT IF HE IS RIGHT?
WHAT IF THIS TRULY IS THE WAY TO MAKE THE WORLD BETTER?

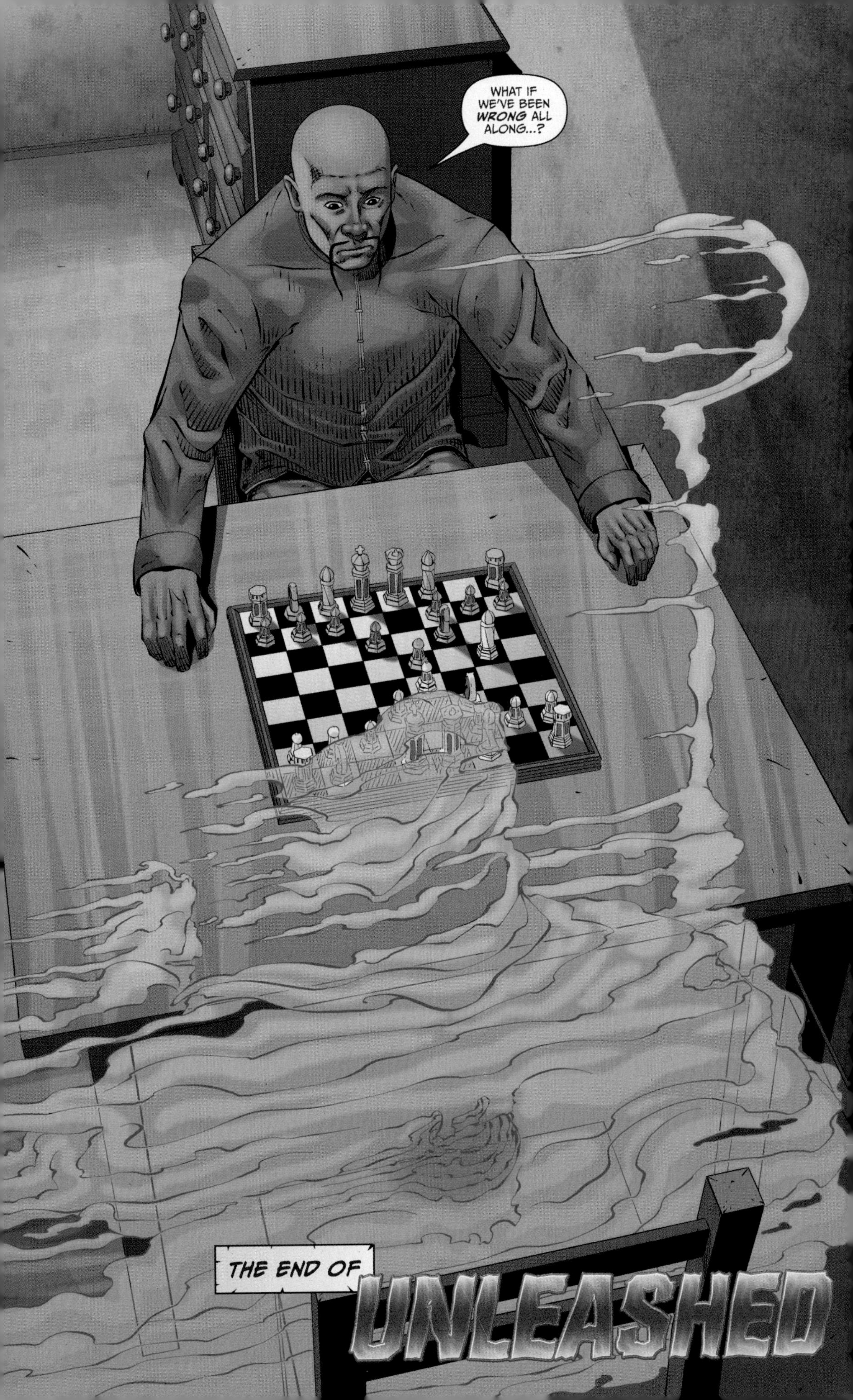
WHAT IF WE'VE BEEN *WRONG* ALL ALONG...?
THE END OF
UNLEASHED

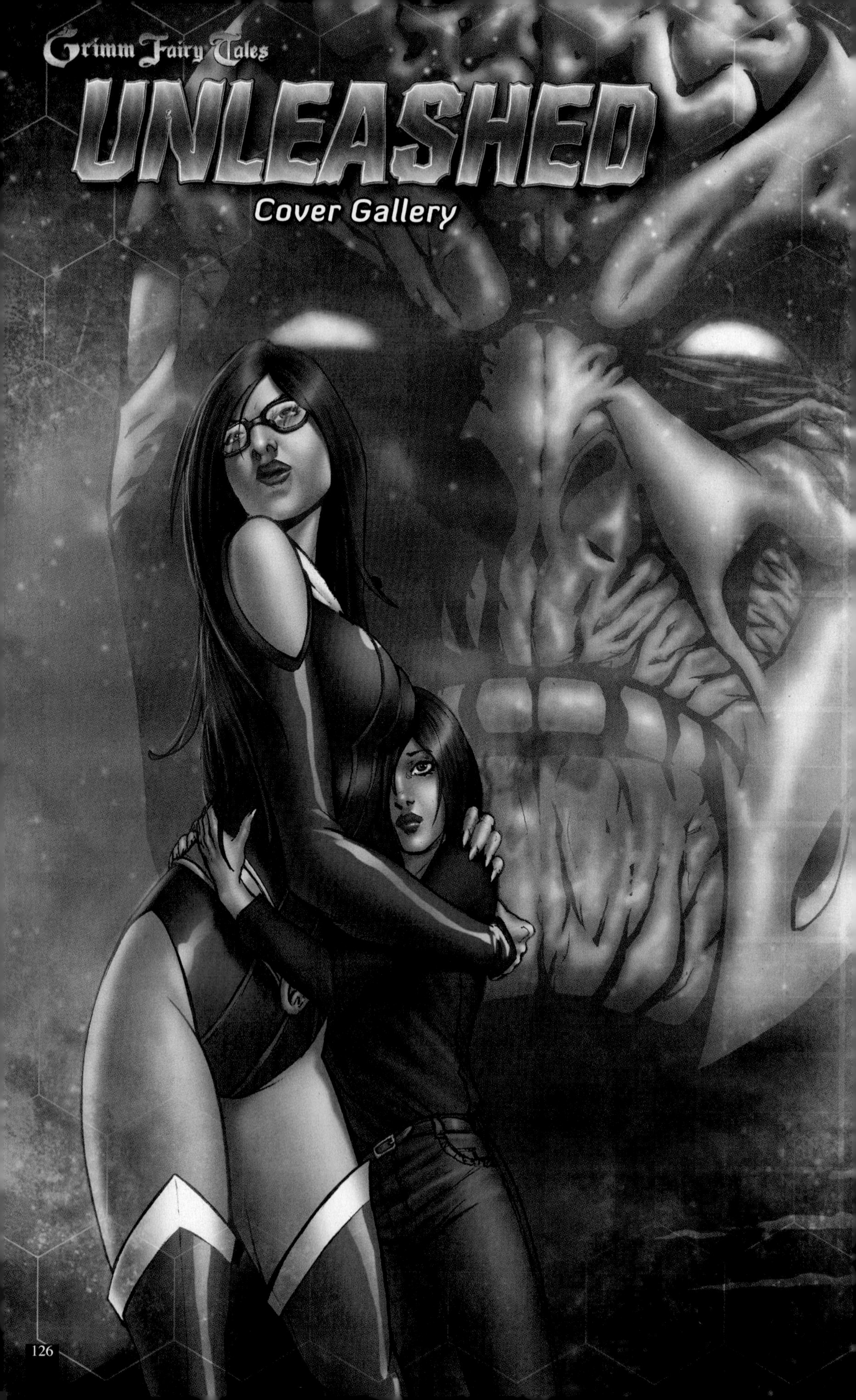
Grimm Fairy Tales
UNLEASHED
Cover Gallery

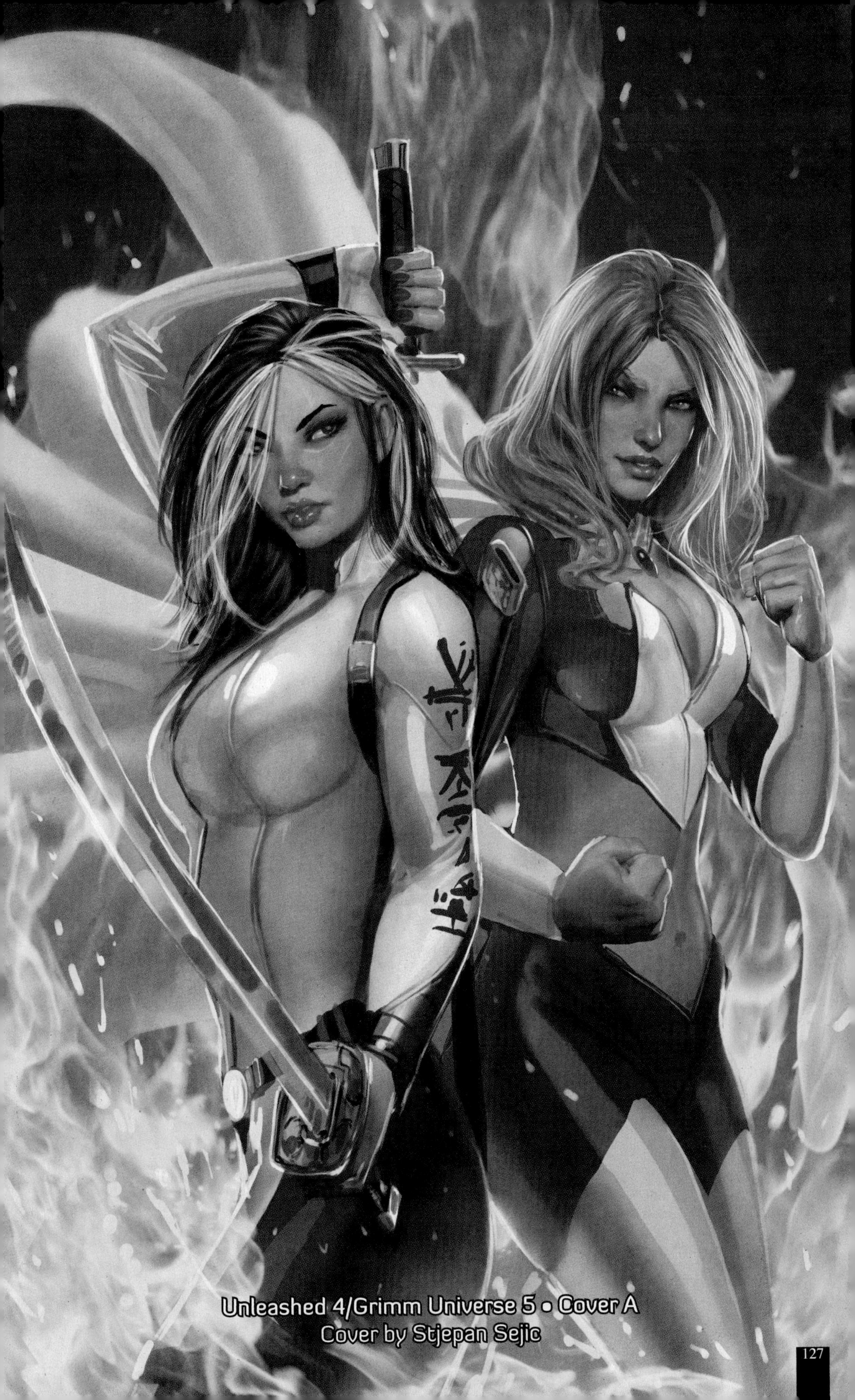

Unleashed 4/Grimm Universe 5 • Cover A
Cover by Stjepan Sejic

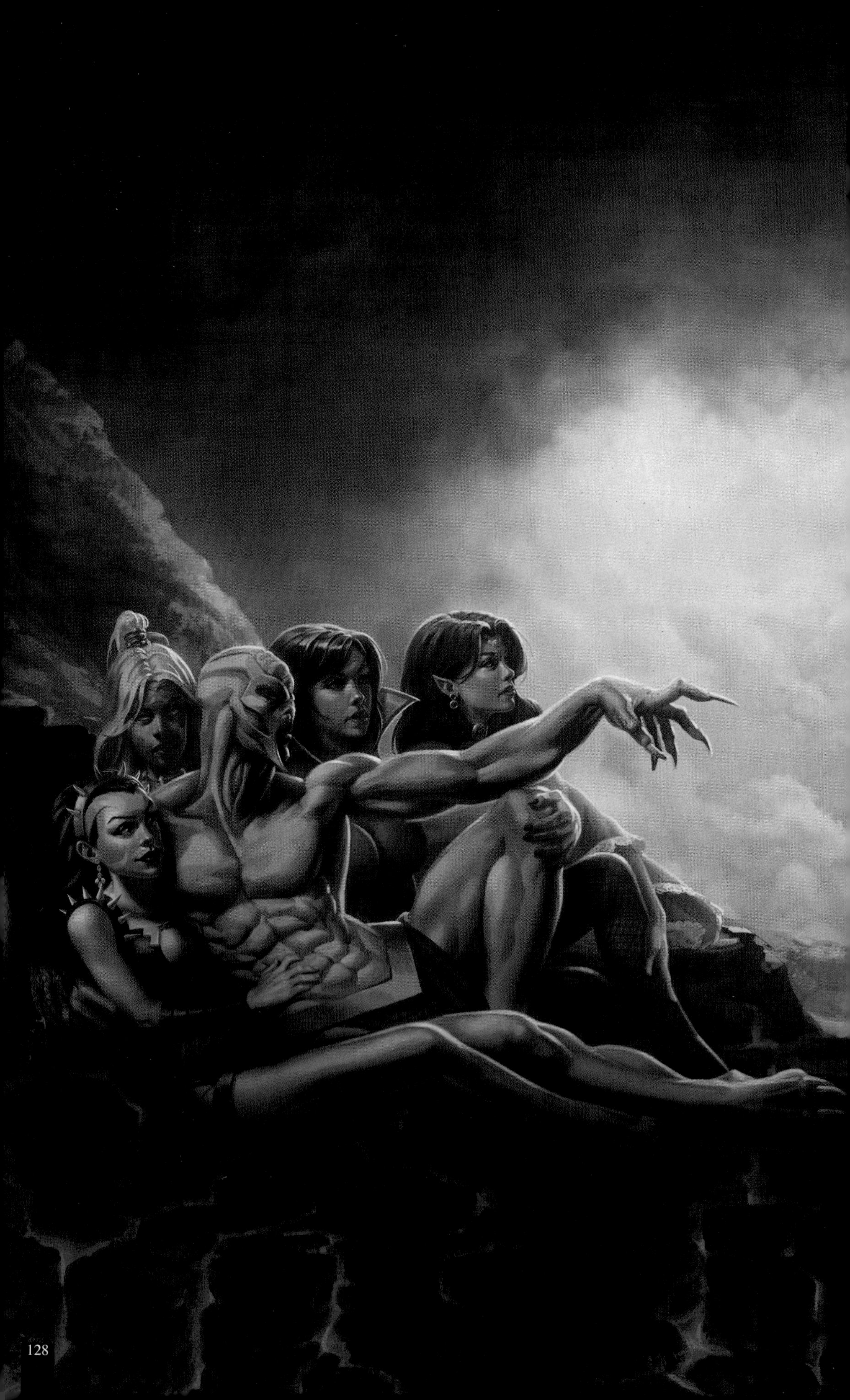

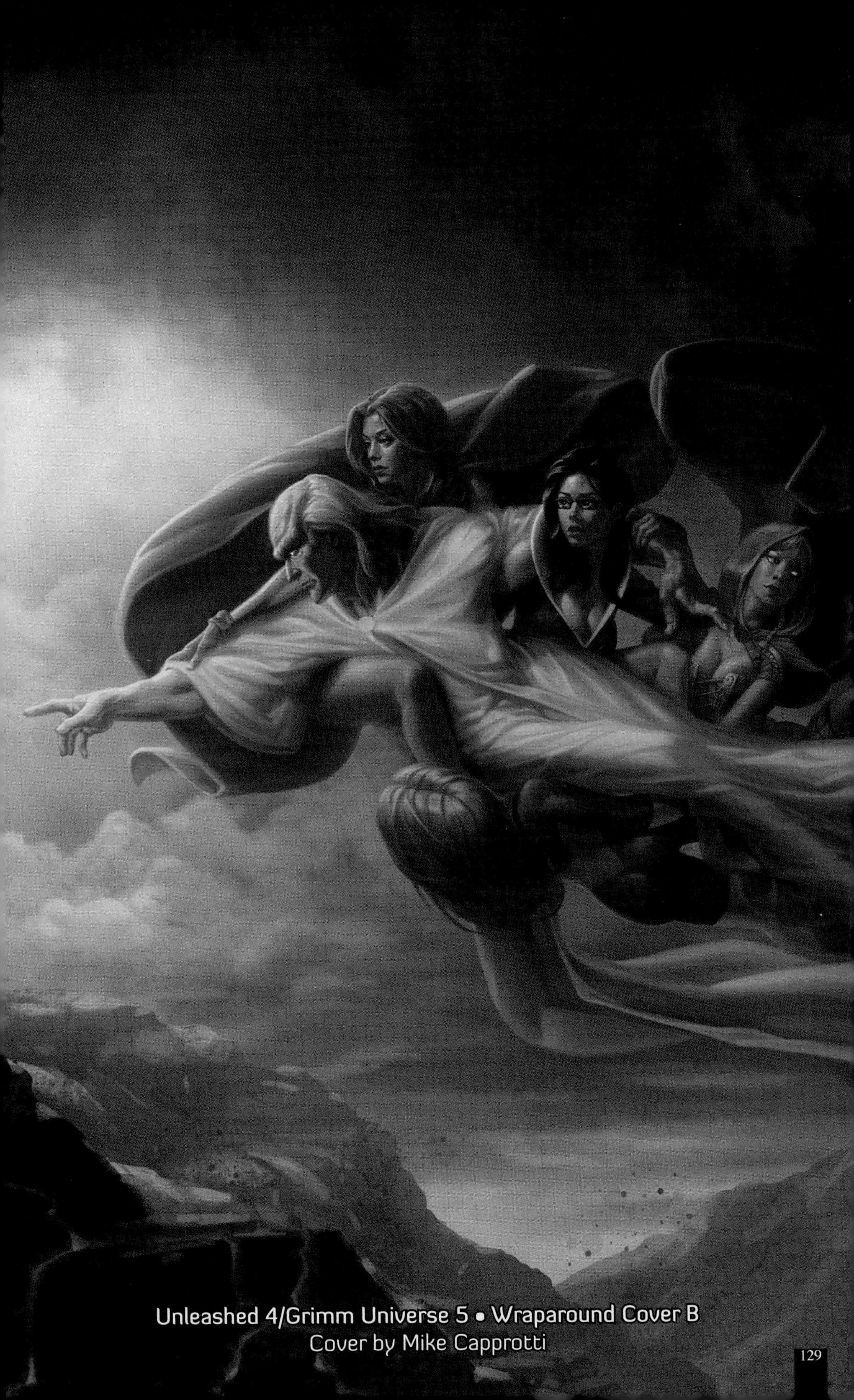

Unleashed 4/Grimm Universe 5 • Wraparound Cover B
Cover by Mike Capprotti

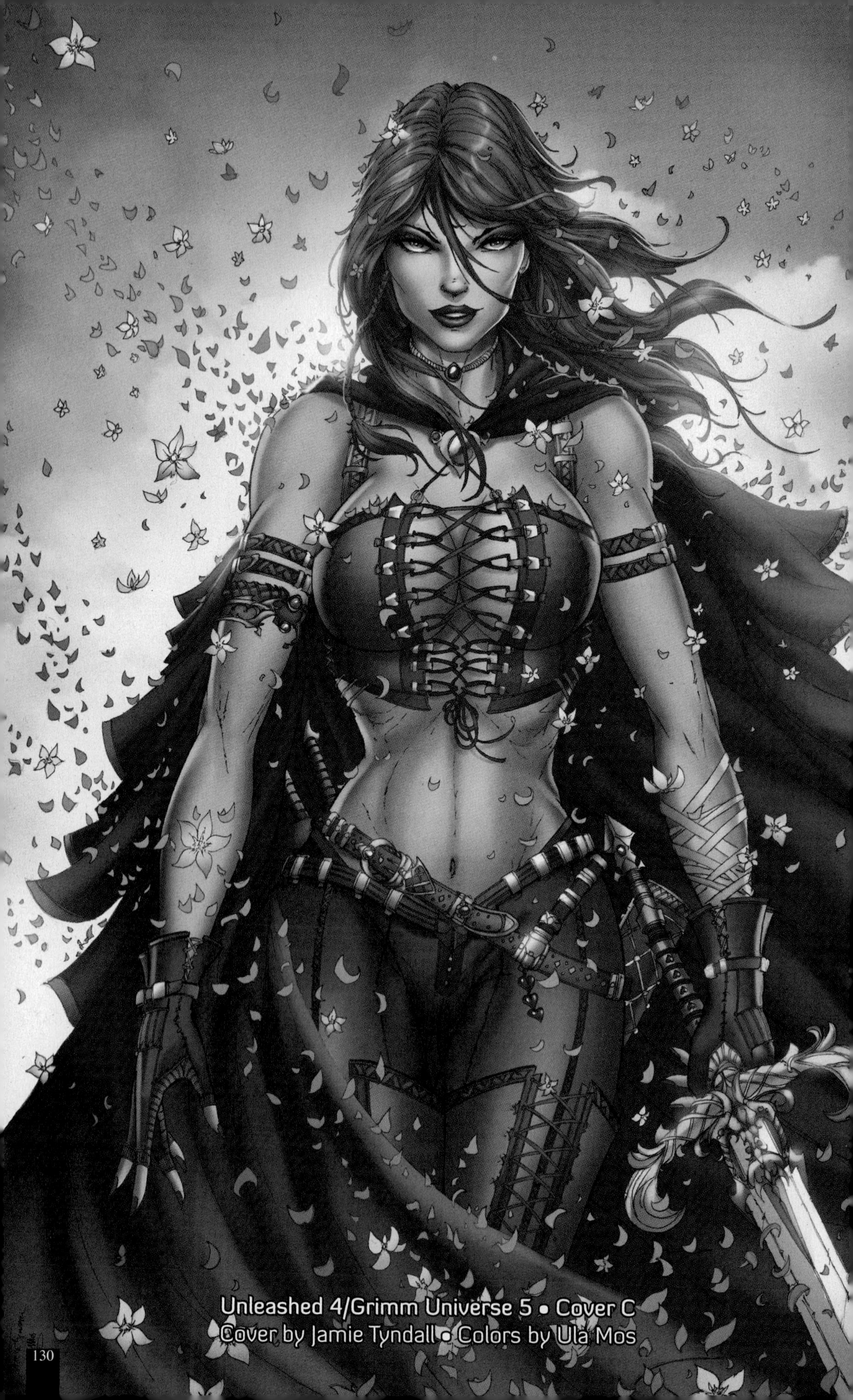

Unleashed 4/Grimm Universe 5 • Cover C
Cover by Jamie Tyndall • Colors by Ula Mos

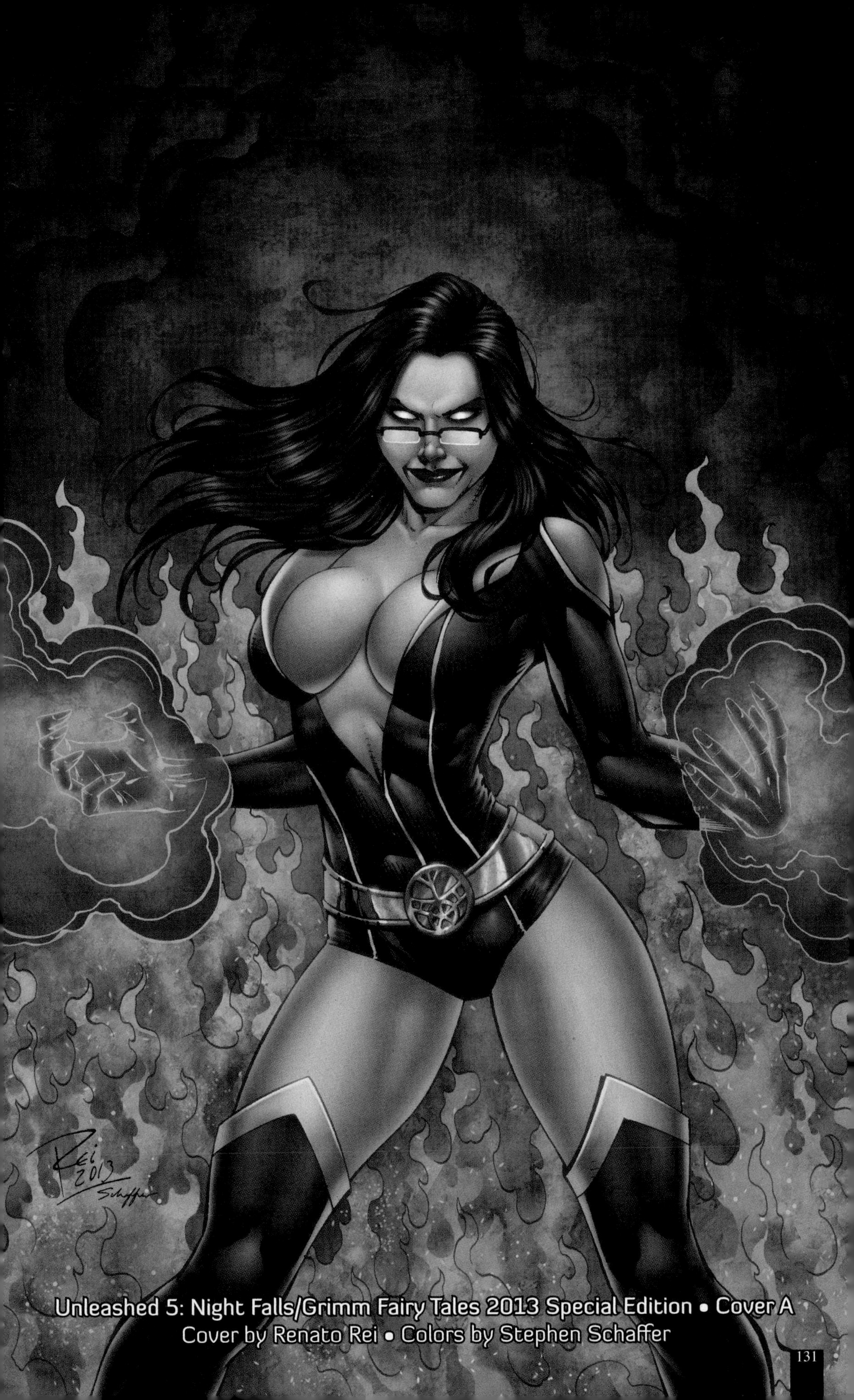

Unleashed 5: Night Falls/Grimm Fairy Tales 2013 Special Edition • Cover A
Cover by Renato Rei • Colors by Stephen Schaffer

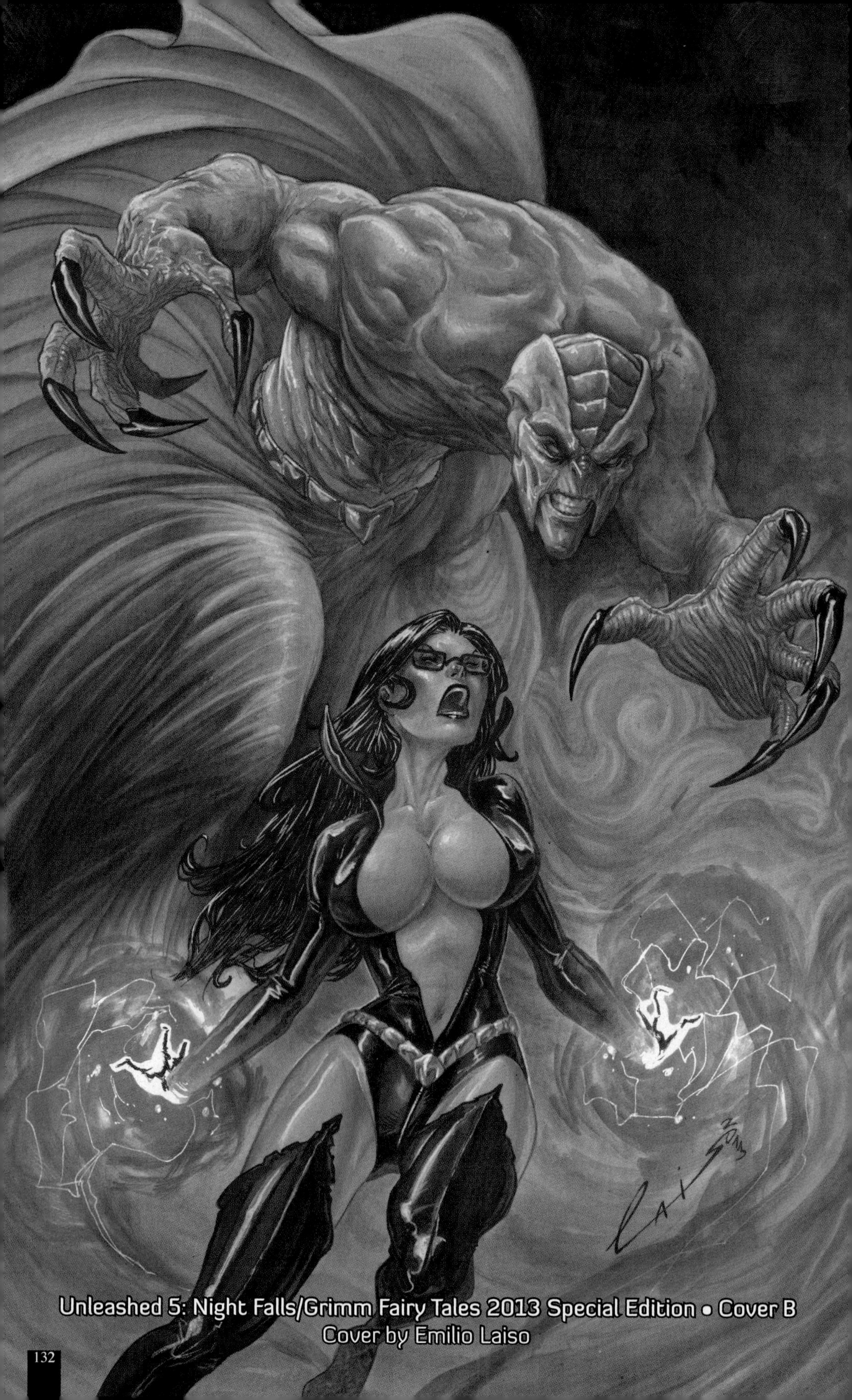

Unleashed 5: Night Falls/Grimm Fairy Tales 2013 Special Edition • Cover B
Cover by Emilio Laiso

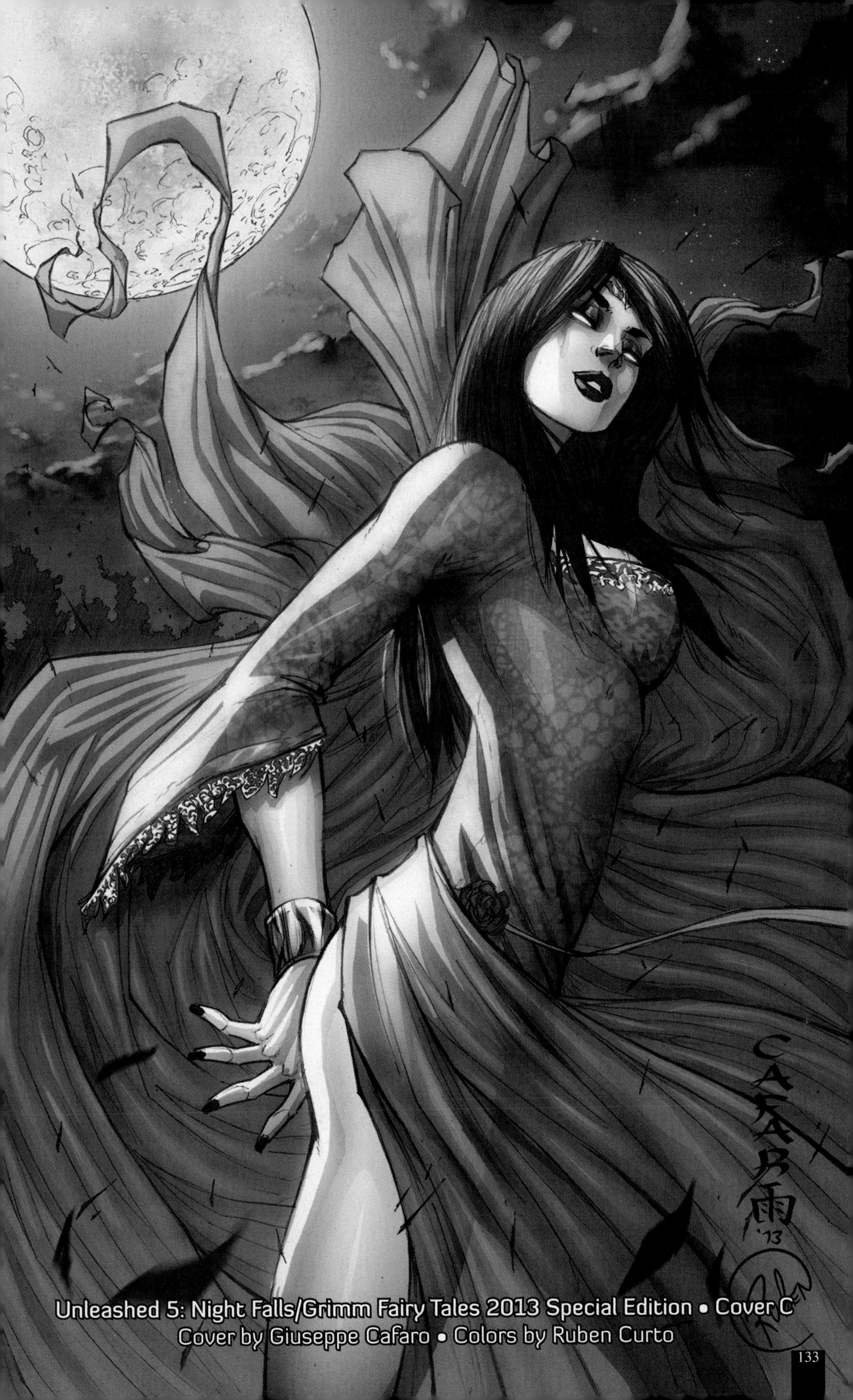

Unleashed 5: Night Falls/Grimm Fairy Tales 2013 Special Edition • Cover C
Cover by Giuseppe Cafaro • Colors by Ruben Curto

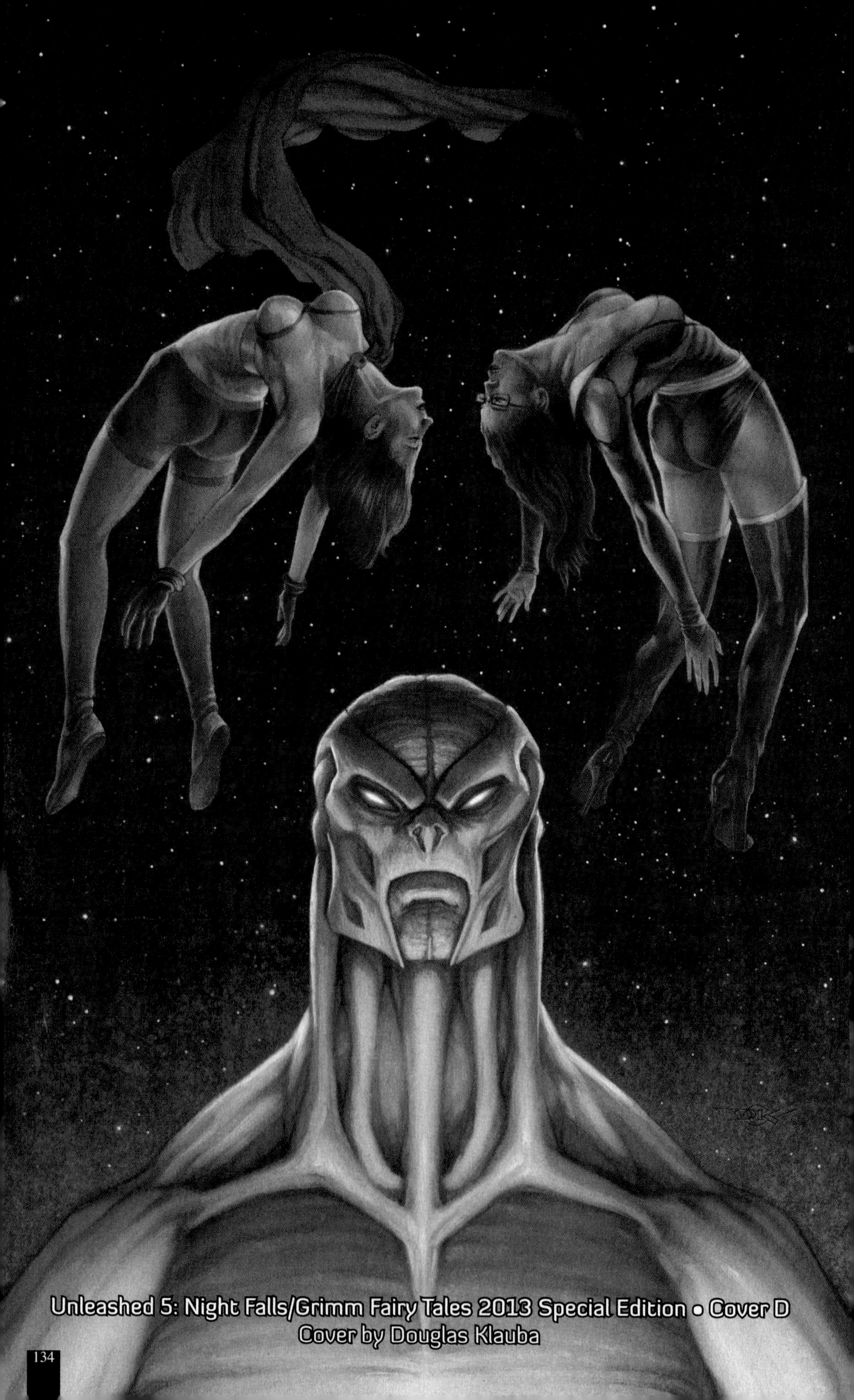

Unleashed 5: Night Falls/Grimm Fairy Tales 2013 Special Edition • Cover D
Cover by Douglas Klauba

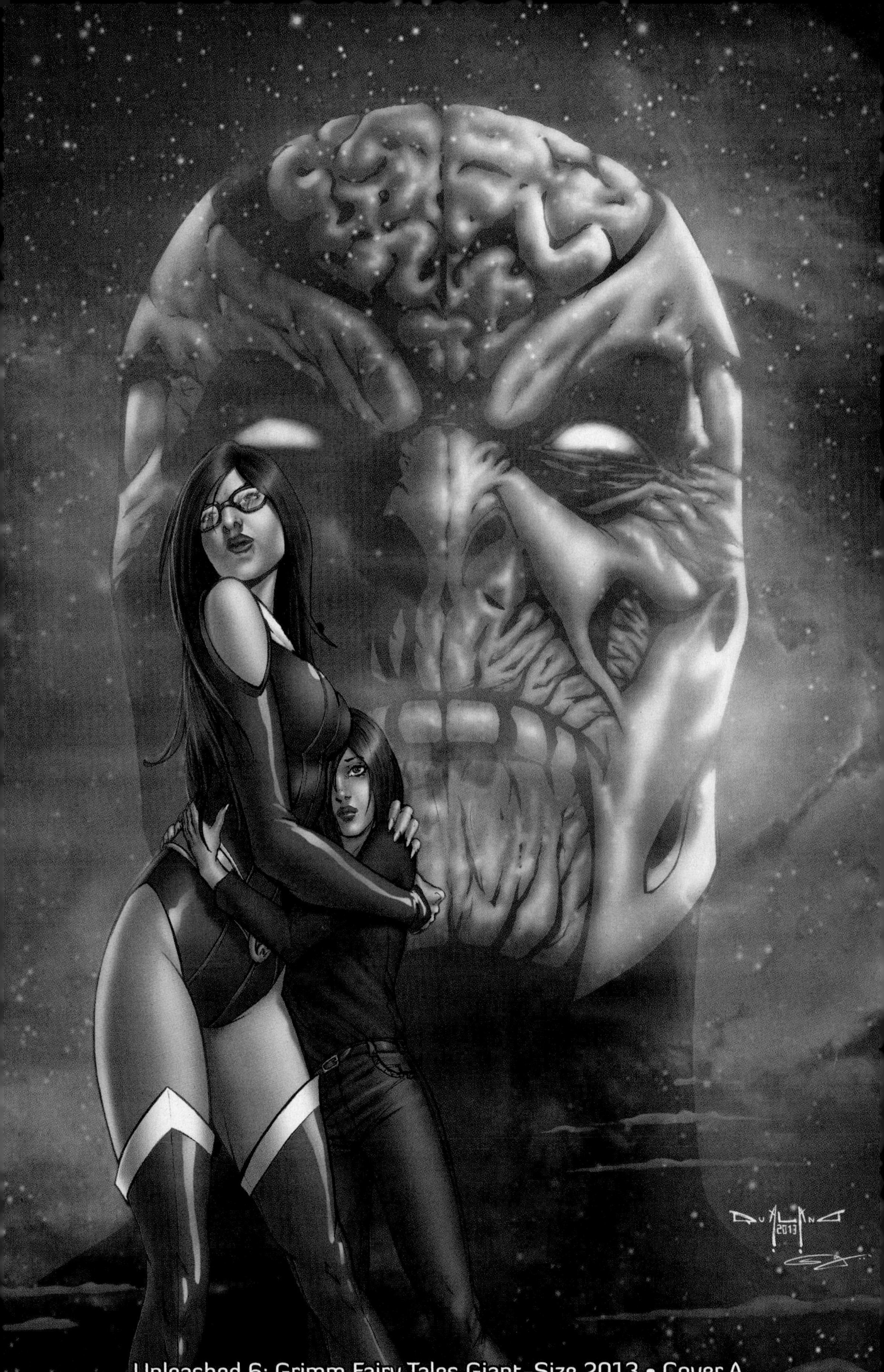

Unleashed 6: Grimm Fairy Tales Giant-Size 2013 • Cover A
Cover by Pasquale Qualano • Colors by Sanju Nivangune

Unleashed 6: Grimm Fairy Tales Giant-Size 2013 • Cover B
Cover by Alfredo Reyes • Colors by Ylenia Di Napoli

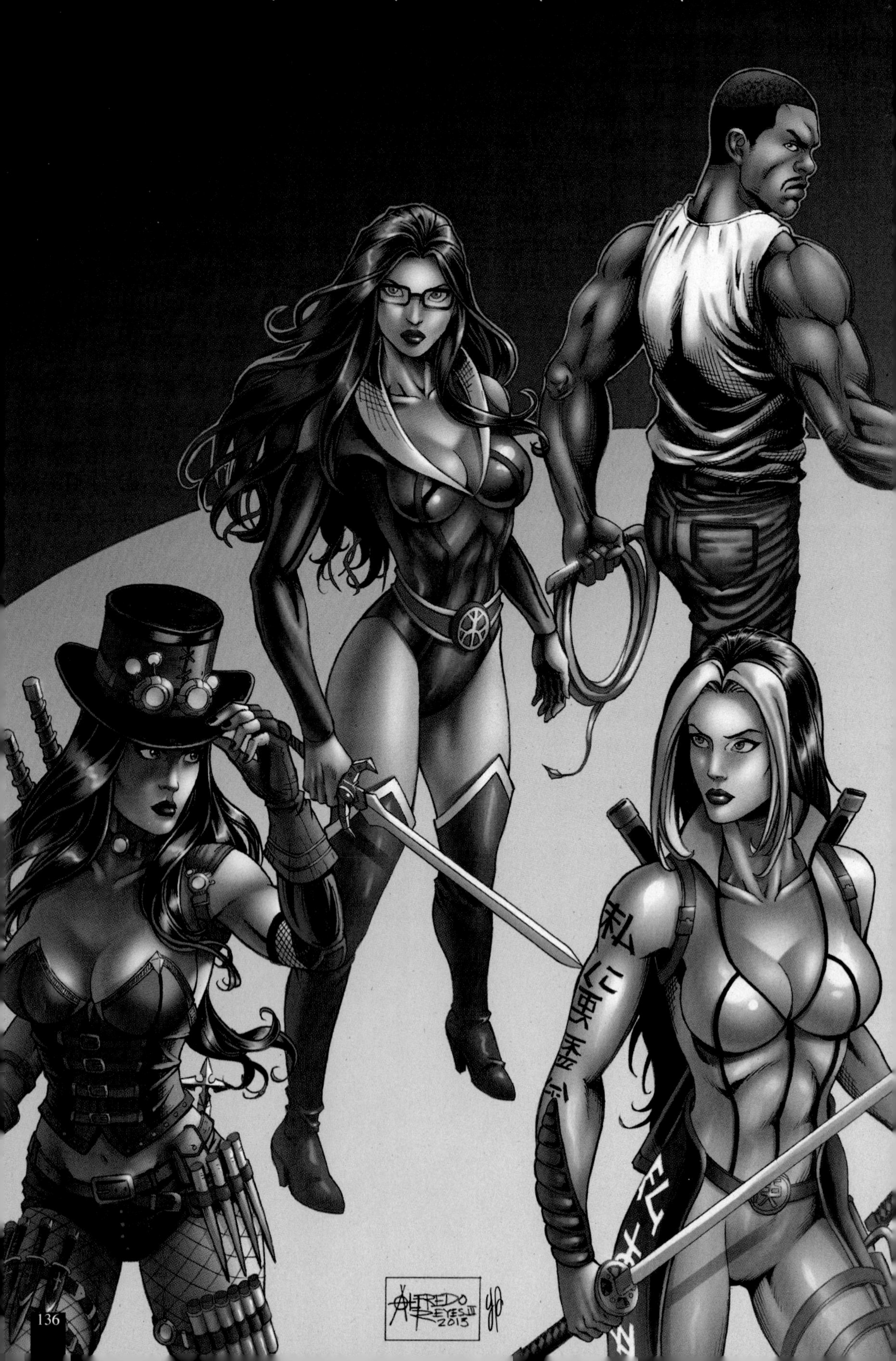

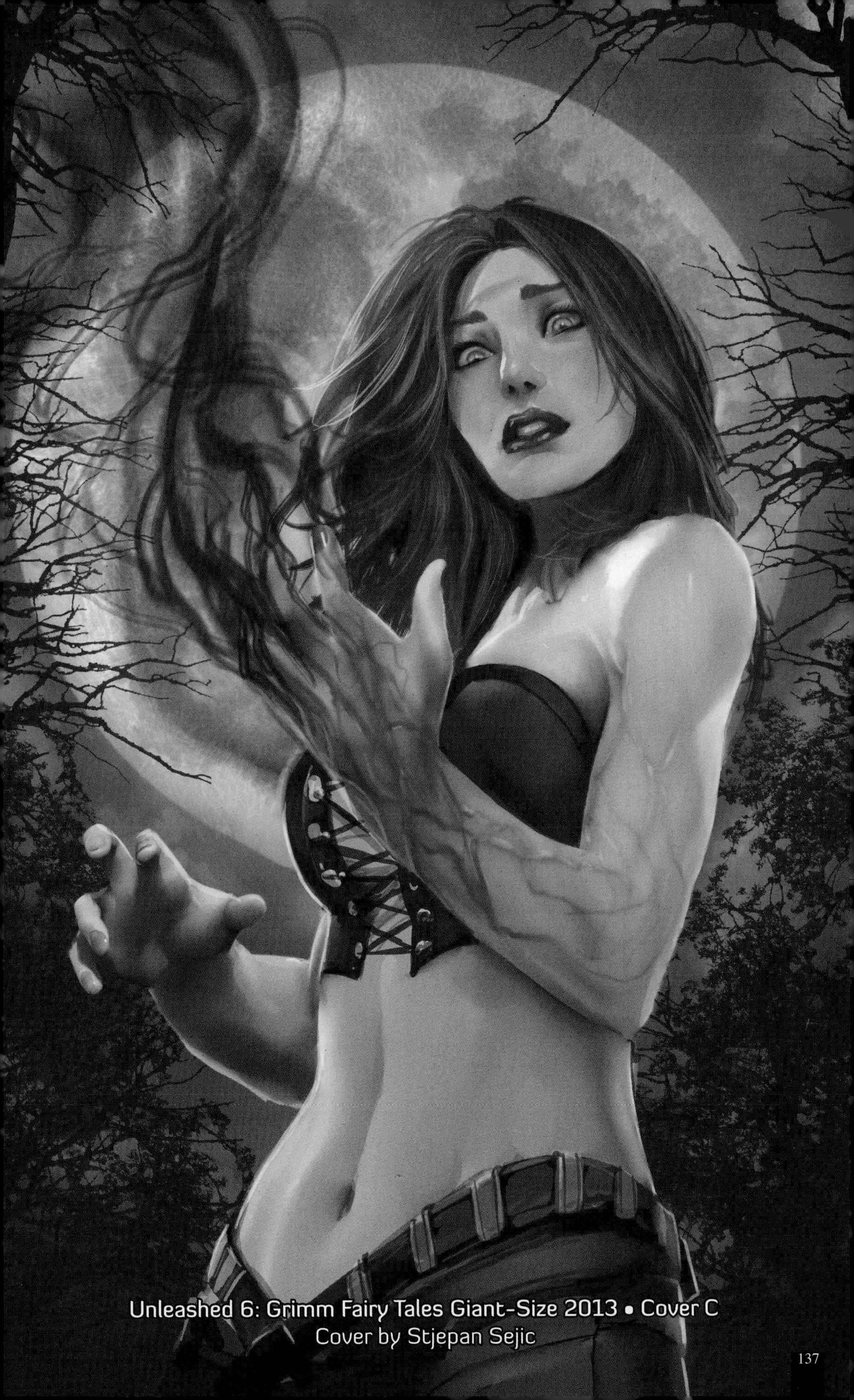

Unleashed 6: Grimm Fairy Tales Giant-Size 2013 • Cover C
Cover by Stjepan Sejic

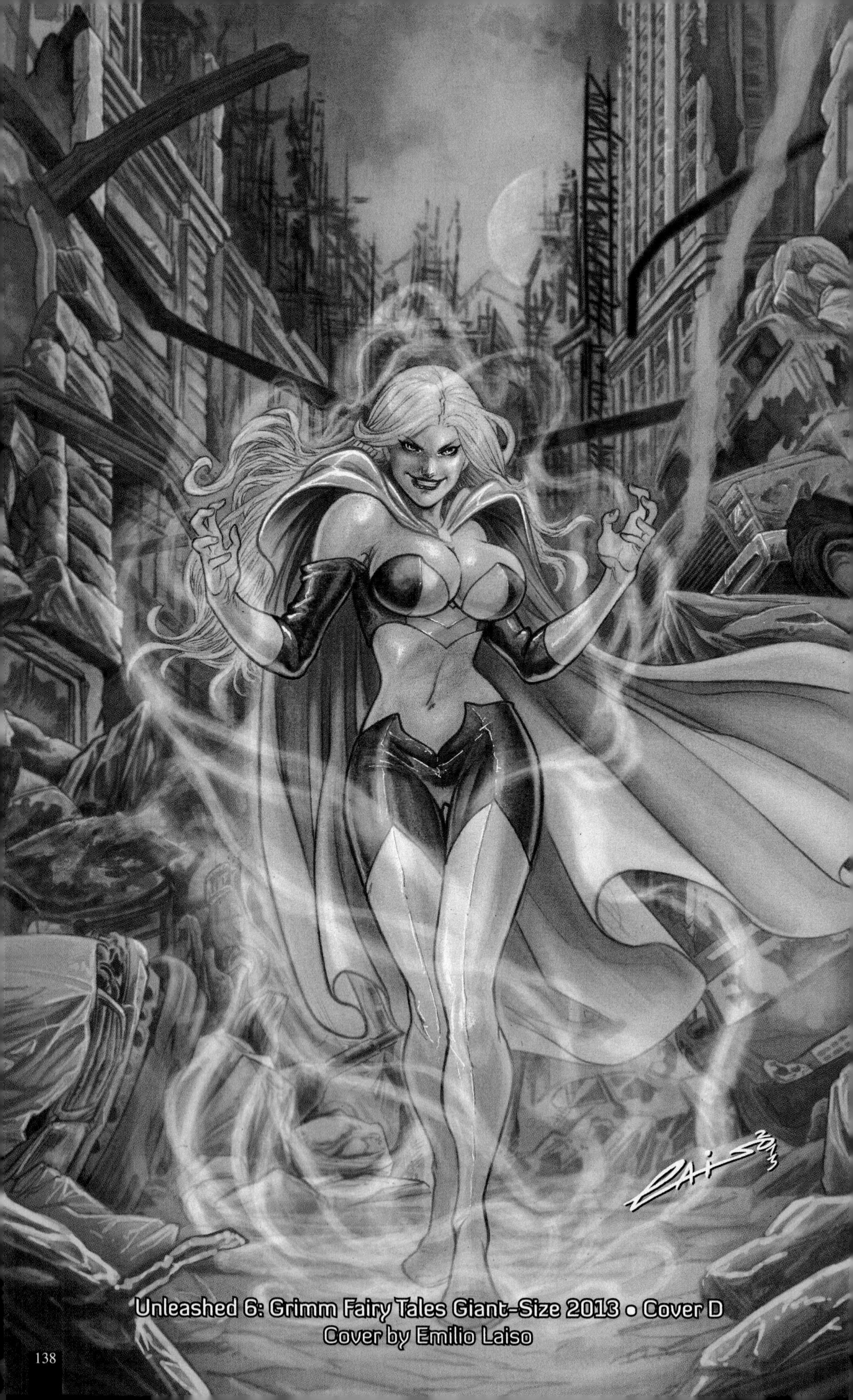

Unleashed 6: Grimm Fairy Tales Giant-Size 2013 • Cover D
Cover by Emilio Laiso

Grimm Fairy Tales
UNLEASHED

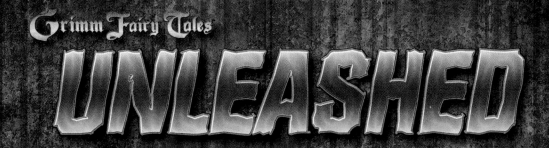

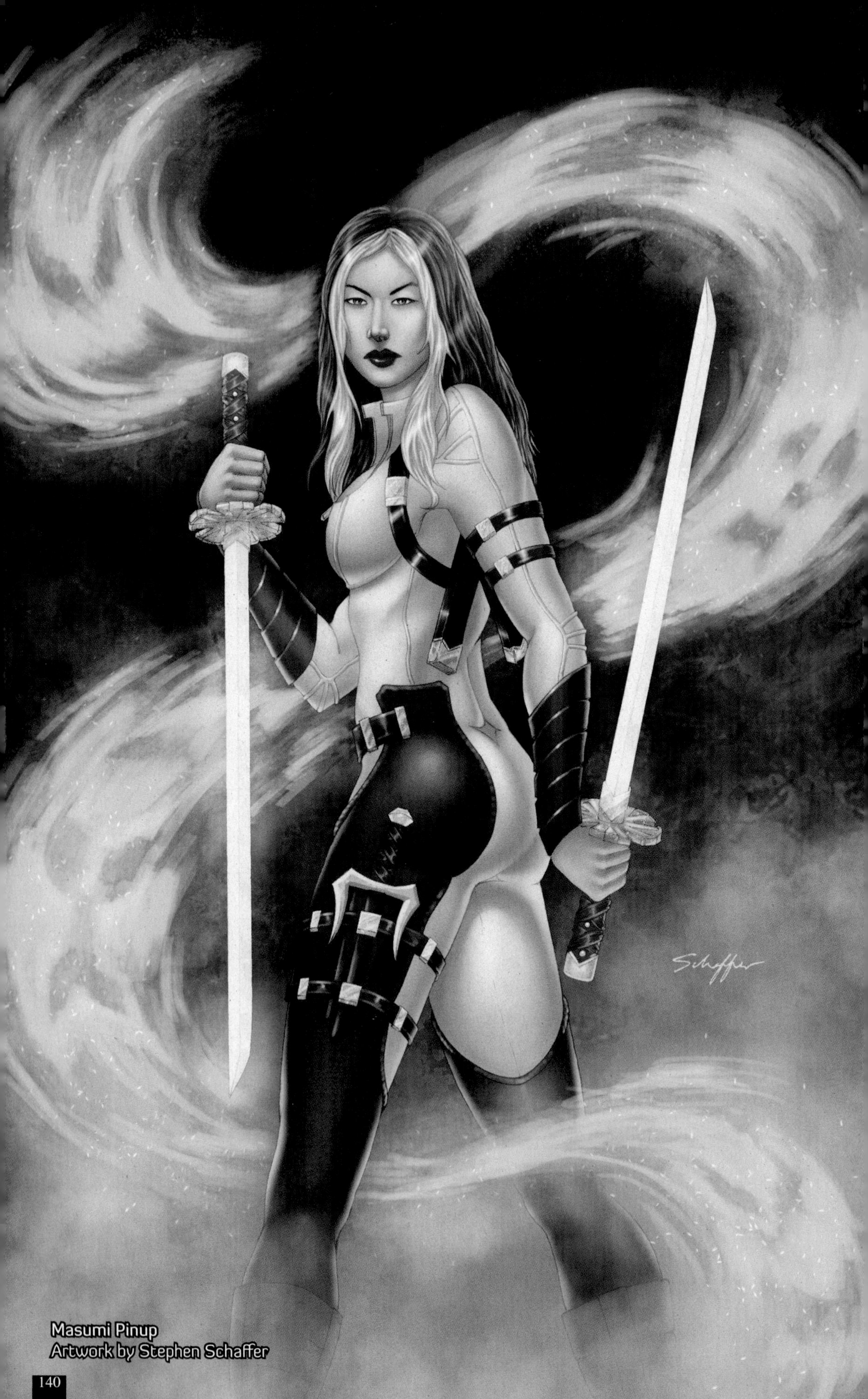
Schaffer

Masumi Pinup
Artwork by Stephen Schaffer